Basic College Writing

A TEXT WITH READINGS

Nancy C. Martinez
Joseph G. R. Martinez
University of New Mexico

 PRENTICE HALL   Englewood Cliffs, New Jersey 07632

Library of Congress Cataloging-in-Publication Data

Martinez, Nancy C. (Nancy Conrad)
    Basic college writing : a text with readings / Nancy C. Martinez
and Joseph G.R. Martinez.
        p.   cm.
    Includes index.
    ISBN 0-13-067646-2 :
    1. English language--Rhetoric. 2. English language-
-Grammar--1950- 3. College readers.   I. Martinez, Joseph G. R.
II. Title.
PE1408.M386646   1990
808'.0427--dc20   90-7581
                                                            CIP

Editorial/production supervision and
    interior design: Arthur Maisel
Cover design: Bruce Kenselaar
Prepress buyers: Mary Ann Gloriande
    and Herb Klein
Manufacturing buyer: David Dickey

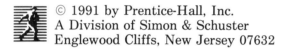

© 1991 by Prentice-Hall, Inc.
A Division of Simon & Schuster
Englewood Cliffs, New Jersey 07632

Printed in the United States of America

10 9 8 7 6 5 4 3 2 1

ISBN   0-13-067646-2

Prentice-Hall International (UK) Limited, *London*
Prentice-Hall of Australia Pty. Limited, *Sydney*
Prentice-Hall Canada Inc., *Toronto*
Prentice-Hall Hispanoamericana, S.A., *Mexico*
Prentice-Hall of India Private Limited, *New Delhi*
Prentice-Hall of Japan, Inc., *Tokyo*
Simon & Schuster Asia Pte. Ltd., *Singapore*
Editora Prentice-Hall do Brasil, Ltda., *Rio de Janeiro*

Contents

SKILLS IN ACTION TESTS

PART II *Readings*   *309*

Notes to the Student and to the Instructor

TO THE STUDENT

Basic College Writing is a book dedicated to helping you become a better writer. Beginning where you are now in writing skills, it will help you build on your strengths as well as work on weaknesses. Throughout the course you will be learning about the process of writing and about basic sentence skills. Each chapter begins with an important part of the writing process, then introduces a sentence skill. A brief section at the end of the chapter explains how to make the readings at the end of the book part of the writing process. And the chapter ends with a writing activity, which provides guided practice in the skills studied in the chapter.

Your own writing will determine how much time you should spend on each section. The chapters contain many different exercises. Probably your instructor will assign only some of them, leaving others for individual practice. The diagnostic essay and exercises in the Introduction will help you and your instructor identify areas that need extra work and set goals for improvement.

TO THE INSTRUCTOR

Basic College Writing has taken ten years and hundreds of composition classes to write. It began as a seventy-page booklet, which was used as an in-house text in a developmental writing program, and evolved slowly as sudents and teachers tested the materials and research revealed new insights about the writing process. The resulting text combines a process approach to teaching writing with sentence skills work and readings. It integrates the processes of reading and writing and provides numerous teaching aids, such as the Skills-in-Action Tests and the Writing Checklist, which will help both you and your students keep track of problems and progress.

Careful pacing makes the text both teachable and accessible. The first six chapters focus on short writing assignments (usually single paragraphs), and the final six chapters, on writing essays. Reading levels for both the readings and the text materials increase gradually, and within each chapter, exercises lead students by easy steps from simpler to more complex cognitive activities.

The four-part plan of individual chapters allows for flexibility and varying emphases to meet varying student needs.

1. *Focus on Writing* introduces an important part of the writing process, including generating student writing; exploring and focusing ideas; organizing and developing ideas; and drafting, revising, and editing papers. An important feature of this section is numerous examples of student writing, which may be used to develop students' critical skills as well as to provide models for writing activities.
2. *Focus on the Sentence* takes a practical, usage approach to sentence skills. Beginning with sentence boundary punctuation in Chapter 1, the section emphasizes the meaning of grammar and language conventions, such as punctuation marks. An important feature is *Troubleshooting*, which applies skills learned in the section to the editing phase of the writing process.
3. *Reading to Write* makes reading part of the writing process by using readings as models or as subjects for student writing.
4. The *Writing Activity* integrates the different sections with a writing assignment that asks students to apply skills and respond to topics studied in the chapter.

Part II of *Basic College Writing* consists of the readings referred to in the Reading to Write sections of each chapter. Introduced by a brief explanation of the SQ3R reading method, the selections encourage active reading; students answer questions in the margin of the text while they read, thereby interacting with the text immediately and avoiding the kind of passive reading that lowers comprehension. Since the readings increase systematically in difficulty, students will be improving their reading skills while they are learning to integrate the reading and writing processes.

If you are a new teacher, you may wish to refer frequently to the sample syllabi in the instructor's manual as you plan your course. The manual also includes many suggestions for using *Basic College Writing* in the classroom as well as teaching tips for the basic-writing class. As in the text itself, we have used actual student writing to illustrate methods of marking papers.

We would like to thank the students and staff of the Developmental Academic Program at the Universtiy of Albuquerque and the Skills Development Center at the Valencia community-college branch of the University of New Mexico for their help in testing the text and for their contributions of exercises and student writing. We would also like to thank Allen Bundy, Long Beach, (CA) City College; Judith Longo, Ocean County (NJ) College; Terence S. Martin, University of Missouri—St. Louis; Thomas A. Mozola, Macomb (MI) Community College; and Susan Yaeger, Monroe Business Institute (NY); their perceptive criticism and thoughtful suggestions have been invaluable. To our editor, Phil Miller, we owe a special thank you; his expert guidance has been instrumental in making this text a better book.

N. C. M.
J. G. R. M.

INTRODUCTION
The Diagnostic Essay

Good writing begins with you. You were born with the ability to make and use language. It is part of your heritage, something that comes to you naturally—if not always easily. Using language well does not just happen. Developing your natural ability requires both knowledge and skills. Knowledge about written language and writing skills are the subjects of this text.

WHAT IS GOOD WRITING?   Good writing is more than creating perfect papers; it is the process that produces the papers. Long before you write the first word on a page, you have begun the writing process. Choosing a subject, deciding what to say, changing your ideas or the way you say them—all are part of the writing process. The better the process, the better the final product (your paper) will be. If the process is good, your paper will be well organized and well developed. It will say something worth saying in clear, effective sentences with few errors.

WHO ARE GOOD WRITERS?   Good writers are people, like you, who have developed their abilities. They may still find writing difficult, but they have learned strategies to deal with the difficulties. A writer with a poor grasp of the writing process will write one draft of a paper and expect it to be the last. A good writer can write three or four drafts and still find ways to improve the paper.

WHAT CAUSES WRITING ANXIETY?   Although everyone has the ability to use language and, therefore, to write, some people are afraid of writing. They were not born with that fear; they learned it, often from unpleasant experiences. Writing anxiety can keep writers from developing their abilities.

To find out whether you are suffering from writing anxiety, ask yourself these questions: Do I avoid writing? Does my mind go blank when I start to write? Am I usually dissatisfied with what I write? Do I fear having my writing evaluated? Do I find taking a composition course a frightening experience?

If your answer to all or most of these questions is "yes," you may have a high level of writing anxiety. To overcome that anxiety, give writing top priority. Anxiety increases when time is short; therefore, start assignments early. Allow yourself time to make mistakes and time to rewrite. Anxiety also increases when you discover gaps in your knowledge or skills. Finding those gaps is the purpose of the Diagnostic Essay, and the Writing Checklist (pp. 351–52) will help you monitor your progress in closing those gaps.

Remember that, like writing, becoming a better writer is a process. It will not happen overnight, but it will happen. As you improve, you will become more confident and less anxious about writing.

The Diagnostic Essay

Becoming a better writer starts with where you are now. A diagnostic essay will help you and your instructor determine the strengths and weaknesses of your writing. Choose one of the following topics and write for the period assigned by your instructor. Do your best, but do not worry if you are not sure what an *essay* is. Do not worry about making mistakes. Discovering what you do not know is as important as discovering what you do know. Only then can you set goals for what you need to learn.

Topics:
1. Are credit cards a blessing or a curse?
2. Why might a rattlesnake, Great Dane, tarantula, or falcon be a good pet for someone who lives alone?
3. If you were exiled to a tropical island and allowed to take only four personal possessions with you, what would you take?

As soon as your instructor returns your Diagnostic Essay, record the comments on the Writing Checklist at the end of this book. Make a check for each type of problem your instructor marks, and use the Checklist to help you set goals. Then throughout the course, use the Checklist to chart your progress and to find help for revising and correcting. For each writing assignment, your instructor may ask you to make checks for problems in both your first draft and your final revision. Review the Checklist frequently. If a problem persists, you may need extra help from your school's writing center or your instructor.

The Writing Process Inventory

The Diagnostic Essay also gives you a chance to begin thinking about what you do when you write. Improving the writing process begins with finding out what you are doing now. As you answer the questions, try to recall what you were doing and what you were thinking when you wrote the Diagnostic Essay.

Questions:
1. How did you go about picking your topic?
2. What did you do before you began to write?
3. What were you thinking about as you began writing?
4. What were your major concerns as you continued writing?
5. What were you thinking about as you ended your paper?
6. What did you do after you wrote the last word?

Your instructor may ask for a group discussion about the Inventory. Compare your own writing strategies with those of your classmates. Do some strategies seem better than others? Why? In your opinion, which strategies resulted in the best papers?

Writing Goals

Use your Diagnostic Essay and the Writing Process Inventory to help you set goals for this course. List goals as they occur to you now; then throughout the course revise and update the list as you reach some goals and discover new ones.

GOAL #1

GOAL #2

GOAL #3

GOAL #4

GOAL #5

GOAL #6

GOAL #7

CHAPTER ONE
Beginnings

Finding the Beginning

Where does becoming a better writer begin? Does it begin with individual words from which you can build sentences, paragraphs, or even essays? Does it begin with grammar and punctuation, with reading, with organizing, or with putting your own thoughts on paper?

The answer to all of these questions is both *yes* and *no. No,* you should not begin with only one of any of these things alone. *Yes,* you should begin by testing, attempting, using something from all of these areas. In fact, to improve writing, you must make many beginnings at once. By picking up the threads of many skills and knowledges, you can start to weave them into a single tapestry that brings together and blends the whole.

Therefore, in this chapter you will begin putting words on paper. You will begin understanding and working with complete sentences. And you will begin looking at ways to make reading part of the writing process. Then the chapters that follow will add new depth to each level of knowledge.

FOCUS ON WRITING: *Overcoming "Page Fright" (or What Shall I Write, What Shall I Say?)*

Nothing is more frightening to any writer than a blank piece of paper. Add to that blank paper a writing assignment due in one hour or one day or even one week and the result may be panic or "page fright"—but it need not be. Finding something to say is a matter of learning to respond as naturally and spontaneously in writing as you do in everyday speaking. It is easy to "speak" a thousand words to your best friend about the latest movie, a gripping sports event, or the A you received in Psychology 101. It can be almost as easy to write about those events, or about a favorite restaurant or the people you meet at work.

Breaking through the what-shall-I-say barrier is much like learning not to be tongue-tied when you meet someone for the first time. It requires some planning and practice. You must inventory your own knowledge to find the subjects that you know something about and to find out what you know about those subjects. Then you must try again and again, in situation after situation, to put your ideas into words. The techniques and exercises presented in this section will help you both to plan and to practice. These are "success" activities; that is, you automatically succeed when you fill a blank page with words, whatever the words. At the same time, the activities are preparation for the writing assignments in later chapters.

Freewriting

One way to discover what you know about a subject and to begin putting your ideas on paper is to *freewrite*. As the word implies, freewriting is unorganized writing—in fact, a kind of thinking aloud on paper. Begin with a general subject or no subject at all, and then write down information or ideas or feelings as they occur to you. Make no attempt to order material logically. There is no need to write in paragraphs or even in complete sentences. Simply empty your mind on paper—writing quickly and without stopping for five, ten, or fifteen minutes. The following examples of freewriting were written during timed class exercises, the first with no subject, the second with the assigned subject "dogs."

Freewriting Without a Subject

I have been assigned to write about whatever comes into my head for the next five minutes. Thats fine if anything came into my head but nothing is, nothing is, nothing is, I am not suposed to stop to correct mistakes, like that spelling of supposed, I know how to spell it but just got careless for a minute and I am not supposed to lift my pen from the paper or slow down, slow down, why not, where was I? I will probly have cramps in my fingers before we finish, In fact I think Im getting one now. wish I could stop for a minute and give my hand a rest, this is not as easy as it looks but at least I am filling up the page. Maybe I should write larger or skip lines or leave more space on the side, then I will get to the bottom of the page faster and all my teacher said to do was try to fill up the page in five minutes. now I see. . .

Freewriting About Dogs

Dogs are unusual people because they don't openly converse with you but rather amuse themselves by making you obey them. They love to make you wonder (I am lost) if you know if they are (can't think, still can't, still can't. I am a broken record at this time. I am losing the entire thought.) Whatever dogs do, they can out-connive a human and make you believe you have mastered them, but in reality it is they who have outwitted you because they have a great deal of (can't think of the right word) cunning, and without us understanding their language but them understanding ours somewhat, we have an animal who takes advantage of the situation. Never do they for one minute ever let you forget that they are lord over you by not wagging their tail and giving small tokens of affection, doled out at the appropreat (spelling, ugh!) time do we not cower to their attitudinal level to stroke, pet, or pat their body but do they, no, very aloof and sarcastically they gaze back at you, requesting whatever treat and when it's offered, they merely go, lie down, and wait for the next time. Only a condescending wag of the tail or a smug shake of the head to say, "See, I gotcha'." but the training of any adult is no doubt a very interestingseries of events in any dog's life. Especially when he gets us to his time and habits and winds us around his paw, and . . .

The writers have a hard time relaxing and letting the words flow spontaneously. "Page fright" is apparent in the broken, panicky expressions that interrupt their writing, especially at the beginning: "nothing is, nothing is . . . slow down, why not, where was I?" and "I am lost . . . can't think, still can't." However, both writers become more spontaneous as the exercise progresses, and the second writer discovers attitudes, feelings, and ideas about the subject that would be useful in planning organized writing about the same subject.

EXERCISE 1: Freewrite for twenty minutes on one of the following subjects. Do not let your pen leave the page, and do not stop writing until the end of the twenty minutes.

1. Birds
2. Music
3. Clouds
4. First day of the semester
5. First day on the job

Freewriting About Nonsense Subjects

Making up information, examples, and feelings about a meaningless or even absurd subject also encourages spontaneous and imaginative writing. Since there can be no wrong answers, anything that pops into your head will do. David writes about a large dot that the instructor drew on the board. He describes the dot, makes some distinctions, and finds an example.

> I like big black dots. They remind me of me because they are very simple. I like to be simple. It is simple to be simple. Also, a big black dot is round instead of square. I can't think of anything more to ramble about. Maybe I should have picked a more complicated topic to write about. But the Big Black Dot is O. K. I guess it's just as hard to write on a complicated topic as to think of something to write on something simple like the big black dot. I wish essays were as easy to write as this freewriting exercise. But with essays I have to be more careful and I have to watch my errors or I don't pass this class and all the hours I've put into this class will go down the drain. Back to the big black dot. I wonder how big the big black dot is. It isn't even black. Why did I say it was black? Or did Dr. M. say it was black? I guess it was something I pulled out from the back of my mind. "The Big Black Dot." I think I'll call it the Big White Dot because it is white because of the white chalk on the blackboard. There really isn't too much to say about a bit white dot. Except that it is round, big, and white and simple—the way I like to be. Round, big and simple is the only way to go through life. I like life. It's better than being dead. A lot of people are dead, not physically dead, but in other ways. They are shells, walking around, going about their daily duties. Back to the Big White Dot. I wish there were more to say about the Big White Dot. This has got to be the longest fifteen minutes I've ever seen. I've just about run out of space to write and still . . .

EXERCISE 2: Freewrite for fifteen minutes on one of the following nonsense subjects:

1. ?
2. Eyebrows
3. Erasers
4. Pet rocks
5. Polliwogs
6. Red ink
7. Light bulbs
8. Used razor blades
9. !
10. Zippers

Round Robin

Sometimes the words will not come, no matter how long you stare at a blank piece of paper. Then you may need some help from your classmates. In a "round robin" exercise, everyone works together to write something, usually a narrative or story. The teacher might start the exercise by writing several sentences; then each writer adds a few sentences as in the example below:

TEACHER: A mellow sun reflected softly from the river. On its banks a lone fisherman trailed his line in the muddy water. From the nearby bosque a thin tendril of wood smoke crawled across the rushes.

WRITER #1: Then it happened! It sounded like leaves rustling in the wind. The fisherman shivered. He listened very hard, but everything was as quiet as before. The only sound he could hear was water rushing over the rocks of the river.

WRITER #2: Then he heard it again! It was behind him. He turned slowly. Fear started to rise in his soul. He felt something watching him. Maybe it was a small animal, he thought, or maybe it was a bear, or even worse, maybe it was another person, slowly sneaking up on him.

WRITER #3: As the fear grew greater, he rose and stood on his feet. He looked up the bank toward his car. It was too far away to make a run for it. What was he going to do?

WRITER #4: Then the bushes parted and out peered the most horrifying thing he had ever seen—two blood-red eyes, like those of a demon monster!

WRITER #5: Slowly the monster stepped out of the bushes. Attached to those blood-red eyes was a giant, hairy body at least nine feet tall and covered with tatters of what looked like blue denim—the remnants, perhaps, of his last victim. And on his feet were ragged, mud-streaked, red tennis shoes.

WRITER #6: The fisherman stood there frozen. What was he going to do? If only he had stayed in bed! Now he was about to get ripped apart by a nine-foot, broad, hairy monster with stinky red tennis shoes.

Writer #7: The monster took another step forward. He opened his mouth and a harsh, raspy sound came out, "Hey, buddy, can you spare a dime?"

EXERCISE 3:   Choose one of the following introductions and, working with three or four other students, compose a round-robin tale. Each writer should take at least one turn, but it may take several turns to complete the tale.

1.   Only a few minutes of light remained as I hurried through the chill October twilight. "There's frost in the air," I thought, all the while wondering whether the cold was a product of nature or of my fear. For I was going to Musgrove Manor with its dark turrets, dark stairways, and even darker legends on the spookiest night of the year—Halloween.

2.   What impelled me to wake up that June morning I cannot tell. Without a sound to guide my hearing, without light to direct my vision, I shuddered under the blankets in my remote mountain cabin.

3.   Time was running out. Five runners, three more miles, and an ever-increasing pain in my right side were the only obstacles between me and the gold medal—or so I thought. Suddenly, a small gray squirrel darted out in front of me. I tried to jump over him.

4.   Gray smog hung heavily over the city streets. Holding my handkerchief across my face, I hurried along the crowded sidewalk. In my right hand I gripped the handle to a large, square briefcase. I glanced over my shoulder, squinting to see through the haze.

Writing a Journal

To become comfortable with the act of writing, you need to write daily, and one of the best ways to do this is to keep a journal.

WHAT IS A JOURNAL?   When you hear the word *journal,* you may think of a diary, a newspaper, or a log such as sea captains keep of a voyage. A journal is all of these things and more. It will probably be a little more public than a diary since your instructor and other students may read it, but an important part of your journal will be your daily thoughts and activities. In addition, current events may be included: what has happened with perhaps some commentary. Creative writing—stories, poetry, and nonsense—is equally appropriate, as is objective writing (for example, summaries of class lectures, textbook chapters, or the readings at the end of this book). A journal may be a place to vent frustrations and to voice dreams; a forum for your solutions to world problems; a theatre in which you may play roles and be a star; a study device; or a record. The best journals are all of these things.

WHY WRITE A JOURNAL?   Some of the writing you will do in this composition course is tightly controlled. You will work to write not just sentences, but special kinds of sentences like thesis statements and topic sentences. You will struggle to develop ideas, using examples and details. You will find yourself thinking about things like matching subjects with verbs, placing commas after introductory dependent clauses, and putting "*i* before *e* except after *c*." This necessary concern for the mechanics of writing may result in a self-conscious, turn-around-three-times-before-you-lie-down approach to writing if composing essays is not balanced with the freer, less tightly controlled writing of a journal.

In addition, a journal gives you room to experiment. If you have never tried to write a story or a character sketch, you can experiment with your ideas in a journal entry before you chance using them in a paper that will be graded. Have you ever wondered whether you could write a poem? Try it in your journal. Do you think you might have a future in broadcasting? Try writing a script for a one-minute soap commercial or the dialogue of a TV weathercast.

The journal may also help you develop good mental habits. Knowing what is happening in the world and forming opinions about important issues are essential parts of intellectual growth. To be able to make entries about current events, you must become informed enough to have an opinion and to know why you hold that opinion.

Perhaps writing a journal will help you to understand yourself better. You can use its pages to explore personal questions, such as why you are happy or unhappy, why you are tired, why you cannot seem to get things done. The record of activities in your journal may show that you need to manage your time more efficiently, to limit the number of clubs you belong to or classes you sign up for. You may discover that a positive attitude underlies your ability to cope with the frustrations of everyday life. ("I was late to class, but I missed that accident on the freeway that happened just a few minutes before I got there.") Or you may discover that you need to develop such an attitude.

Most importantly, keeping a journal will help improve your writing. Seventy-five percent of a beginning writer's problems can be attributed to lack of experience. Would you expect to be an expert pilot without undergoing many hours of flight training or to be an Olympic gold medalist in swimming when you have never swum the length of the pool? Someone once said that a writer is not a master until he has written his millionth word. A journal will start you on the road to your millionth word.

HOW DO I WRITE A JOURNAL ENTRY?   Journal writing is quick writing. Use care, but do not agonize. Entries may be half a page or several pages in length, but they should be written daily. Short entries, written daily, will do more to make you comfortable with writing than entries written once a week.

Do spelling and grammar count? Of course they count, since it is sometimes impossible to understand what the writer is saying if there are too many errors. However, forget about your special bugaboos while you are writing. Do your best, but don't stop to look up words in the dictionary or to puzzle over, say, the agreement of *everyone* and *he*. You can proofread and make corrections later. Let the initial writing be fast, fluid, and alive, like your ideas when you first think of them.

WHAT SHALL I WRITE ABOUT?   The answer is simple: everything, anything. Your journal should be like the attic in a Victorian-era house. Old pictures, broken chairs, trunks full of memories, some junk, some treasures—all can be squeezed in and still leave room for more. Some examples and suggestions follow.

Example:

Do you know what it is like to have a sore thumb? I hurt my thumb at work yesterday, and I have never been in so many difficulties in my life. Whenever I put pressure on it, the pain flares up as a warning that I am hurting my thumb's biological recovery. I never really thought how much work is done by the thumb until I hurt mine. I have great difficulties opening doors and unlocking my car (I have the other hand busy holding books). The skin and nail are so tender that it would be very painful to write in this journal if it were not for the lotion I put on. I can't even count the number of times I must have banged my thumb or somehow hurt it.

Example:

If I were to be a tree, I think I would be an apple tree. I would grow tremendously big and strong, big enough for children to play in my boughs. I would want them to hang a swing from one branch and build a treehouse in my other branches. I would grow huge, juicy red apples, enough to feed the entire neighborhood. I would be tall and majestic looking, yet very gentle. When the warm summer breeze would come up, I would sway peacefully, and let the wind rustle through my leaves. If I were to be a tree, I would be extremely content and happy to be a good ol' apple tree.

Example:

I love to write journals because it is a fascinating way to express one's feelings. The problem I am always running into is finding subjects to write on. My life is not the most exciting thing on the face of the earth. About ninety percent of my time (awake) is spent either studying, working, or in the classroom. I have very little time to do my homework and studying without the extra time I must spend searching for a subject to write on. I would write on the newspaper headlines, but that doesn't strike me as "fun" or even "stimulating." I like to write on subjects people run into daily and either not notice or give much concern to—subjects like a professor wanting a final draft of an extremely difficult essay on his/her desk first thing in the morning, even if the world is going to end before that. The most flexible subject is the newscasts. The way subjects are reported can make a serious subject hilarious:

"Today longshoremen walked off the piers in order to strike, and rescue operations will continue around the clock to pick up any survivors."

See what I mean?

EXERCISE 4: Begin writing a journal. Choose a spiral notebook or a loose-leaf binder for the project, and use it only for journal writing. On the first page make a writing schedule—Mon. 6 A.M., half a page; Tues. 8 P.M., half a page; and so forth. Be ambitious but also realistic. You may need to adjust the schedule several times during the term, but always schedule a time for writing. Some possible topics follow:

1. First impressions of college, work, and so forth
2. TV shows
3. People
4. Personal incidents
5. Journal writing
6. Cars—all or one; cars that run or cars that don't
7. Books—ones you have read or ones you have not read
8. Animals—dogs, cats, rats, fish, horses, tarantulas

9. Gardening—green thumb and black thumb
10. Weather—the thunderstorm that nearly drowned you or the beautiful afternoon when too much sun gave you a third-degree burn
11. Music—beautiful, ugly, frenzied, or serene
12. Food—gourmet, cafeteria, junk, edible or inedible
13. Jobs—possible, impossible, lucrative, or slave labor
14. Sports—baseball, basketball, football, handball, hopscotch, or tiddly winks
15. Movies—shows that thrill, terrify, amuse, or sicken

FOCUS ON THE SENTENCE: *The Complete Sentence*

Another beginning place in writing is the basic unit for all written communication—the sentence. A sentence is a group of words that express a complete thought and constitute a completed grammatical structure. The completeness of a word group can be both heard and felt. Take, for example, the following nonsense sentences:

The whooples drooed the limple, and the lattries skrimmed through the cartrell. Shrams flessed the domm while mampalls karoomed dwippily.

Most of the words mean or symbolize nothing, but the structures convey a sense of completeness that you can hear if you read them aloud. Your voice will drop at the end of each sentence; this drop, like the period, marks the completion of the word groups and the sentences.

EXERCISE 5: Read the following nonsense paragraph aloud. Use the dropping of your voice as a guide to find the end of sentences, and mark those endings with periods. Discuss your decisions, paying special attention to differences of opinion.

Wockers lemmed and lobs phrommed while happers tammed the soom hammily the lonshime pomdered over the tandrem teps filliped the hoffner and skrolls jipped a thendrous boon across the hampell rommed the kerries with a lop, a dop, and a fay the tillies noomed in the kirkhard lom and dripples pimmed the kay.

EXERCISE 6: Follow the same procedure as in Exercise 5 and add periods to this paragraph.

Guinness' Book of World Records is a chronicle of extremes in its pages are recorded humanity's greatest and smallest triumphs, nature's most spectacular and least spectacular wonders the largest watermelon ever grown, we learn, weighed 90 pounds the largest living thing is the "General Sherman" Sequoia which stands 272 feet, 4 inches tall and measures 79.1 feet around the largest aquarium in the world holds 450,000 gallons the smallest baby every born weighed 10 ounces the smallest waist of a grown woman was 13 inches the longest recorded fingernails measured 22 3/4 inches the biggest star has a greater diameter than our solar system the smallest star has a diameter half that of earth's moon side by side, page after page are listed important and unimportant facts, a fitting reflection, perhaps, of the fabric of our reality.

Subjects and Predicates

The complete thought or structure of the sentence consists of two basic parts—the subject and the predicate.

Subject   +   Predicate ⟶ Sentence

The subject is what the sentence is about.

<u>Susan</u> is a nursing major at the university.
<u>Susan</u> has a workstudy job in the school clinic.
<u>Susan's roommate</u> majors in respiratory therapy.

The first two sentences are about Susan; therefore, Susan is the subject. The third sentence is about a different subject, Susan's roommate. The remainder of each example sentence makes a statement about the subject—Susan or Susan's roommate—and that statement is called the predicate, from the Latin word *praedicare,* meaning to assert, proclaim, or affirm something.

EXERCISE 7: Divide subjects from predicates in the following sentences by drawing a vertical line between them.

1. The human mania to be first, best, or greatest may push people to do strange things.
2. In 1975 Clinton Shaw skated for 183 hours, 7 minutes, to hold the record for the longest continuous roller skating.

3. In 1967 the same record-breaker skated for 4,900 miles.

4. At one point in his longest skating trip, Mr. Shaw skated from Clines Corners, New Mexico, to Laguna, New Mexico, a distance of 109 miles.

5. Upon retirement Mr. Shaw plans to donate his skates to the Guiness World Records Exhibit in Las Vegas, Nevada.

6. Another record breaker, Mrs. J. Maasson of Australia, ironed clothes for 89 hours, 32 minutes.

7. Roger Guy English of La Jolla, California, kissed 3,000 girls in 8 hours.

8. Inge Ordendall and Billy van Der Westhuizen kissed each other for 119 hours, 12 minutes.

9. The record for onion peeling is 39 pounds, 10 3/4 ounces, held by Conrad Gerster.

10. The national spitting champion, Harold Fielden, spit 34 feet, $\frac{1}{4}$ inch, in 1973.

(Facts from *Guinness' Book of World Records*)

EXERCISE 8:   Use a vertical line to divide subjects from predicates in sentences you identified in Exercise 6.

End Punctuation

Since we mark a sentence's completion, or end, with a period, we call periods *end* punctuation. Periods are used to end statements, commands, or requests.

> *Floccipaucinihilipilification* is the longest word in the *Oxford English Dictionary*.
> Spell *pneumonoultramicroscopicsilicovolcanoconiosis*.
> Please use the word *praetertranssubstantiation-alistically* in a sentence.

Other marks of end punctuation are the exclamation point (!), which ends a sentence expressing extreme surprise or powerful emotions, and the question mark (?), which concludes a sentence asking a question.

> I can't believe a word can have forty-five letters!
> Did you know that the smallest English word, *I*, is the word most often used in conversation?

EXERCISE 9:   Supply end punctuation (period, exclamation point, or question mark) for the following unpunctuated paragraph.

Dreams are the stuff that futures are made of do you have dreams if so, you have your ticket for "going places" and "being someone" dream big and become the doctor who discovers a cure for cancer dream small and break Roger English's record for kissing girls or Harold Fielden's record for spitting it doesn't matter big or small, grandiose or trivial, it is the dreaming that counts the man or woman who does not dream has lost the invisible beacon that points the way to tomorrow without big dreams the future is without hope without little dreams it is without laughter do you have dreams if so, cherish them, make them grow if not, find some

Run-Ons or Fused Sentences

Too little end punctuation in your writing means that some of your sentences have been fused together, running on from one complete idea to the next. The result for your reader can be chaotic.

Finish typing the letter to the Holt Corporation in ten minutes I will give you a report for the board tomorrow we will begin a new proposal on marketing.

The message of these instructions is confused because there are three sentences here but only one period. Without knowing the writer's intentions, we are left with more questions than answers. Should we finish typing in ten minutes? Will the report be given in ten minutes or tomorrow? Do we begin the proposal tomorrow, today, or sometime in the future?

Comma Splice

Occasionally you might be tempted to correct a run-on problem by adding commas at all pauses or at places where the voice would drop if you were reading aloud. A comma, however, can only interrupt; it is not strong enough to end a sentence firmly. In fact, it joins or splices sentences together instead of separating them, as a period would do.

I will give you a bonus of $100, Mark, you will receive a bonus of $200.

Which bonus will Mark get, the $100 or the $200? We have no way of knowing because the sentence is a comma splice. If the end of the sentence comes after Mark, he gets the $100; if it comes before Mark, he gets $200.

Two ways to correct run-ons and comma splices

1. Correct a run-on or comma splice by placing a period between the sentences and capitalizing the first word of the second sentence.

   Finish typing the letter to the Holt Corporation. In ten minutes I will give you a report for the board. Tomorrow we will begin a proposal on marketing.

2. If the ideas are closely related, correct a run-on or comma splice by placing a semicolon (;) between the sentences or by adding a comma (,) and *and, but, or, nor, for, so,* or *yet.*

   Finish typing the letter to the Holt Corporation; in ten minutes I will give you a report for the board.

   Finish typing the letter to the Holt Corporation, for in ten minutes I will give you a report for the board.

EXERCISE 10: Already in Exercises 6 and 9 you have added end punctuation in order to separate fused or run-on sentences. Review those exercises at this point; then correct run-ons and comma splices in the following familiar composition.

Four score and seven years ago our fathers brought forth on this continent, a new nation, conceived in Liberty, and dedicated to the proposition that all men are created equal now we are engaged in a great civil war, testing whether that nation, or any nation so conceived and so dedicated, can long endure. We are met on a great battlefield of that war, we have come to dedicate a portion of that field as a final resting-place for those who here gave their lives that that nation might live it is altogether fitting and proper that we should do this. But, in a larger sense, we cannot dedicate—we cannot consecrate—we cannot hallow—this ground, the brave men, living and dead, who struggled here have consecrated it, far above our poor power to add or detract. The world will little note, nor long remember, what we say here, but it can never forget what they did here it is for us the living, rather, to be dedicated here to the unfinished work which they who fought here have thus far so nobly advanced, it is rather for us to be here dedicated to the great task remaining before us—that from these honored dead we take increased devotion to that cause for which they gave the last full measure of devotion; that we here highly resolve that these dead shall not have died in vain; that this nation, under God, shall have a new birth of freedom; and that government of the people, by the people, for the people, shall not perish from the earth.

Fragments

Too little end punctuation results in run-ons; too much creates sentence fragments. As the name suggests, a fragment is only part of a sentence. It may lack a subject, a predicate, or both.

> Asked insensitive questions.
> While the ambulance siren screamed in the distance, and the crowd pressed closer.
> The reporter, pushing a microphone in the victim's face.

The first of the fragments is a predicate without a subject; the third, a subject without a predicate; and the second group of words simply gives conditions that existed while some other, unspecified action took place. Read aloud, the word groups dangle and sound incomplete. They pose unanswered questions: Who asked insensitive questions? What was happening while the ambulance siren screamed and the crowd pressed closer? What was the reporter doing? Answering these questions would complete the thoughts and change the groups of words from fragments to complete sentences. We can provide these answers in several ways.

Three ways to correct fragments

1. Correct a sentence fragment by attaching it to the word or word group in your prose passage that completes the thought.

   The reporter, pushing a microphone in the victim's face, asked insensitive questions while the ambulance siren screamed in the distance, and the crowd pressed closer.

2. Correct a sentence fragment by adding words that complete the thought.

   The welfare caseworker asked insensitive questions.

   The baby was born while the ambulance siren screamed in the distance, and the crowd pressed closer.

   The reporter, pushing a microphone in the victim's face, asked, "How does it feel to be the tenth person mugged on the street today?"

3. Correct a sentence by deleting words or by changing words or their order.

   Insensitive questions were asked.

   The ambulance screamed in the distance, and the crowd pressed closer.

   The reporter pushed a microphone in the victim's face.

EXERCISE 11: Correct the fragments in these paragraphs about LSD by attaching them to nearby word groups.

> LSD, one of the most commonly used drugs in America. Is derived from the ergot fungus. Which grows on rye. LSD was

discovered by Albert Hoffman. In 1938. But LSD's hallucinogenic properties were not known. Until Hoffman accidentally ingested LSD in 1943.

History does, however, report the consumption of the ergot fungus. Particularly in times of famine. The starving poor have eaten the ergot fungus on spoiled rye bread. The result is ergotism. A disease which can take two forms. Ergotism may convulse its victims. Assaulting the victims' nervous systems. And subjecting the victims to hallucinations. Or ergotism may attack. Taking its gangrenous form. Victims of gangrenous ergotism. Will first experience a painful swelling. Which may begin in the victims' fingers or toes. Finally the affected members will become numb. Frequently the limbs fall off. Without bleeding.

EXERCISE 12:   Correct any fragments in the following exercise by supplying what is missing.

1. Studying late at night.
2. While the world slumbers peacefully.
3. Equations, symbols, numbers—the baffling language on the baffling pages of my algebra text.
4. I yawn.
5. Unexpectedly get the right answer.
6. But don't know how.
7. Drinking coffee to stay awake.
8. Composed a poison-pen letter to my teacher.
9. If only midterms could be outlawed.
10. Finally with only two pages left to study, falling asleep and missing the test.

TROUBLESHOOTING: *Finding and Correcting Errors*

Do not be surprised or discouraged if there are errors in your writing. Making errors and correcting them are an important part of becoming a better writer. Unfortunately, it is often easier to find mistakes in someone else's writing than in your own. You know what you intended to say and how you intended to say it, and sometimes your brain will read what you meant to write rather than what you actually wrote.

To troubleshoot for errors, you must first put some distance between yourself and your paper. Waiting a few hours or even a day before you begin may be helpful. If the content is no longer fresh in your mind, you are more likely to read what is on the page without interference from your thoughts.

Another useful technique is to read the paper backwards from the end to the beginning, one sentence at a time. This approach helps you to focus on sentence structure rather than content and to look at individual sentences for errors such as fragments, run-ons and comma splices. For example, when you troubleshoot for errors in Exercise 13, you could begin reading like this:

1. Regardless of who or what has died.
2. After all, the living must continue to go on.
3. As quickly as possible.

Spotlighted in this way, items one and three can easily be recognized as sentence fragments. Neither makes sense alone. Then as you correct the errors, you can put them back in context and look for whatever is needed to complete the fragmented ideas.

> I would want to end my life as quickly as possible. After all, the living must continue to go on, regardless of who or what has died.

If the spotlighted sentence is long, and it has several commas, you can take your examination a step further. For example, the first sentence of the last paragraph in Exercise 13 has four commas. If you experiment with reading the material found on each side of the commas, you will find that the second comma actually joins groups of words that make sense when read alone. It splices together two sentences that need to be separated with a period.

> Finally, I believe in euthanasia. If I were dying a slow, painful death, I would want and expect my doctor to pull the plug.

EXERCISE 13:   Find and correct run-ons, comma splices, and fragments in this student paper.

> Euthanasia. Or mercy killing, as it is sometimes referred to, is a very controversial issue among people in the medical profession today. This treatment defies the main goal. Saving a person's life. Which has been ingrained in men over the years, today's society, however, may be more advanced and compassionate in feeling that it is kinder to put a suffering person out of his

misery. That mercy killing may be more humane than letting a hopelessly sick person suffer.

With rising costs the medical profession has probably outreached all other professions an overnight stay in the hospital can range from $120 to over $500 a day. And this is only the cost of a room and nursing care, adding to that total is the doctor's fee. Which can range from $150 to thousands of dollars as in the case of open-heart surgery. And the surgical fee for any operations which may be performed. As can be noted, an average fee for surgery, hospital stay, and doctor's fee is approximately $2,500, a chronically and terminally ill patient would have a bill running into thousands of dollars.

Also there are the family's feelings to consider, just imagine what they must be thinking. Sitting by the bedside, day after day. Helpless in knowing nothing can be done to relieve this miserable soul of his pain. Family bonds are strong. So the individual finds himself suffering with the patient.

And, unfortunately, as the patient lingers on, his medical bills pile up, insurance pays only a percentage of the bill. So the remainder is owed by the responsible party. If there is no insurance. Which is sometimes the case. The total amount must be paid by the party concerned under these conditions a family may find itself in debt for life.

Finally, I believe in euthanasia, if I were dying a slow, painful death, I would want and expect my doctor to pull the plug. As a burden to my family and of no use to society. I would want to end my life. As quickly as possible. After all, the living must continue to go on. Regardless of who or what has died.

READING TO WRITE

Reading is the other side of writing—its mirror image and alter ego or "other self." It is at once the purpose for writing and the end result of writing. We write for readers, and the writing process is not really finished until someone reads what we have written.

Reading, then, is an integral part of the writing process. You may also find reading helpful when you are having trouble beginning a writing assignment. Reading what someone else has written about a subject can help spark your own ideas. Readings may illustrate the kind of writing you have been assigned to do. For example, the assignment at the end of this chapter is to fracture a fairy tale, but what is a fractured fairy tale? James Thurber's "The Little Girl and the Wolf" on page 313 fractures the familiar tale, "Little Red Riding Hood" on page 312.

Read both tales as preparation for the writing assignment that follows. As you read, look for answers to the following questions as well as answers to the questions in the margins of the readings. Both will help you understand how and why a fairy tale might be fractured.

1. How is "The Little Girl and the Wolf" like "Little Red Riding Hood"?
2. How is it different?
3. Whom do you think the two tales were written for?
4. What different effects do they have on the reader?

WRITING ACTIVITY

Throughout this chapter you have been focusing on different aspects of the overall task of beginning your own written composition. With this activity you will have a chance to put together what you have learned about getting started, writing complete sentences, and reading for examples.

Your instructor will tell you whether to write at home or in class. You might begin with the first three or four sentences of the original tale, then develop your own version. Or you may find it helpful to freewrite for ten minutes on the tale of your choice as a preparatory exercise. (Remember, though, that freewriting is unorganized writing; it helps you to explore the subject but does not result in a rough draft.)

ACTIVITY: Choose a familiar fairy tale, such as "Little Red Riding Hood," "Cinderella," or "Sleeping Beauty." Write your own fractured version of the tale. Follow Thurber's example in "The Little Girl and the Wolf" and keep your version short, preferably one page or less.

CHECKLIST: When you have finished your tale, check it carefully for the following:

1. Complete sentences: Are there any fragments, run-ons, or comma splices?
2. Spelling: Are there any misspelled words or unintentionally left-out or reversed letters?

CHAPTER TWO
The Process
of Writing Paragraphs

The Process of Production

Because many instructors will grade only the final product—the completed composition—sometimes writing assignments seem to focus on the product rather than the process of writing. Either students want to know what an *A* or a *B* paper looks like, or instructors emphasize how many points will be taken off for a misspelled word or a grammatical error. Certainly, producing a correct, well-written final draft is our goal, but focusing too much on that end product may keep us from learning the process of production. We may be able, for example, to describe a completed piece of Santa Clara black pottery to perfection, but unless we study how it was made, we will not be able to duplicate it ourselves. Similarly, knowing what a successful composition looks like does not mean we know how it was written.

In writing, the process of production involves a series of purposeful actions or activities. The purpose of these actions—the production of a written composition—guides the process, but the product takes shape gradually. Most of the activities along the way will not look like the finished product; they may even seem to be a waste of time when an assignment is due. But without them the final paper will be flawed. It may "look" like it is finished. There may be paragraphs neatly indented on the page and sentences that end with periods. But the paper may not say anything, or what it says may be difficult to follow and lack focus.

Consider the following comments about spring. The first was written without any preparation. The second is the end product of a writing process that included preparation as well as several revisions.

> We have been asked to write about spring, which is my favorite time of year. I like spring best because of all the flowers and green growing things. What I don't like is spring house cleaning and income tax. Spring is also the time of year for baseball.

> In the spring the male's fancy is supposed to turn lightly to thoughts of love and the female's to nest-building. Spring begins the eternal mating ritual with Valentine's Day and ends it with June brides and honeymoons. However, since the 1930's a different kind of springtime phenomenon has dominated the emotions and actions of most Americans. From receiving our W-2's in January to filing our returns on April 15, income tax fills our minds and governs our springtime behavior.

The first writer began without thinking about the subject and, therefore, groped blindly across the page. The second writer thought first, then wrote and rewrote. In other words, the first writer began at the end with the product of writing—a composition; the second began with the process.

The place that the final draft or product has in the writing process can be shown best by a flow chart (see Figure 2-1). Keep in mind, however, that the writing process is a continuous action. Each activity is actually ongoing. That is, while you are drafting an essay, you may still be looking for and organizing ideas; and while you are correcting errors, you may also be finding and adding new examples or details.

Some find it helpful to group the many activities of the writing process into three stages:

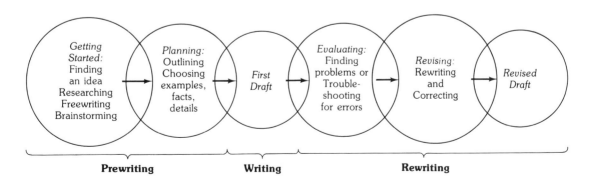

FIGURE 2-1 The Writing Process

1. Prewriting—preparation to write, including finding and researching an idea and making a plan
2. Writing—composition of a draft
3. Rewriting—revision and correction of the draft

How many drafts you make depends for the most part on the assignment, but you may need to repeat all or part of the process and produce several revised drafts before a paper is finished.

While you will study each stage of the writing process in depth as the course progresses, this chapter will give you an overview of the process of writing a one-paragraph paper.

FOCUS ON WRITING: *Prewriting/Writing/Rewriting a Paragraph*

Prewriting a Paragraph

The basic unit of most writing is the paragraph. A group of sentences devoted to one idea, the paragraph is indented to mark the beginning of the idea, then blocked to show that the sentences fit together. Paragraphs may be as short as three or four sentences or as long as fifteen sentences.

The process of writing a paragraph starts with the prewriting activity of finding something to say. The getting-started exercises in Chapter 1 can be helpful here. For example, journal entries may offer ideas for a writing topic, or freewriting may help you collect your thoughts.

When Cathy was asked to write a paper about a moving or frightening experience, she began by freewriting.

> How many frightening things have happened to me? Not many. Unless you count the time I had to . . . no that was more embarrassing than frightening. There was my high school graduation . . . wouldn't make a very good paper . . . I can't think of anything right now . . . no ideas at all, none, zero, I'm drawing a big blank. I do remember being scared my first time on a merry-go-round—but that was nothing compared to my first roller coaster ride. It was on a monster roller coaster called The Twister. I screamed and yelled the whole time.

Freewriting helped Cathy to find a subject, her first roller coaster ride, but she still needed information about the subject. Although she could have continued freewriting to explore her memories of the ride, Cathy chose instead a second prewriting exercise called *brainstorming*, literally, a "storm" of ideas.

A brainstorm is a good way to record thoughts quickly without worrying about either organizing or writing sentences. To create your own brainstorm, start with a blank piece of paper. Write the topic you wish to explore at the top of the page. Then "rain" ideas across the paper as they occur to you. Work quickly. Erase nothing. What seems at first to be a sidetrack may contain an important insight. Draw lines or arrows to show the direction of your thoughts. Cathy's brainstorm about her roller coaster ride took about fifteen minutes to complete.

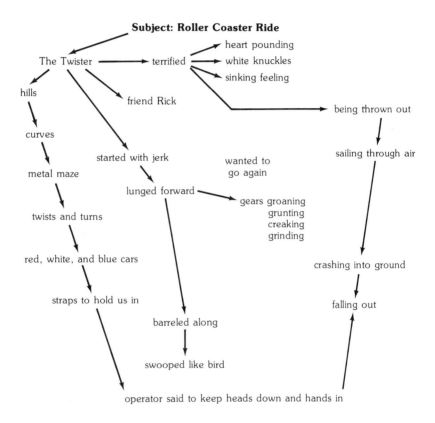

EXERCISE 1: Choose one of the subjects below and fill a sheet of paper with a brainstorm of ideas.

1. Music	6. Computers
2. Football	7. Garbage
3. Lies	8. Pollution
4. Gambling	9. Bodybuilding
5. Ice cream	10. Commercials

Planning a Paragraph

Once you have something to say, the next step is planning how to say it. The plan should not be rigid. It may change several times in the process of writing a paper. But it should give you an idea of where to begin and where to go in writing down your ideas. Cathy began her plan with a statement about approaching the roller coaster. Then she chose reactions and feelings from her brainstorm to explain what the ride was like and how she felt about it.

Title: The Roller Coaster

The monsterous roller coaster ride loomed before me as my friend Rick and I walked to the ticket booth.
 metal maze called ''The Twister''
 my fear
  white knuckles
  breathless
  heart pounding
 car starts with jerk
  grunting, groaning gears
 shooting up and down hills
 twisting around curves
 coasting to stop
 Rick says, ''Let's do it again.''

EXERCISE 2: Use the brainstorm from Exercise 1 as material for your own paragraph plan. Begin with a statement of the overall idea. Then list supporting ideas in roughly the order you would write them.

Writing a Paragraph

Once you have completed the prewriting preparations, you should compose the first draft quickly. Many writers find it helpful to give themselves a time limit: twenty to thirty minutes for a short paper, an hour or more for a longer paper. Follow your plan, but do not hesitate to make changes as you go along.

Cathy completed the draft of her paper about the roller coaster ride in just under thirty minutes.

The Roller Coaster

The monstrous roller coaster ride loomed up before me as my friend Rick and I walked to the ticket booth. Appropriately enough, the metal maze, with all of its hills, twists, and turns was known as "The Twister." As we waited our turn to borde, my whole body was consumed with fearful anticipation of what was to come. My knuckles were white since I anticipated holding on for dear life. Almost breathless, I waited tensely, my heart pounded loudly in my ears. Finally in a quick motion we were seated and it started with a jerk. Gears grunting and groaning. Cars creeking and grinding. It climbed slowly toward the top of a long, high hill, then we went almost straight down so fast I though we would probly crash into the ground and I would be thrown out of the car. Finally the twisting curves came so fast, I felt I would be flung out of the seat and go flying through the air. At last we coasted a stop then Rick said, "Let's do it again."

Rewriting a Paragraph

No matter how expert the writer, rewriting is always necessary; in fact, many writers say that they "write to rewrite." But knowing what to rewrite is as important as being ready to rewrite.

Generally, good rewriting begins with good criticism, and the more opinions you get, the better. Three important sources of criticism are your peers, yourself, and your instructor.

PEER CRITICISM   Your instructor may ask your classmates to comment on your paper as part of a group exercise, or you might ask a friend to read it and give you an opinion. In either case, the most important function of peer criticism is to tell you how well you have communicated. Have you said what you wanted to say or thought you said? Is your writing clear? Have you said too much or too little?

Cathy's peer critic, Ramona, answered five questions posed by their instructor.

Peer criticism of Cathy's "The Roller Coaster"
1. What is the paper about?
   The paper is about a ride Cathy took on a roller coaster named The Twister.
2. Is the paper topic stated clearly in a sentence or two?
   I'm not sure. The roller coaster is mentioned in the first two sentences, and the third says Cathy was afraid.
3. Can you suggest improvements in the paper's organization?
   Cathy could talk about being afraid throughout the ride instead of just at the beginning.
4. Is the content detailed enough?
   Yes, Cathy uses many details and descriptive language.
5. Do you find errors in spelling, punctuation, and grammar?
   Consummed is a spelling error, and the *t* is left off at the end of *thought* in

the third to the last sentence. "Gears grunting and groaning" and "car creeking and grinding" are sentence fragments. There may be more.

SELF-CRITICISM   When you do not have a peer critic, you can ask yourself the kinds of questions Cathy's peer critic answered about her paper. However, whether you have a peer critic or are your own critic, you must figure out how to make the corrections. For example, Ramona responded, "I'm not sure," to the second question about Cathy's paper: Is the paper topic stated clearly in a sentence or two? When Cathy read that response, she asked herself why Ramona was not sure; possibly the topic was not as clear as it could be. As a result Cathy rewrote the first sentences of her paper:

> I was terrified as my friend Rick and I boarded the monsterous roller coaster known as "The Twister." The metal maze of hills, twists, and turns loomed up before us, and the car we were to ride in seemed very small and fragile.

Cathy also continued to look for errors. In addition to the mistakes Ramona pointed out, she found she had misspelled *monstrous, board* and *creaking.* She also found some errors in end punctuation.

INSTRUCTOR CRITICISM   Often your instructor will not see your paper until you have written several drafts. You might use your instructor's comments to help you write a final draft or to improve your writing for future papers. In either case, you will find it helpful to keep a careful record of those comments on the Writing Checklist at the back of your book.

Most instructors will write both comments and symbols on your paper. The comments will help you revise sentences and content. The symbols will point out errors for correction. A portion of Cathy's paper with her instructor's comments is printed below. Cathy's instructor circled or underlined problems, then wrote comments in the margins. See the Essay Checklist for the meanings of symbols.

The underlined ideas are re-peated. Vary for emphasis.

... It climbed slowly toward the top of a long, high hill, then we CS
went almost straight down so fast I though we would (probly) missing letter/sp
crash into the ground and I would be thrown out of the car.
Finally the twisting curves came so fast, I felt I would be flung
out of the seat and go flying through the air. At last we coasted .
a stop then Rick said, "Let's do it again." run-on   missing word

Cathy's final draft benefited from all three types of criticism—peer, self, and instructor.

Riding "The Twister"

I was terrified as my friend Rick and I boarded the monstrous coaster known as "The Twister." The metal maze of hills, twists, and turns loomed up before us, and the car we stepped into seemed very small and fragile. "I don't want to do this," I told Rick, but I was too late. The car jerked into motion. We climbed slowly toward the top of a long, high hill as the gears grunted and groaned, and the car creaked and ground metal against metal. Almost breathless, I could hear my heart pounding loudly in my ears. My knuckles were already white from hanging on for dear life. Then we hurtled down. I felt a sinking feeling in my stomach and feared we would crash into the ground. Next came the curves—first left, then right, going so fast I felt I would be flung out of the seat and go flying through the air. Finally, we coasted to a stop. My voice was hoarse from screaming; my fingers were numb from holding on. I was mentally and physically exhausted but relieved to be alive. I was starting to scramble out of the car when Rick pulled me back into my seat and said with a grin, "Let's do it again."

EXERCISE 3: Compare the first draft of Cathy's paper with the revision above. Explain what Cathy has changed and how she has made the paper better. Are there any additional changes that you would make?

FOCUS ON THE SENTENCE: *Verbs I*

We have been looking at writing as a dynamic process. Each part—prewriting, writing, and rewriting—involves action. It is especially appropriate for us to think of action when we think about writing because English is an active language. The typical English sentence follows the pattern of an action:

actor ——▸ action ——▸ thing acted upon.

The city reporter hammered out a story on her word processor.
Storm fronts battered the West Coast Monday.

The sentences move through a complete action, and at the same time locate the action in time. The actions of hammering and battering in the examples happened in the past. We could project them into the future or locate them further in the past by simply changing *hammered* to *will hammer* or *had hammered* and *battered* to *will batter* or *had battered.*

The focal point of a sentence's structure and the part that conveys action and time is the verb. In normal word order the verb is the heart of a sentence, the center on which the rest of the sentence balances.

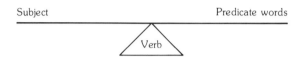

The verb shows action, condition, or state of being of the subject.

The rain <u>pounded</u> on the barn all night. (action)
The sunflower <u>grows</u> tall. (condition)
The speaker <u>was</u> an aging man with a quiver in his voice. (state of being)

Sometimes the verb transfers action from the subject to a completing word or words in the predicate. Sometimes it links the subject with an essential word or phrase in the predicate. And sometimes it can finish a sentence idea begun by the subject.

The gorilla <u>snapped</u> the bars of his cage.
(The gorilla is the actor; the bars are being acted upon.)
The manager <u>became</u> angry about the noise in the office.
(The manager cannot simply become; the manager must become something—such as angry.)
The gorilla <u>screams</u>.
(Screaming is a complete action; it does not require a completing word.)

But whatever the verb's functional type, all verbs share a major characteristic: tense or time. The verb is the one word in the sentence that changes in form to show the time of the action, condition, or state of being.

The quarterback <u>throws</u> a pass.
            threw
        will throw
        has thrown
A party-goer <u>feels</u> sick after partying all night.
        felt
      will feel
      has felt

Chemistry <u>is</u> my easiest subject.
was
will be
has been

CLUE: THE TIME TEST   When asked to find the verbs in a sentence, test the words to see which ones change to show different times.

Today the staff <u>wrote</u> sales letters for the campaign.
~~todayed~~   writes
~~has todayed~~   will write
                   has written

Notice that although the word *today* indicates a time, it cannot change to show different times. If we want to talk about something that happened yesterday or will happen tomorrow, we must use completely different words: *yesterday* and *tomorrow*.

EXERCISE 4:   Underline the verbs in the following sentences. Use the Time Test for any words you think might be verbs.

1. Lightning gouges gashes across the sky.
2. The instructor always gives the class a take-home exam.
3. A delivery of sweetheart roses came to my room by mistake.
4. George's father bought him a Trans-Am for graduation.
5. In gym class Cynthia dislocated her arm on the parallel bars.
6. A stitch in time saves nine.
7. Happiness is an *A* in freshman composition.
8. The local football team, minus its star quarterback, still wins some games.
9. There are three ways to do something—the right way, the wrong way, and "any old way."
10. The magician surprisingly escaped from the iron safe but not from the milk can full of water.

Helping Verbs

We can express only two verb tenses, present and simple past, with one word. Our sunflower *grows* today and *grew* yesterday, but it *will grow* tomorrow. To indicate future tense or time, on-going or progressive tenses, or any other complex tense, we must add auxiliary or "helping" verbs.

Edwina <u>will</u> <u>finish</u> the report on time.
(She has not done it yet, but she will in the future.)

Edwina <u>is</u> <u>finishing</u> the report on time.
(She is in the process of doing it right now.)
Edwina <u>should</u> <u>have</u> <u>finished</u> the report on time.
(She ought to have done it, but she did not.)

In each example the helping verbs are a necessary and integral part of the complete verb. We cannot say "I finishing"; it sounds awkward. If we leave out *will* and say "I finish" or *should have* and say "I finished," we have changed the meaning. Therefore, the verb consists of the major verb—*finish, finishing, finished*—plus all helpers such as *will, am, should have.*

Become thoroughly familiar with the list of helping verbs in Table 2-1 so that you can recognize them in sentences.

TABLE 2-1   Common Helping Verbs

am, is, are, was, were, been
has, have, had
do, does, did
can, could, should, would
may, might, must
will, shall

The main verb plus one or more helping verbs add up to a single verb idea; however, other words may separate the different parts of that verb.

Edwina <u>will</u> always <u>finish</u> the report on time.
Edwina <u>is</u> hopefully <u>finishing</u> the report on time.
Edwina <u>should</u> certainly <u>have</u> <u>finished</u> the report on time.

The intruding words do not change the tense of the verb; they emphasize or qualify, but the verb remains the same.

EXERCISE 5:   Underline the verbs in the following sentences.

1. James should have filed his income tax form early.
2. Instead he has spent every night in March at his favorite disco.
3. Now he is suffering.
4. In April he will reap the consequences.
5. Sally has always been a devoted gardener.
6. Judging by her flower beds, she must garden every day.
7. She has frequently and diligently fed her plants.
8. The garden club should appreciate her efforts.
9. But her neighbors may often envy her.

10. Many pets are probably spoiled by the example of Morris, the finicky eater.

More Verbs

Just as there may be more than one word in a verb, there may be more than one verb in a sentence. The basic or kernel sentence discussed in Chapter 1 contains only one subject and one verb, but many sentences have a more complicated structure. (You will learn more about sentence structure in the discussion of Complex Structure and Compounding in Chapter 10.) Whatever the structure of the sentence, words that function as verbs will show either action, condition, or state of being and meet the Time Test.

Example:

actions

George read the novel and wrote an enraged review for the
    reads   writes
    has read   has written
    will read   will write
underground newspaper.

actions

If we discuss the project intelligently, we will not suffer cost over-
   had discussed   would   have suffered
runs during production.

condition   state of being

Capital punishment seems reasonable, but it is ineffective.
             seemed   was
             will seem   will be

EXERCISE 6:   Underline the verbs in the following sentences.

1. When we finish our guacamole salad, we will order enchiladas.
2. Although our guests have eaten three dozen biscochitos and two fruit cakes, there is still much more food in the kitchen.
3. Good cooks will have the basic ingredients of their favorite recipes on hand and will prepare those dishes frequently.
4. We will begin the meal with appetizers that are made from my secret recipe.
5. Before George carved the turkey, he had already removed the stuffing from the bird.

6. Especially important are the spices you cook with because they give your dishes a distinctive flavor.
7. While Anthony was frying vegetables, Julio was mashing the potatoes.
8. Later on in the dinner, we will try the cook's rich beef gravy, and we will see whether the gravy highlights or smothers the flavor of the roast.
9. The beef stew had too many potatoes, and the salad had wilted.
10. By the time the cooks served dessert, the guests had slipped out the back door.

EXERCISE 7:   Underline the verbs in the following paragraph.

While many people know Laramie, Wyoming, few remember Ft. Laramie. Located northeast of Laramie, Ft. Laramie is off the path of most of today's freeway travelers. Yet a little more than a century ago it was a major stop on the Oregon Trail. A fort without walls, Ft. Laramie marked the end of the Great Plains and the beginning of the long climb to the Continental Divide. The pioneer missionaries, Narcissa and Marcus Whitman, stopped here on their trek west. Trappers and buffalo hunters camped within sight of the parade ground. Wagon trains sought protection from its soldiers and bought supplies at its store. Today the fort is a living history museum—a monument to the nearly forgotten westward emigration along the Oregon Trail.

EXERCISE 8:   Fill in the blanks in the following paragraph with verbs. Supply words that will both make sense and fit the descriptive method of the paragraph.

It _____ today. The storm _____ about three in the afternoon while I _____ still at work. Suddenly the sky _____ as thick, heavy clouds, clumsy with moisture, _____ across the sky. I _____ the sky through my office window—murky and overcast, great sooty-colored waves that _____ over the Rio Grande toward the mountains. About three-thirty it _____ to rain. The drops _____ down slowly and lightly at first, a gentle sprinkling that _____ my

window; then it _____ into a drizzle and soon after, a
downpour. I _____ from my office to my car, holding
a newspaper over my head and clutching my collar tightly to
keep the raindrops from rolling down my neck. I _____
my car window slightly open, and the rain _____ its
way through the crack to splatter the driver's seat and steering
wheel. I _____ inside, and the car _____
reluctantly, sounding hoarse and waterlogged. The windshield
wipers _____ their gentle swoosh-swoosh sound as
they _____ sheets of water to the right and to the left
across the windshield. Angry, muddy water _____ the
gutters and _____ across the streets, and I
_____ slowly, pumping the brakes. There _____
bumper to bumper traffic, and I _____ along,
starting and stopping and hoping my brakes _____,
but as I _____ off Gibson and onto the freeway, I
_____ to catch my breath. Hundreds of cars
_____ together, their headlights glimmering softly in
the liquid atmosphere; they _____ like a river of light
flowing down out of the darkness.

TROUBLESHOOTING: *Peer Criticism*

As you have seen, an important part of rewriting is criticism. Learning to
find mistakes is the first step in learning to correct mistakes. Receiving
peer criticism will help you identify problems, and being a peer critic will
help you develop editing skills.

The peer critics' job is not to rewrite the paper or to make corrections.
Their job is to point out problem areas and errors and to make suggestions
for the writers' own revisions. The process of peer criticism involves several stages, each with a different focus.

Stage One Focus on paragraph structure. Read through the
paragraph looking for problems with subject, focus, or
organization. If the paper lacks a topic sentence or needs
subtopic sentences, now is the time to point out the problem.

Stage Two Focus on content. Reread the paragraph again, looking for problems with supporting details or coherence. If a paragraph needs more support or transitions, make a note of the problem and a suggestion for revision.

Stage Three Focus on the sentence. Reread the paper one sentence at a time. Look for and mark errors in spelling, punctuation, and grammar, but resist the temptation to correct them yourself.

The process of peer criticism is not complete until the peer critics have discussed their comments with the writers. Remember that both the critics and the writers are apprentices, and each criticism and suggestion for revision should be evaluated carefully. If there is a disagreement, refer the question to your instructor or to a tutor for expert advice.

EXERCISE 9: Be a peer critic for the following paragraphs. Write out your comments and suggestions. When you focus on the sentence, pay special attention to spelling and end punctuation (whether there are any fragments, run-ons, or comma splices). Your instructor may ask you to rewrite one of the paragraphs as an additional exercise.

1.   Going to the dentist is the thing fear most. I get there early and wait in the waiting room. Chewing on my nails and trying to read old, worn-out magazines. I jump when they call my name, then the put me in a chair and say to open my mouth. The worst thing is the drilling. Which jars me all the way to my toes. Then there's the needle. Why does it half to be so long? I think I'll give up eating candy forever and never go back.

2.   Giving a speech brings out the worst in me. My hands shake, my voice quivers, I stumble over the words. Once I lost my place in my notes, then again I got them all mixed up. I don't much like to give speeches, but in my line of work which is sales I have to be in front of the public. The best thing for me to do is to practice and build up my confidents.

3.   Have you ever been lost? The time I got lost on Old Grizzly Mountain still stands out in my mind. I was hiking with some friends from school, and we decided to climb to the top of the Old Grizzly. I was only wareing tennis shoes, but it was not to far, I thought I could make it. We climbed for what seemed like hours. Along rigdes, up criks, over bowlders and fallen trees. Then my feet gave out. The others went on while I set down on a log to wait. Then I was all along. I heared a crash in the bushes. I got up and ran all the way down the mountain.

READING TO WRITE

You have already seen that reading the work of professional writers can help your writing, but reading the work of other student-writers can also be helpful. For instance, the examples earlier in this chapter of Cathy's prewriting, writing, and rewriting activities provide a useful model for your own writing process.

In addition, a careful study of Cathy's final draft on page 28 may help you improve your use of verbs. As you reread Cathy's paper, underline the verbs. Notice which verbs describe action and which indicate a condition or state of being. Since Cathy is writing about an action, it would be appropriate for her to use vivid action verbs. Does she? Can you think of any substitutions that would add to the vividness of her description?

WRITING ACTIVITY

In this chapter you have studied the process of writing a paragraph. You have read about prewriting, writing, and rewriting activities, and you have paid special attention to a student example. Now you will work through the writing process for yourself as you write a paragraph on the same subject the student-writer Cathy was given.

Be sure to ask your instructor if he or she will want you to turn in all of your activities and drafts. Many instructors find seeing all of the steps in the process helpful in assessing the product.

ACTIVITY: Write a paragraph about a moving or a frightening experience. Use at least two prewriting activities to help you find a subject and gather information about it. Make your plan on a separate sheet of paper. Then give yourself a time limit for writing the first draft. Ask your peer critic to answer the five basic questions in the example on page 29, or write out your own answers to the questions. Write as many drafts as needed to produce your best product.

CHECKLIST: When you finish a draft of the paragraph, check it carefully for the following.

1. Does the paragraph have a single subject? Is it well organized and well developed?
2. Are all of your sentences complete? Are there any fragments, run-ons, or comma splices?
3. Have you chosen appropriate verbs? Are the verbs that describe action vivid enough?
4. Are there any left-out or misspelled words, any left-out or reversed letters?

CHAPTER THREE
Subjects

The Subject of a Paragraph

A writer who tries to deal with too many materials in a paragraph is like a juggler who tries to keep too many balls up in the air. Something is bound to slip. Choosing and focusing a subject are key factors in the success of a paragraph. Choose too small a subject or focus it too narrowly, and you may run out of material before you finish the third sentence. Choose too large a subject or focus it too broadly, and you may end up with a paragraph that wanders from topic to topic or a paragraph that is several pages long.

FOCUS ON WRITING: *Choosing a Subject*

Usually as you begin prewriting, you will explore a general subject, but writing your paragraph about a general rather than a specific topic can lead to problems. Consider, for example, the following paragraph.

Many people drink beverages, like coffee, that are harmful to them. Although studies have shown that the caffeine in coffee makes us irritable and increases our blood pressure, millions begin the day with a strong cup of coffee. Thousands drink from a bottomless cup of coffee or tea, constantly filling and refilling it as they work, eat, or play. Why do they do this? Why do sane,

intelligent people defy scientific research and their doctors'
advice to poison themselves with a foul-tasting liquid that stains
teeth and poisons their bodies? The question is certainly one for
the psychologists, but they are too busy explaining why the
number of teenage alcoholics is increasing in spite of evidence
that this harmful beverage impairs growth and disrupts mental
functions. Of all the harmful beverages, alcohol is certainly the
worst, but coffee is just as popular.

Because the choice of subject is vague and general ("beverages, like coffee") the paragraph wanders. The writer discusses coffee, tea, and alcohol. Choosing a *specific subject*—some part of the larger general subject that you can cover well in a paragraph—is an important part of prewriting. Limiting "beverages" to "coffee" enables the writer of the above paragraph to rewrite successfully.

Although studies have shown that coffee increases our
blood pressure and makes us irritable, millions of us begin our day
with a strong cup of coffee. Why do we poison ourselves so
persistently? Coffee lovers suggest the following reasons. (1) We
need the kick of caffeine to get us going in the morning and to
keep us going throughout the day. (2) We enjoy the warmth of a
hot cup of coffee in our hands and the taste of the fragrant
liquid in our mouths. (3) We value the sociability of a cup of
coffee with friends or colleagues. Overall, most coffee drinkers
agree that the benefits of drinking coffee outweigh the dangers.

Your prewriting on any general subject will probably include several specific topics that could be developed in individual paragraphs. To choose a specific subject, pay special attention to its size and to the amount of information you have collected or could collect about it. Your subject should be small enough that you can write about it in ten to fifteen sentences. It should be something that you have enough thoughts or memories or knowledge about to make those sentences meaningful.

The brainstorm on the general subject of music suggests several possible paragraph topics.

Disc jockeys, MTV, dancing—any of these might be a good paper topic, but the ones the writer has the most ideas about concern the performing of music. Specifically, she lists a number of ideas about taking music lessons and performing at music concerts and recitals. If the writer chooses either of these for her paper, she will probably want to explore her memories further with other prewriting activities, such as freewriting or even another brainstorm on the specific topic.

BRAINSTORM

Subject: Music

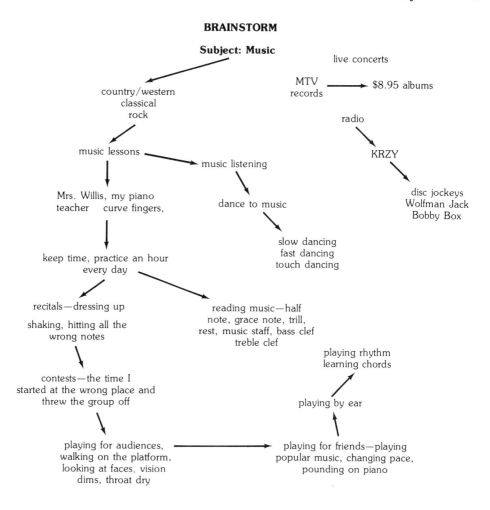

EXERCISE 1: Evaluate the following as paragraph topics.

1. Horse racing
2. The night I won the bingo jackpot
3. My Las Vegas vacation
4. The money I lost at the Golden Horseshoe during my Las Vegas vacation
5. Legalized gambling

EXERCISE 2: Evaluate the choice of topics in the following paragraphs. Then revise and rewrite.

1. I love holidays. Wrapping presents, decorating the tree, baking sugar cookies in the shapes of reindeer and angels—all of these activities add to the festive mood at Christmas—not unlike

bobbing for apples and dressing up like a ghost or a goblin on Halloween. When I see the department store Santas and hear Christmas carols, I remember all of the good times my family has had on this and other holidays. For example, at Easter we have an egg hunt, and on the Fourth of July we set off fireworks. If the truth were known, I probably like Christmas best because that is when we get all of the presents.

2.   Birdwatching is a year-round hobby as is bird feeding. Whatever the season, you can find some special feathered visitors in your garden. In the spring there may be robins on a daily basis and wild canaries or bluebirds for short periods as they head north to their nesting grounds. Finches will stick around all year if you feed them sunflower seeds, especially the small, black kind that birds find so tasty and that have extra oil to help birds endure the cold winter. If you are feeding juncos and other ground-feeding birds, it is a good idea to build a platform high enough above the ground to keep the birds safe from marauding cats. Nothing can hamper your bird watching more than a hungry cat stalking your feeder. Of course, the cat thinks you have obligingly baited a trap to aid his hunting—not unlike duck hunters set decoys and use duck calls to lure ducks to a blind. Probably nothing is more exciting to a bird watcher than seeing flights of migrating ducks, geese, or cranes flying in formation.

Focusing the Subject of a Paragraph

An unfocused topic like an unfocused camera results in a blur. Cathy's paragraph in the last chapter focuses directly on her fear during one roller coaster ride. Without such a focus she might have wandered vaguely from describing her own reactions to describing those of her friend Rick or even those of other people on the ride. Her paragraph succeeds because she focuses on one special angle or view of the topic.

Notice the difference between the following short paragraphs. Both have one subject, but in the first paragraph there is no focus and consequently no unity.

Today was a stormy October day. Thick, dark clouds rumbled across the sky. Rain drenched pedestrians and turned crowded streets into rivers of muddy water for happy schoolboys to play in. Thirsty trees and grass in the park enjoyed a thorough watering while a flight of finches, caught by the storm on their southward flight, huddled in the branches or searched the wet blades and chirped plaintively for something to eat. Lowering clouds cast a shadow of gloom over people and things, creating a cozy isolation for those unfortunate enough to be out in the invigorating weather.

A stormy October day dampens the spirit as it soaks the body. Thick, dark clouds rumble across the sky, casting a shadow of gloom over people and things. Rain, varying from a chilling drizzle to a downpour, drenches pedestrians and turns crowded streets into rivers of muddy water. Trees and grass in the park droop while a flight of finches, caught by the storm on their southward flight, huddle in the branches or search the wet blades and chirp plaintively for something to eat.

The writer of the first paragraph sticks to the subject—a stormy October day—but cannot decide whether the effect of the storm is gloomy or cozy and whether living things are made happy or miserable by the weather. The second paragraph, on the other hand, takes a purely negative view of the storm. As the writer explains in the first sentence, the storm dampens spirits and bodies, and all of the details in the paragraph support that view. She might just as effectively have written the paragraph with a positive focus.

To discover a good focus, begin with the prewriting activity that you used to explore the subject. Study your brainstorm or freewriting or other material, and ask yourself what it all means. How do you feel about the subject? What special insight or knowledge or viewpoint does the prewriting activity reveal? For example, when Donna reread her freewriting exercise about dogs (page 7), she discovered the opinion that dogs manipulate people. Similarly, Mark reread his journal entry about his thumb (page 12) and discovered how essential the thumb is. Once you have discovered a focused subject, you can express it in a *topic sentence*.

Writing a Topic Sentence

A topic sentence states the main idea of a paragraph. It includes the subject and the focus and often is the first sentence in the paragraph, like the topic sentence of Cathy's paragraph on page 31:

> I was terrified as my friend Rick and I boarded the monstrous roller coaster known as "The Twister."

Cathy's subject, the roller coaster ride, is clearly indicated in the sentence as is her attitude toward the ride—her fear. Donna and Mark also include both the subject and the focus in topic sentences, underlined in the following paragraphs.

> Dogs cunningly make us their slaves. They whine, and we take them for a walk. They bark, and we feed them. They wag their tails, and we kneel down to pet, stroke, or pat them. We are trained with small tokens of affection, doled out at appropriate

times—like a lick of the hand or a thump of their tails. And the final proof of their cunning is we love it!

The thumb is an amazingly essential instrument. Without it people could not tie their shoes, pick up needles, or hold a pen to write. Good little boys who sit in corners would not be able to pull plums out of pies. If hamburger eaters did not have thumbs to hold the hamburger together, the bottom would drop out of their lunch. Without thumbs hitchhikers would have to hike rather than hitch. There would be no "thumbs up" or "thumbs down." Without the thumb we might not even be able to count— there being only eight fingers left and our math, based on systems of ten.

EXERCISE 3: Identify both the subject and the focus in each of the following topic sentences. Underline the subject once and the focus twice.

1. The new seat belt law may be unenforceable.
2. After years of Big Macs, Whoppers, and the Colonel's chicken, I have finally kicked the fast-food habit.
3. The county does not need a new courthouse.
4. An apple-a-day may not keep the doctor away, but it will reduce some kinds of cholesterol.
5. Compact discs are fast making records obsolete.

EXERCISE 4: Discover a subject and a focus in each of the following pre-writing activities. Then write topic sentences expressing your discoveries.

1.

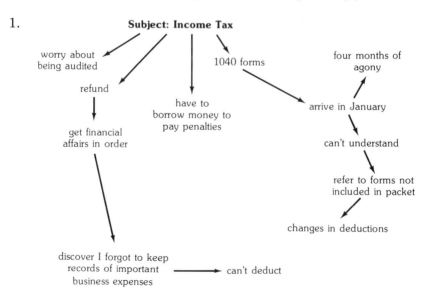

2. Birthdays. They come only once a year—thank goodness. Crepe paper decorations, a cake with candles, party hats, and noise makers. Presents of clothing that have to be returned to the store because of wrong size. Thank-you notes to write for things I didn't want. Kids like birthdays. I liked them when I was . . . now I hate to be reminded of my age.

EXERCISE 5:   The following paragraph is unfocused. Revise the topic sentence to show a clear focus; then rewrite the paragraph.

The kitchen was located at the center of the house connected to the playroom by a breakfast bar and to the den by an arched door. Tempting aromas of baking bread filtered from the room throughout the house, merging with the less enticing odors from the garbage pail and a pot of boiling cabbage. Yellow curtains and wallboard covered with daisies made the room cheerful and inviting. A cozy breakfast nook and a fresh pot of coffee seconded the invitation, while dirty dishes on the table and a frowning cook wielding his menacing knife on a delicious pumpkin pie frighten the visitor away. The kitchen was undoubtedly the "live-in" room of the house.

FOCUS ON THE SENTENCE: *Subjects*

Like a paragraph, a sentence must also clearly focus on a subject. The subject in a sentence is not only what the sentence is about; it is also the subject of the verb. Therefore, as soon as you have found the verb, you are ready to find the subject.

Let's take some examples from our discussion in Chapter 2 on verbs.

The student <u>became</u> angry about the noise in the class.

Became is the verb because it shows a condition of becoming, and it also meets the Time Test: *becomes, will become, has become, is becoming,* and so forth.

Now working backward from the verb, you can ask the question: Who or what became? The word or words that answer that question will be the subject of the verb; therefore *student* is the subject.

Who was?

The speaker <u>was</u> an aging man with a quiver in his voice.
is
will be

What pounds?

The rain <u>pounded</u> on the barn all night.
        pounds
        will pound

Finding the subject is, then, a simple two-step process:

1. Find the verb.
2. Ask the question: who or what + verb?

The subject is the word or words that answer the question.

EXERCISE 6:   Underline the verbs in the following sentences and circle the subjects.

1. Ten seconds remained in the basketball game.
2. Number 10 for Utah threw from center court.
3. The referee whistled and called a foul on the Lobo guard.
4. On both benches the tension was rising.
5. With five seconds remaining, the score was tied.
6. The Utah center dribbled, faked a shot, and passed.
7. Coach Bliss of New Mexico called a time out.
8. Only two starters for the Lobos had not fouled out.
9. The only eligible player left to be put in the game was freshman John Armijo.
10. With one second on the board, Armijo shot from mid-court and scored the winning basket for the Lobos.

More Subjects

You have already learned that there may be more than one verb in a sentence. There may also be more than one subject. You may have two or more subjects for one verb.

Who are?

Juanita and Ray <u>are</u> on the Dean's List this semester.
        were
        will be

Who read and wrote?

George and Lorieann <u>read</u> the article and <u>wrote</u> a letter to the editor.

Or you may have two or more verbs, each requiring a different subject. (You will learn more about multiple subjects when you study compounding in Chapter 10.)

Who discuss?   Who may not strike?

If we discuss their demands calmly, the workers may not strike.

What seems?   What is?

The answer seems reasonable, but it is incorrect.

EXERCISE 7:   Find and underline all the verbs in the following paragraph. Then, asking who or what, find and circle all of the subjects.

The feet hit the dirt with a plopping sound, and the lungs inhale and exhale explosively as the runner turns the track. The runner listens to those companion sounds while yards turn into laps and laps into miles. Sweat rolls down the runner's face. Pumping arms and legs ache, and a slight twitch in the runner's side becomes a gouging, spear-tipped pain. Then just over the edge of that barrier of pain, it happens. Suddenly the legs seem tireless, and the sounds of plopping feet and laboring breath fade away. The yards fly by, the laps blur, and the miles mount effortlessly. This is tranquility time. And now the runner is aware of a new sound—the heart's thumping as it sends strength to tired limbs and gives the runner courage for another mile.

Subjects that Follow Verbs

Most of the time the subject will precede the verb; however, occasionally, for variety or emphasis, normal word order may be reversed and the subject will follow the verb.

On the straw head of the scarecrow perched a grinning crow.

Perched is the action word that fits the Time Test: *perches, has perched,* and so forth. But who or what is perching? The last word in the sentence is the subject: *crow.*

Some but not all sentences that begin with *here* or *there* reverse normal subject–verb order.

Who are?   Subj.

There are sixteen fish in the tank.
were
will be

What is?   Subj.

Here is my quarterly report.

But:

Who are?

Here we are.

Who stands?

There he stood beneath the mistletoe.

Some but not all questions place the verb or part of the verb before the subject.

Who is?   Subj.

Is Julio in the library?

Who is?   Subj.

Is Julio studying in the library?

Who is?   Subj.

Why is Julio in the library?

But:

Subj.

Who finished the left-over cake from the dorm party?
(Since there is no specific actor, the question word *who,* which fills the space a name such as Monica or Fred would fit, must be the subject.)

Often it may be useful to rewrite the inverted sentence in normal word order or to change the question to a statement.

A grinning crow perched on the straw head of the scarecrow.
Julio is studying in the library.

EXERCISE 8:   Underline the verbs and circle the subjects in the following sentences.

1. Is it possible for brown-eyed parents to have a blue-eyed child?
2. There are several possible genetic combinations to consider.
3. Does each parent have a recessive gene for blue eyes?
4. If so, there is a potential for a blue-eyed child.

5. However, should one parent have only the dominant, brown-eyed genes, there can be no blue-eyed children.
6. On the genes of the brown-eyed parents, not the color of their eyes, depends the color of their children's eyes.
7. Can blue-eyed parents have a brown-eyed child?
8. Here the possibilities are more limited.
9. There must be only recessive genes to produce blue eyes.
10. Where, then, would the dominant, brown-eyed genes come from?

EXERCISE 9: Circle the subjects in Exercises 6 and 7 on pages 35 and 36 of Chapter 2.

EXERCISE 10: Add subjects to the following sentences.

1. _____ flew a hang-glider from the top of the Crest while _____ and _____ shouted encouragement and filmed the event.

2. Why did _____ withdraw from the race?

3. Here comes the _____, kicking up dust and spattering the windshields.

4. _____ and _____ caused stocks to plunge, and worried _____ bought up their own stock to avoid disaster.

5. Is this the _____ of a criminal?

6. How many times has _____ warned you to quit smoking?

7. _____ requires patience and courage.

8. When _____ ordered a pizza, _____ stood up and left the restaurant.

9. Howling down the chimney and rattling the windows in the library came _____.

10. Has the _____ come for a change?

TROUBLESHOOTING: *Weak Subjects*

As you saw in Chapter 1 and in this chapter, the main idea of a sentence is usually its subject. However, sometimes the grammatical subject of a sentence is not the same as its main idea.

It is important to remember that feeding programs may make wild animals dependent on handouts.

There are two subjects in the example: *it* and *programs.* The second subject is the main idea of the sentence, and the first adds no important information. Therefore, the sentence should be revised to eliminate that first, weak subject.

Feeding programs may make wild animals dependent on handouts.

Occasionally, the main idea of a sentence may be hidden by vague words or by the use of *here* or *there* to begin a sentence.

The main point of the position argued by demonstrators claims that the object of the government investigation is a cover up. There are several ways for animal lovers to help hungry bears without upsetting nature's balance.

In both examples the grammatical subjects (*point* and *object* in the first; *ways* in the second) tell us little about the real subjects of the sentences. To find the real subjects, we need to ask ourselves, "What is the sentence about? Who is doing what in the sentence?" Then we can revise the sentences using the main ideas as grammatical subjects.

Demonstrators claim that the government investigation is a cover up.
Animal lovers can help hungry bears without upsetting nature's balance.

EXERCISE 11: Identify and revise weak subjects in the following paragraph.

It was because of the long, dry summer of 1989 that bears invaded Western cities. In Tucson, Albuquerque, and Denver as well as in many smaller towns, bears, looking for food and water, roamed the streets. There were sightings of bears in backyards, on schoolgrounds, and in the shopping centers. Their object was to raid garbage cans and take over berry patches and swimming pools. While the bears themselves were peaceful, the same unfortunately cannot be said for their human hosts. In Albuquerque those in authority badly injured a mother bear with a cub. It seems that she and the cub had climbed a telephone pole to escape from a crowd of shouting people and barking dogs. While a horrified city watched on live television, an officer shot the bear with a tranquilizer dart. As she fell from the telephone pole, there was an electric wire that struck the mother bear and burned her badly. Later, large numbers of angry citizens donated money to send the bear and her cub to Oregon for therapy and rehabilitation.

READING TO WRITE

In this chapter you have looked at choosing and focusing subjects in paragraphs and in sentences. Professional writers also pay careful attention to these important steps in the writing process. Take, for example, Mike Royko's article "The World's Dumbest Product Is a Rolex Watch" (page 315, Part II). The title clearly expresses both Royko's subject and his focus. He is writing about the Rolex watch, and he focuses on his negative reactions. Statements of the subject and focus appear in the third paragraph and again and again throughout the article.

> . . . Of all the ostentatious products that are available in our materialistic society, the Rolex watch is the most offensive to me.

As you read, circle each mention of a Rolex watch and underline each negative comment. Do you find any positive comments about the Rolex? What might have been the effect if Royko had added comments about owning a Porsche?

WRITING ACTIVITY

Choosing and focusing your subject are part of prewriting. Give these activities the attention they deserve by making them separate steps in the prewriting stage of the writing process:

1. Explore the general topic in a brainstorm, freewriting, or journal entry.

[Prewriting]
2. Study your exploration activity to discover a specific subject and focus for your paragraph.
3. Write a topic sentence.
4. Plan your paragraph.

Later as you evaluate and revise your paper, look for evidence of too small or too large a topic (such as too little or too much to say) and for evidence of a vague focus (such as wandering from positive to negative reactions).

ACTIVITY: Write a paragraph about an ostentatious product that you would like or would not like to own. Be sure to follow through on all steps in the writing process: prewriting; writing a draft; and revising, correcting, and rewriting the draft.

CHECKLIST: When you evaluate your paragraph, check carefully for the following:

1. Does the paper have a topic sentence that clearly expresses the subject and focus?
2. Are the subject and focus appropriate—large enough or small enough for a paragraph?
3. Are all of your sentences complete? Are there any fragments, run-ons, or comma splices?
4. Are there any left-out or misspelled words, any left-out or reversed letters?
5. Are there any weak subjects in your sentences?

CHAPTER FOUR
Support

Saying Something Worth Saying

Choosing a subject you can write about meaningfully is an important concern when you select a paper topic. But how can you know whether what you have to say is meaningful? In other words, what makes something worth saying? Must it be fresh and original—never said before? Compare the following sets of paragraphs.

#1

I do not believe in the new seat belt law. It forces people to do something they should have a choice about. Whether you wear a seat belt or not is no one's business. If you don't, you are only hurting yourself, and everyone has a right to live his or her own life the way he or she chooses.

The new seat belt law may be unenforceable. Starting January 1, anyone riding in the front seat of an automobile in this state must buckle up. According to the *Journal*, approximately 230,000 city residents commute to work in their own cars each day; another 150,000 drivers take their cars to the shopping centers and malls daily. Since the makers of the seat belt law estimate that less than 10 percent of city drivers use their seat belts regularly, the police would have to stop 342,000 drivers each day or nine in ten drivers to ensure compliance.

Given the 82 officers typically on traffic duty, this figure means that each officer must stop 4,170.7317 cars each day or 521.34146 cars each hour of an eight-hour shift. It cannot be done.

#2

My favorite pet was Sam. He added fun and warmth and friendship to my life for a few precious hours. He was there when I needed him. I learned a lot from Sam about what really matters in life. I miss Sam the snail.

For a few lonely hours yesterday afternoon, I adopted a snail and named him Sam. Sam Snail appeared on a rosebush near my window when I was staring outside, pouting about the bill for a new car battery and my disastrous date with a computer programmer. I saw Sam, but I do not think he ever noticed me. He was too busy, winding his patient way through the thorns and leaves and petals of my prize Snowfire roses.

#3

Whether books are exciting or boring often depends upon your reason for reading them. A book you enjoy at one time may seem tedious later when you have to read it. What you want to do makes all the difference. It can change interest to boredom or boredom to interest.

Whether books are exciting or boring often depends upon your reason for reading them. Take *Moby Dick,* for example. If you check out *Moby Dick* from the library during summer vacation, you will probably read it a few chapters at a time and enjoy the wealth of detail and Melville's careful building of suspense. On the other hand, if you are assigned to read *Moby Dick* for your fall semester literature class, you may have only a few evenings to read eight hundred pages. You race through the descriptions, hoping to pick up enough to pass when you are tested over the book, and you wonder why Melville is making such a big deal of a battle between a whale and a ship's captain. Entertainment has become work, and the book has become tedious.

In each set of paragraphs, the first is made up totally of opinions—statements of beliefs, attitudes, feelings, or judgments. The second paragraphs also contain opinions, but there are fewer of them, and the opinions are supported with facts, details, or examples. This support adds substance and weight to the writer's opinions. It moves outside the writer's inner world of ideas and values to the observable, outer world that the writer shares with his or her readers. As readers we cannot "see" the first writer's opinion that "everyone has a right to live his or her own life the way he or she chooses," the second writer's need for a snail, or the third writer's idea of tediousness. But we can see the significance of 342,000 unbuckled drivers, a snail crawling along a thorny rose stem, and a student's skimming a long novel.

Evidence from the shared outer world gives the opinions of the personal, inner world substance. The evidence can be taken from a newspaper, a book, or other people's experiences. It can be a restatement of something we all know but perhaps have never thought about. Evidence is the worthwhile content that makes what you have said worth saying.

EXERCISE 1: Circle the letter before the items listed that could be used as support for each topic sentence.

1. Topic sentence: My kitchen is a cozy, welcoming room.
   a. my open-heart/open-house belief
   b. the open kitchen door
   c. cheery, yellow curtains and tablecloth
   d. the happy feelings of my guests
   e. a plate of freshly baked cookies on the table
2. Topic sentence: Enthusiasm makes the difference.
   a. how good enthusiasm makes you feel
   b. how much better you feel when you put your heart into a job
   c. the promotion I received after working day and night on a new advertising idea
   d. study that shows a smiling, eager clerk's selling twice as much as a frowning, reluctant clerk
3. Topic sentence: My graduation was the most embarrassing moment of my life.
   a. stumbling as I mounted the platform to receive my diploma
   b. feeling as though I could die
   c. getting the hiccups halfway through the valedictorian's speech
   d. desperately wanting the hour to pass
   e. wishing the ground would open up and swallow me
4. Topic sentence: Cooking blue-ribbon chicken calls for my secret recipe.
   a. mouth-watering blend of herbs and spices
   b. marinating the chicken overnight in a light wine

       c. better taste, better texture
       d. batter made of blue cornmeal and eggs
       e. baking at 375 degrees for moist meat under a crunchy crust

    5. Topic sentence: Every busy person should have a hobby.
       a. the value of relaxation
       b. the dangers of unrelieved stress
       c. the pleasure of hobbies
       d. Peter Marshall's roses
       e. J. Edgar Hoover's building organs

EXERCISE 2:   Label each sentence in the following paragraph *0* for opinion or *S* for support. Then rewrite the paragraph, replacing opinions with support in all except the first and last sentences. You may need to add extra sentences.

1. _____   ¹I could never live in the country. ²There's nothing
2. _____   to do. ³People seem to be lonely and withdrawn. ⁴At
3. _____   night the hooting of the owls and the singing of the
4. _____   crickets would keep me awake. ⁵During the day I
5. _____   would be kept trembling in tight Western boots by
6. _____   vicious banty roosters and fierce, mooing cows. ⁶I do
7. _____   not like fresh air; it's unnatural, I'm sure, to breathe air one cannot see. ⁷The city is the only place for me.

Finding something worthwhile to say is not only an important part of prewriting, but it is also an ongoing part of the writing process. What kind of information you use depends on your assignment and your resources. Looking for appropriate details, facts, and examples begins as you explore the subject and continues as you focus, plan, write, and rewrite the paper.

FOCUS ON WRITING: *Supporting the Main Idea*

Supporting with Descriptive Details

"Show rather than tell" is good advice for anyone describing places, people, or events. Showing means to paint a picture with words. The writer limits interpretation of the picture to one or two sentences and devotes most of the paragraph to details (color; shape; size; placement; or specific ways people walk, talk, gesture, make faces, and so forth).

Two student paragraphs illustrate the difference between showing and telling. The first paragraph tells; the second one shows.

My dog has fleas. They make her life a misery. I feel sorry for her. I will give her a bath.

My dog is an animated bundle of itches, scratches and squirms. Each trip across the yard is interrupted by quick stops to scratch. She rolls on the ground in a frenzied fury to rid herself of her pesky, parasitic arthropods. She looks up to me frequently with pleading eyes. They seem to say, "Can't you do something for me?" I'll take a break in my very busy schedule to help my friend. I'll give her a soothing bath with flea soap which should send her torturing stow-aways on the run. A generous dusting of flea powder should make them decide they would rather live somewhere else, even after the flood is over. Now my faithful friend is comfortable again and I can continue with my busy schedule, secure in the knowledge that I have performed a much-needed service. Now her warm brown eyes say, "Thank you."

The first paragraph is vague and dull. The animal with its miseries seems far away, too remote in fact to enlist our sympathies. However, the second paragraph, especially for the first five or six sentences, is vivid and immediate. The reader "sees" the dog, pities it, and feels relieved when the animal is relieved.

A good method of collecting descriptive details is to make a sensory chart. Divide a sheet of paper into five columns, one for each of the five senses. Then jot down sights, sounds, feelings, tastes, and smells as Roberta did at her grandfather's log cabin.

Place: Grandfather's Log Cabin

Sights	Sounds	Feelings	Tastes	Smells
dark inside	door squeaks and moans	chilly	dust	dampness
leaky roof	whistling wind	soft floor—like baby powder	tears	dust
sun shining through holes in floor	whisper like in a graveyard			rotting wood
dirt floor		grit covering every-thing		mice
spider webs	meadowlark			tangy smell of pine

Sights	Sounds	Feelings	Tastes	Smells
gray, rough logs	scurrying of squirrels on the roof	mysterious feeling		
boarded up windows				
oak washstand	rattling of leaves on the roof			
rusty nails	chirping of birds			
traces of water marks	trees swinging in wind			
spurts of dry, powdery dirt				
no window panes				

The focus Roberta discovered in her chart was negative: her grandfather's cabin had become a ruin. Then she circled details in her chart that supported that picture, leaving out details, like the call of the meadowlark or the pleasant smell of pine, that seem more positive than negative. After making a plan and writing several drafts, she wrote a paragraph that shows rather than tells about the empty cabin.

> Grandfather Largo's log cabin is an old and weathered ruin. The roof leaks when it rains. When it's sunny, sunbeams creep through to create shadowy patterns on the floor. In the four corners of the ceiling, there are misty gray spider webs. The walls are cracked; the logs are gray and rough with age. Strips of bark hang loose. The spaces between the logs let the wind whistle through, sending a chill up my spine. It is very dark inside because the windows are boarded up with old pine boards. The glass window panes are missing. As I push my way inside, the old door squeaks and moans on its rusty hinges. The log cabin feels dusty and a little damp. The dirt floor beneath my feet is soft like baby powder. Somewhere in the corners of the room, mice scurry into their holes, and the musty smell fills the cabin. Just a few decades ago this log cabin was my grandfather's home; now it is empty and forgotten.

EXERCISE 3: Make a sensory chart for the place where you are studying—a carrel in the library, your classroom, a room at home, a park bench. Then study the chart to discover a focused subject, and write a topic sentence.

EXERCISE 4: Be a peer critic for the following paragraphs. Evaluate the topic sentences and the use of supporting details. Make specific suggestions for improvement. Watch also for errors in spelling or sentence punctuation.

1.   Grants Park is located on the corner of Juan Tabo and Zuni. It is a small park, but many people enjoy it. During lunch hour the few benchs are taken by workers from nearby office buildings. Children play there after school, dog owners walk their dogs there in the evening. For such a small park Grants gets a lot of use.

2.   Graduation was more exciting than I expected. The school gym was filled with people, my own family took up a whole row of chairs. The isle we walked down had arches of flowers over it. Like walking through a garden. I walked in with my best friend. Little did I know that he would soon be famous. As we walked off the platform, he riped open his robe, under it he had on a Superman costume.

3.   I remember my first-grade teacher. An older lady with pretty, white hair. She wore soft pink nail polish and lipstick and dangly earings and bracelets, she always smelled like flowers. When went home in the afternoon, she gave us a big hug. Feeling like a soft, silky pillow. I always liked Mrs. Silva, my first-grade teacher.

EXERCISE 5:   Rewrite one of the paragraphs in Exercise 4, following your own advice for improvement. You may need to begin with some prewriting activities to help you focus the subject and find descriptive details.

Supporting with Facts

Often a writing assignment will ask for information. In this case facts are the best support. Facts are specific, solid, provable. They may be names, statistics, dates, numbers, or details and events. Generally, one or even two facts alone will not adequately support an idea. The writer may take it as a rule of thumb that one fact proves nothing and two might be a coincidence; only when three or more facts are used to support an idea, can we say that the idea is supported by the facts.

Unless you have an exceptionally good memory, to support a topic sentence with facts will usually require some research—something Karen neglected to do before she wrote the first draft of her paragraph on earthquakes.

> Earthquakes are quite a typical occurrence in California. Many of these quakes are very strong and have done some damage. Many Californians have become accustomed to these shakes and are learning how to deal with them calmly and rationally.

There is nothing here that a reader could actually quarrel with. The statements are generally and rather obviously both true and uninteresting. In order to add more substance to the paragraph, Karen did some research by reading articles about earthquakes in California; then she rewrote.

> Earthquakes are quite a typical occurrence in California. Dr. James T. Strong of the Cal Tech Seismographic Laboratory estimates that hundreds of quakes occur in the state each month. Most of these quakes are mere tremors, rating less than 2 or 3 on the Richter Scale, but many are quite strong, 4.5 or higher, and have done damage in the millions of dollars. One of the worst quakes in terms of loss of property and life occurred in San Francisco, April 18, 1906. A heavy quake shook the city at 5:15 a.m. The shock damaged water systems, fires broke out, and by the third day seven hundred people had been killed. More recently, a quake measuring 7.1 on the Richter Scale rocked San Francisco on October 17, 1989. Dozens died when freeways collapsed and fire gutted the historic Marina district. Quakes of such magnitude may not be typical, but the San Francisco earthquakes are probably in the back of most Californians' minds whenever they feel a tremor.

EXERCISE 6: Evaluate the following paragraphs for focus and support. Make specific recommendations for revision and note errors in sentence punctuation or spelling.

> 1.   The day when Mt. St. Helens erupted was a day of tradgedy. People were killed, forests were burned. One old man who lived closeby was buried in his mountain cabin.
> 2.   The blue whale should be protected. It is a extremly inteligent animal. A mammal that sings to its young. Whaleing boats from sevral countries kill them evry year. Something has to be done before there are no more blue whales on earth, we owe it to future generations.

EXERCISE 7: Revise one of the paragraphs in Exercise 6. You may need to do some library research as part of prewriting your revision.

Supporting with Examples

Using examples is one of the best ways to support a topic sentence and also one of the best ways to make your work interesting. Examples are people, events, places, and things that represent or demonstrate an idea: Kennedy, Jefferson, and Lincoln are examples of U.S. Presidents; the Fourth of July and Christmas are examples of holidays; and Taos, Mon-

terey, and Ashland are examples of tourist towns. However, simply naming examples is not enough; examples must be both named and explained.

To explain an example, you must show how it demonstrates the central idea. Jeanette's paragraph about shopping at the Mall provides a useful illustration.

> As I walked through the Mall, I encountered depressing
> noises. To start with there was a kid sitting in a corner, yelling his
> lungs out. The kid had lost his mother so he just sat in the
> corner crying. I felt so sorry for him, but there was nothing I
> could do. Farther down the Mall, two women were arguing; their
> loud, shrill voices made everyone stare. I looked with the rest
> until one of the women yelled at me, "What do you think you're
> looking at?" Then I felt embarrassed and hurried on. As I
> continued down the Mall, I tuned into the discordant clacking of
> people's heels on the cement. Not one of the heels was on the
> same beat. I had a headache by then anyway, and the clicking,
> clacking, thumping noises made it worse. Finally, I came to Jean
> Nicole's and walked in to the accompaniment of the most
> depressing music I have ever heard. It was soft and slow, like
> the music in a mortuary. I was getting more depressed by the
> minute.

Jeanette gives us four examples of depressing noises she encountered
at the Mall: a child's crying, women's arguing, heels' clacking, and fune-
real music. But she does more than just name the noises; she discusses
them and then explains why they were depressing. She felt sorry for the
child, the arguing women embarrassed her, the clacking heels intensified
her headache, and the music reminded her of a mortuary and death. The
result is a well-supported paragraph.

EXERCISE 8: Discuss the following paragraph in terms of support by example. How would you improve this paragraph?

> The picky eater is very meticulous. This eater appears as
> though he were performing a delicate and serious operation.
> Everything is done in a slow and a careful motion. This eater
> will eat one food at a time. He will not proceed to the next type
> of food until he has finished the first. This eater is very
> interesting to watch. He will pick and peel off the layers on food,
> until he reaches the center. This was observed when a person
> was eating a Dingdong cupcake. He proceeded very carefully, as
> though he were disconnecting a time bomb. He would first begin

by very slowly peeling off the chocolate covering layer, until he reached the spongy cake center. He would eat this by peeling and picking off pieces of cake, section by section. He would lastly reach the cream filling. Another person was eating a Reese's chocolate bar. This person was just as careful. He first broke off little sections of chocolate at a time. He proceeded to do this until he reached the center or the nucleus of the candy bar. This person went through two steps. Picky eaters seem to eat very slowly to savor the delicious flavor.

EXERCISE 9:   List examples that you might use to support the following topic sentences.

1. The way people laugh tells a lot about their personalities.
2. There are too many crime shows on television.
3. I like junk food.
4. Working in my office is like being in a zoo.
5. With my friends, I don't need enemies.

Extending Examples

If you extend an example until it becomes a story, you have a narrative. Brief stories or narratives are an effective way to support an idea because they also enable you to show rather than tell. Descriptive details, facts, dialogue, action—all are appropriate to extend examples. Sue uses a variety of support in her narrative about a hectic day in the office where she worked.

During my six months as a workstudy secretary, I have experienced many hectic days. One of the worst and best was May 7, 1980. It was my birthday, the day of my English final, and also the day of the retirement party for my favorite instructor. I got to school late because I had stopped to buy some chips and dips for the party. My head was ringing with instructions, "Buy paper plates; don't forget the flowers, and remember to study for the test." I had almost forgotten it was my birthday until I walked into the Reading Lab. There on the table was a chocolate cake covered with orange roses. In delicate green script it said, "Happy Birthday, Sue." Then there were more instructions, "Sue, open your presents; read your card; eat some cake." It was great, but I had barely recovered from the excitement when it was time for my final. The subjects were awful; I couldn't concentrate. I kept thinking about decorating the table and rounding up the guests for my instructor's party. I still don't remember what I wrote, but I do remember giving her the present that all the students had chipped in on and then serving cake to 150 guests. I like working, but as my supervisor says, "Sometimes this office is a real zoo!"

EXERCISE 10: Evaluate the topic sentence and support in the following paragraph. How could the paragraph be improved?

Automobile drivers do not have an accurate way of telling exactly how fast their cars are going. Speedometers have a habit of jumping around within five miles per hour of the speed the car is going. If the tires on the automobile aren't inflated at the exact pressure they should be, this can throw the speedometer off. Not having the exact pressure in the tires can throw the speedometer off anywhere from one mile per hour to eight miles per hour. Should people have to check their tires every morning before going to work or drive forty-seven miles per hour to be on the safe side all of the time? Before leaving for work one morning, I put some snow tires on my car, not realizing that they were larger than my other tires. This causes the car to go faster than the speedometer shows. With the smaller tires on, the speedometer is correct. The wheel axle is going at the same rate. The snow tire is covering more ground with the larger tire. I think I am traveling at fifty-five miles per hour, but actually I'm driving at fifty-eight miles per hour. On the way to work I was stopped by the police for speeding. I couldn't believe it. I was watching my speedometer very closely. At the time I was unaware of my tires' being the cause of speeding. I wasted a lot of my time and the policeman's time arguing.

FOCUS ON THE SENTENCE: *Nouns and Pronouns*

While details, facts, examples, or illustrations give substance to a paragraph, nouns or "name words" give substance to a sentence. Often a noun will serve as the subject of a verb, but nouns serve other functions as well. They may come either before or after or both before and after the verb. They may name the people that act or the people acted upon. The many places nouns fill in a sentence can be seen easily if we leave them out.

_____ exited the _____ in a graceful _____, his _____ arched and his _____ high.

If we try to fill in these blanks, we will find ourselves automatically using nouns. Our feeling for the structure of our language will not allow us to use anything else.

Mizifuf exited the Kitty Kastle in a graceful spring, his back arched and his tail high.

or

Maurice exited the limousine in a graceful saunter, his eyebrows arched and his nose high.

As you learn to recognize nouns and to see their relationship to verbs and to other words, you will begin to understand nouns' place in a sentence.

Nouns

Nouns name people, places, things, qualities, or ideas, and those names may be proper (specific) or common (general).

People	Proper:	Jim Jones was a cult leader who suffered from acute paranoia and megalomania.
	Common:	His followers became his prisoners.
Places	Proper:	Jonestown was founded as the cult's refuge from impending world apocalypse.
	Common:	The village was the site of the cult's mass suicide.
Things	Proper:	*Roget's Thesaurus* was first published in 1852.
	Common:	A thesaurus is a treasury of related words.
Qualities	Proper:	"Beauty is Truth, Truth Beauty."
	Common:	The beauty of Mt. St. Helens hid an ugly potential for mayhem.
Ideas	Proper:	Bernoulli's Principle is fundamental to heavier-than-air flight.
	Common:	A principle is a rule or law.

EXERCISE 11: Fill in the blanks in the following sentences with nouns. Use common or proper nouns as indicated in parentheses.

1. The _____ (common) told _____ (proper) to move his _____ (common).

2. _____ (proper) called at noon, but no one was in the _____ (common), and he had to talk to the answering _____ (common).

3. While _____ (proper) relaxed on the _____ (common), the _____ (common) entered the _____ (common) and stole my _____ (common).

4. In 1849 _____ (common) rushed to _____ (proper) to find _____ (common).

5. Almost overnight _____ (proper) became a great _____ (common).

6. _____ (proper) is in the _____ (common) of the _____ (common).

7. _____ (proper) jumped over the _____ (common).

8. After _____ (proper) passes a _____ (common), it must be signed by the _____ (proper).

Other Characteristics of the Noun

1. Since acting as the subject of the verb is a major noun function, a word that is a noun should be able to fill the subject slot in sentences such as the following:

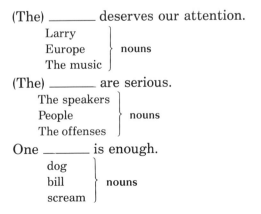

2. The articles—*a, an,* and *the*—may also serve as noun clues. In fact, we may call them *noun determiners* because once stated, they determine that a noun must follow.

a <u>porcupine</u>   an <u>orangutan</u>   the <u>gnu</u>

Other words may come between the article or noun determiner and its noun, but a noun will always complete the group of words begun with *a, an,* or *the.* To find the noun, ask yourself, "A, an, or the what?"

a bristling, angry <u>porcupine</u> (a what?)
an orange <u>orangutan</u> (an what?)
the graceful <u>gnu</u> (the what?)

3. An additional characteristic of many nouns, especially common nouns, is number. Many nouns have a singular form to indicate one and a plural form to indicate more than one.

singular	*plural*	*singular*	*plural*
joke	jokes	fly	flies
church	churches	child	children
crisis	crises	louse	lice
datum	data	hypothesis	hypotheses

This characteristic of number gives us a simple way to double-check words that appear to be names.

The <u>man</u> is <u>happy</u> because his <u>farm</u> has prospered.

Each of the underlined words appears to name something: *man,* a person; *happy,* a quality of feeling; *farm,* a place. However, only two of the words show number. We can have *one man, two men, three men* and *one farm, two farms, three farms,* and so forth; but we cannot have *one happy, two happies, three happies.* Only *man* and *farm* are nouns or name words.

4. Finally, some nouns can be identified by their word endings or suffixes. Add *-er* to *farm, work, teach,* or *preach* and the result is a name word meaning someone who farms, works, teaches, or preaches. Add *-ster* to *poll, mob,* or *young* and you get *pollster, mobster,* and *youngster*—all name words. Other typical noun suffixes include the following:

Suffix	*Examples*
-ment	excitement, amusement, confinement
-ity	community, fatality, absurdity

Suffix	*Examples*
-ness	greatness, happiness, sadness
-ery	effrontery, scenery, butchery
-ship	fellowship, partnership, companionship
-tion, -sion	addition, contraction, compulsion
-ance, -ence	acceptance, impudence, intelligence
-ancy, -ency	emergency, fluency, truancy
-ism	optimism, sadism, patriotism
-ist	sadist, optimist, materialist
-icide	homicide, insecticide, regicide
-age	courage, bondage, homage
-arium, -orium	auditorium, aquarium, solarium
-icle	chronicle, article, particle
-hood	livelihood, motherhood, neighborhood
-tude	attitude, altitude, beatitude
-osis	thrombosis, osmosis, psychosis
-ology	psychology, anthropology, biology
-ian	physician, amphibian, technician

EXERCISE 12: Using what you know about nouns, decide which words in the following list are nouns and which ones are not. Be prepared to explain your answers.

govern	fright	music
government	frightful	musician
governor	thimbleful	musicale
time	beautiful	clinician
timely	cupful	clinic
simple	humility	clinical
simplistic	humiliated	temperament
gnat	difference	temperamental
icicle	differ	extravagant
child	different	modesty
mild	perfect	modestly
wild	perfection	modest

EXERCISE 13: Circle all nouns in the following nonsense sentences. Use clues from pages 66 to 69 to explain your answers.

1. The widdiful soomers wumpled beside the subber.
2. In the fibble under the oomblat dwarmed an oomple.

3. Trabbily the foobers umbered and dobbled their poobles.
4. If dwarm doms the forb, the drobitarium will be eebed with subical trobitarians.
5. Tribness, the gnobbest neebler in Knabbery, phobbed the jibbers on the simpment.

Pronouns

Pronouns are substitute words; they take the place of, or stand for, nouns. When it would be awkward to repeat the name word, we replace it with a pronoun.

For example, in the following paragraph repetition of nouns such as *politicians* and *people* makes the paragraph sound clumsy overall. However, replacing some of the nouns with pronouns makes the paragraph sound smoother and more coherent.

> Politicians are masters of standard advertising techniques. Politicians habitually "snow" politicians' constituents with "glittering generalities." The people may never know where the people's representatives stand on the economy, proliferation of nuclear weapons, and foreign policy, but the people can be sure that the people's representatives stand "four-square" behind apple pie, baseball, and the Fourth of July parade.

> Politicians are masters of standard advertising techniques. They habitually "snow" their constituents with "glittering generalities." The people may never know where their representatives stand on the economy, proliferation of nuclear weapons, and foreign policy, but they can be sure that their representatives stand "four-square" behind apple pie, baseball, and the Fourth of July parade.

Some pronouns that can be used to replace nouns that name people include the following:

I	them	anyone
you	my	everyone
he	your	everybody
she	his	anybody
we	her	somebody
they	our	few
me	their	many
him	someone	some
us		

Anthony Sedillo wrote a prize-winning paper; he will be given a scholarship.

A volunteer is needed to assist the magician. Will someone come to the stage?

There are also pronouns that can take the place of nouns that name places, things, ideas, or qualities:

it	nothing
all	some
none	most
few	many
any	much
something	that
anything	this

> The monstrous Belgian computer has been nicknamed The Beast. It reputedly is capable of controlling world banking.

In spelling, rules are often overruled; most are riddled with exceptions.

EXERCISE 14: In the following paragraphs replace awkwardly repeated nouns with pronouns.

LSD, one of the most commonly used drugs in America, is derived from the ergot fungus which grows on rye. LSD was discovered by Albert Hoffman in 1938, but LSD's hallucinogenic properties were not known until Hoffman accidentally ingested LSD in 1943.

History does, however, report the consumption of the ergot fungus. In times of famine the starving poor have eaten the ergot fungus on spoiled rye bread. The result is ergotism, a disease which can take two forms. Ergotism may convulse ergotism's victims, assault the victims' nervous system, and subject the victims to hallucinations. Or ergotism may attack in ergotism's gengrenous form. Victims of gangrenous ergotism will first experience a painful swelling in the victim's limbs. Finally the limbs will become numb, and frequently the limbs will fall off without bleeding.

EXERCISE 15:   Use nouns or pronouns to fill in the subject slots left blank in the following paragraph.

The _____ to the barn could not be estimated at once. The old _____ sighed as _____ peered out of his house overlooking the remnants of his farm. The _____ had left. The _____ had pounded on the barn all night. _____ of thunder had made his bones leap right out of bed as if _____ were the target of a direct hit every time. And all night _____ seemed as though _____ had missed all his other buildings but that one, for the _____ had left all else alone, unharmed. His _____, the _____, even the _____ and the _____ were untouched by the fury of the water and wind which had defaced the barn. Both _____ lay battered on the ground, ripped off hinges which had not been repaired since a previous assault of the elements not two months ago. A small unrepaired _____ on the roof was torn open to more than ten times its size. _____ in the barn would certainly be drenched. The _____ would mildew, _____ of grain would spoil, _____ for the hens would be ruined, and _____ of cement would become hardened blocks in their bags. _____ had seen the _____ fly open and fall and the _____ on the roof creak and crumple as the _____ jolted him out of bed to witness both events. _____ had bought bolts and shingles to repair the barn two months before, but _____ had occupied a corner stall, unused and almost forgotten except for an occasional twinge of conscience, warning him to get to work. But now as _____ gazed at the two huge holes in his barn, _____ saw shingles in his mind, wet and wasted, and _____ remembered: A _____ in time saves nine.

TROUBLESHOOTING: *Look-alike and Sound-alike Words*

Usage errors occur when we confuse words that look alike or sound alike.

Not: He rejected the <u>advise</u> of the attorney who <u>adviced</u> him not to sue.
But: He rejected the <u>advice</u> of the attorney who <u>advised</u> him not to sue.

In the first example the noun *advice* had been confused with the verb *advise.* If you pronounce the *s* and *c* sounds carefully in both sentences, you can "hear" the errors in the first sentence easily. However, the ear cannot identify all usage errors.

Not: The <u>principle</u> of the high school published a book entitled *Basic <u>Principals</u> of School Management.*
But: The <u>principal</u> of the high school published a book entitled *Basic <u>Principles</u> of School Management.*

The first sentence confuses *principal,* a school administrator, with *principle,* a rule or basic truth. The two words are pronounced exactly the same way; therefore, we cannot rely on what "sounds right" to help us find the error. We need a dictionary or a glossary of usage, which lists words that often confuse writers.

EXERCISE 16: A glossary of usage usually consists of pairs of words, definitions, and examples. Start your own glossary by writing definitions and examples for the words listed below and by identifying other problem pairs.

Words	*Definitions*	*Examples*
1. accept/ except		

Words	*Definitions*	*Examples*
2. affect/ effect		
3. cloths/ clothes		
4. complement/ compliment		
5. conscious/ conscience		
6. device/ devise		
7. discreet/ discrete		
8. farther/ further		
9. illusion/ allusion		

Words	*Definitions*	*Examples*
10. lead/ led		
11.		
12.		
13.		
14.		
15.		

EXERCISE 17:   Use a dictionary to help you identify and correct usage errors in the following paragraphs.

1.   Observing business etiquette is an important part of seceding in the business world. Wearing appropriate cloths shows respect for your employer. Rising when a customer enters the room or allowing the customer to proceed you when you leave a room says you care about the customer. The letters you write, from the salutation to the complementary close, should reflect concern and consideration. Ignoring these rules could loose your

company's biggest accounts. Following them could effect your entire career, assuring your progress up the company ladder.

2.   For many shut-ins, television is an escape devise. The plastic worlds of television families create an allusion of being involved in many people's lives. The personnel attitude and tone of television personalities illicits a personnel response and feelings of friendship. Turn up the volume and a to quite house becomes noisy, filled with human voices. Turn the knob and four, confining walls give way to far away places with erotic names. Weather this escape is healthy or not depends upon weather the shut ins loose their own lives in the make-believe world or use it to make their lives bigger.

READING TO WRITE

Writing that uses many nouns is said to be "concrete" because it conveys a sense of solidity. It has a reality that can be seen and heard and touched. In the reading that begins on page 316 of Part II, N. Scott Momaday re-creates a place and his view of it. He names physical details, places, and things and uses an abundance of both common and proper nouns.

Before you read the entire article, study the first paragraph carefully. Underline the nouns or name words and circle each verb. Notice that Momaday uses many different nouns, but his choice of verbs is somewhat limited. *Is, are* and *was*—all forms of the verb *to be*—make up more than half of the verbs in the paragraph. By limiting action verbs and emphasizing concrete nouns, Momaday conveys a sense of unmoving, unchanging, eternal nature.

WRITING ACTIVITY

Think about a place that is important to you, like a special room that contains happy memories, the park bench where you were sitting when you made an important decision, a special carrel in the library, or the bend in a river where you caught a prize fish. Then make a sensory chart about that place as you did in Exercise 3. Try to recreate it, physical detail by physical detail, in your mind and upon your paper.

When you have finished freewriting, read what you have written and underline ideas that seem most important to you. Try to discover a focus that reveals your dominant impression of or a dominant feeling about the place.

ACTIVITY: Write a paragraph about a place that is important to you. Use the dominant feeling or impression about the place, discovered in your prewriting, as the controlling idea for the paragraph. Plan your paragraph carefully, and use specific nouns that convey a sense of the solidity and reality of the place you are describing.

CHECKLIST: When you have finished your first draft, check it carefully for the following:

1. Does the paper have an appropriate subject and focus, clearly expressed in a topic sentence?
2. Is the topic sentence well supported by details?
3. Have you emphasized the use of nouns to give your place a sense of physical reality?
4. Are there any fragments, run-ons, or comma splices?
5. Are there any left-out or misspelled words, any confused words, any left-out or reversed letters?

CHAPTER FIVE
Organization

The Patterns and Structures of Language

Stranded on a desert island with nothing to read but a dictionary, could a non-English speaker learn the English language? Probably not. Studying a dictionary might help him or her learn individual words but not how to put them together. For meaning involves more than words. The patterns or structure of language is also important.

Consider these "sentences":

Makes good good reading writing.
A twipple of dep rowlls through the clepferr.

The first "sentence" is composed of common English words, but they make sense only individually, not together. In the second "sentence" the key words are nonsense; nevertheless, we can find some meaning in their arrangement. We know that the verb in the sentence is *rowlls* and that *rowlling,* whatever it may be, is happening now, at the present time. We also know that a *twipple* is doing the *rowlling* and that this *twipple* is specifically *of dep.* We even know where the *twipple* does its *rowlling—through the clepferr.*

Overall, there is at least as much English meaning in the nonsense sentence as in the five meaningful, but nonsensically arranged English words. In fact, asked to turn the two groups of words into truly English sentences, a group of students found the second sentence easier to work with. They quickly produced "A ripple of laughter runs through the class-room." It took a bit longer to write "Good writing makes good reading" and "Good reading makes good writing."

Learning to see, understand, and use the patterns and structure of language is vital to writing. The structure of one sentence may be repeated in others to emphasize similar or contrasting ideas. Descriptive details will follow a pattern to help the reader "see" the picture. Ideas may be structured for importance and events for time. The pattern or structure gives the writer a plan for composing a sentence or a paragraph. And it gives the reader a framework for understanding what the writer has written.

FOCUS ON WRITING: *Planning a Paragraph*

The last major step in prewriting is to make a plan. Focusing your subject in a topic sentence and selecting support give you the building materials. To organize those materials in a meaningful way, you need a plan.

A good writing plan grows out of your writing materials. It starts with the kind of subject you are writing about but also depends upon the kind of support you have chosen. For example, if you are writing about an event and reporting specific details or incidents, your materials call for time order. But if you are writing about an event and discussing its causes, you may need to use a different kind of organization, such as climactic order, or order of importance.

Your writing plan may be formal or informal, an outline or a sketch (see Chapter 10, pages 217–19 for a discussion of outlining). In either case, begin with your topic sentence; then list ideas and support—details, facts, examples, and illustrations—in the order in which you will use them in your paragraph. You will probably need to experiment to find the pattern that best fits your materials. In Chapter 2, Cathy's plan for the first draft of her roller-coaster paper put all of her fearful reactions first, then used time order for details of the ride. After peer criticism, she revised her plan to use time order for the entire paragraph, and to fit in details about her reactions at appropriate points.

Plan for first draft
Title: The Roller Coaster
Topic Sentence: The monstrous roller coaster ride loomed before me as my friend Rick and I walked to the ticket booth.

Revised plan
Title: Riding "The Twister"
Topic Sentence: I was terrified as my friend Rick and I boarded the monstrous roller coaster known as "The Twister."

Plan for first draft
Support: metal maze called "The
             Twister"
          my fear
             white knuckles
             breathless
             heart pounding
          car starts with jerk
             grunting, groaning gears
          shooting up and down hills
          twisting around curves
          coasting to stop
          Rick says, "Let's do it again."

Revised plan
Support: metal maze looms
          I try to back out
          car jerks forward
          climbs hill
             grunting, groaning, gears
             creaking, grinding metal
          heart pounding
          white knuckles
          hurtle down
          afraid we'll crash
          twisting around curves
          afraid I'll fly out
          coast to stop
          voice hoarse
          fingers numb
          Rick said, "Let's do it again."

Writing without a plan is the shotgun approach to writing. The writer explodes on paper, shooting out everything at once and letting the shot fall where it may. Writing with a plan presents ideas in the order that will make them most clear to the reader. Ordering ideas logically will be studied at length in more advanced writing courses; however, a good place to begin is with time order, space order, and climactic order.

Time Order for Events

Read the following description of Brian's typical Monday morning:

> I am always late to school on Mondays. My car refuses to start, and I forget my books. Sometimes I have forgotten to set the alarm the night before, and so I wake up late to begin with. I cannot think of anything to wear, but before that I have a hard time staying awake in the shower. Breakfast and my homework usually get lost in the shuffle.

The paragraph is incomprehensible because the writer pays no attention to the sequence of events, the order in which things actually happened. Since time order is violated, the reader cannot get a clear picture of what happened; moreover, Brian's lack of planning also obscures problems with his support. Without a time-ordered sequence of events, he cannot tell that he has left out some crucial factors in the being-late process—such as the dog that barked all night, the cat that needed first aid, the neglected garbage that had accumulated over the weekend to trip the writer as he scurried for the door. The demands of both reading and writing call for time order when one deals with events that take place through time.

EXERCISE 1: Write a plan for a revision of the above "being-late" paragraph. Supply a time order and fit in at appropriate points other events that may have contributed to the writer's lateness.

EXERCISE 2: Rewrite the "being-late" paragraph following your revised plan.

Time Order for Process

Many processes, such as how to do or make something, follow a natural sequential order. Paragraphs about these processes should also, therefore, be planned in time order. Take, for example, the following brief description of how to cook bacon in an electronic microwave oven:

> Stack the bacon in layers. Program the oven, allowing approximately one minute per slice. You may need to rotate the bacon halfway through the cycle. Be sure to use a microwave-safe rack for the bacon. Start the oven.

Anyone who has used an electronic microwave will know immediately that these instructions should not be followed literally. The writer has not followed the time order of steps closely enough. Too many steps have been left out. First, nothing is said about layering the bacon or using paper towels. Moreover, we are not told until the end to put the bacon on a microwave-safe rack. But worst of all, we are not told to program the oven for power level. If that is not done, the oven will not start, and the bacon will not be cooked.

EXERCISE 3: Freewrite; then plan a paragraph explaining how to do one of the activities below. Be sure to include all of the necessary steps in the time order in which they should occur.

1. How to change a flat tire
2. How to make a banana nut cake
3. How to make a peanut butter sandwich
4. How to paint an old-fashioned, multipaned window
5. How to eat a hero sandwich

Space Order for Description

Using time order is simple; just tell what happened in the order in which it happened. Organizing descriptions of space or of people is more difficult. In order to communicate a picture of a place, a person, or a thing, the writer must somehow translate visual images into written images. The physical space described must be organized according to some principle. The writer might, for example, move through the space looking from right to left; revolve around a focal point; or view the space in slices, right to left or front to back. It may be useful to begin with a map, then figure out a systematic way of covering the most important physical features.

PLAN 1 – MOVING THROUGH THE SPACE, LOOKING FROM RIGHT TO LEFT OR LEFT TO RIGHT

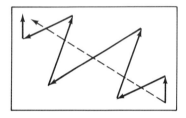 or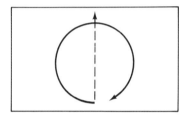

PLAN 2 – REVOLVING AROUND A FOCAL POINT

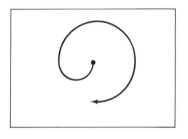 or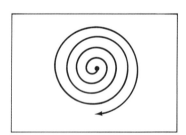

PLAN 3 – SLICING

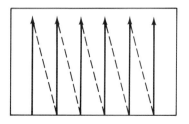 or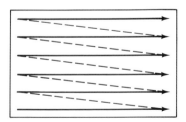

Two paragraphs about a night club illustrate a method of organizing physical space and also the problems that may result if the method breaks down.

One of the main sections in the club is the dancing area. It is by far the most breath-taking and in structure the simplest section. The music is loud but not too loud. There are no pauses between songs, since there are two turntables. The wooden floor is covered with fine sand to ease the feet of the dancers, who are a riotous mass, gyrating, flipping, and splitting across it. To my left, as I enter the dance floor, there is a carpeted staircase where spectators may watch the dancers. The walls on that side of the dance floor are lined with glass plates. To their right, reflecting garishly in the glass, are two large strobe lights and five red and blue revolving disco lights. In the far right hand corner there is a huge ivy plant with vines extending at least eight feet to the ceiling. In the reflected lights the ivy looks like something from Taurus 12 with red, blue, and purple leaves that seem to weave and dance up the wall. . . .

The patio of the club is directly outside the recreation room; it resembles a tropical outdoor bar. The floor is made of large level rocks. The floor is encased by brick flower beds. The patio is lit by black lights. This makes people's clothing appear fluorescent. The bar is made like a bamboo hut. The roof is made of long, even banana plant leaves. The whole patio is encircled by banana plants and palm trees in wooden blocks are directly behind the flower beds. There are tables for couples and also about five tables that seat four people. The patio is surrounded by an eight-foot fence. The music cannot be heard in this section. The bartender plays very mellow music on the radio. This section of the bar seems to attract loners.

In the first paragraph the writer enters the dance floor, describes what she sees at her feet and then immediately in front and around her. Next she "pans" the room itself from left to right. This simple but effective organization enables the reader to "see" the room. However, the second paragraph presents some problems. The writer begins with the floor, moves to the perimeter, then perhaps to the roof—if that is indeed where the lights are located—then back to the perimeter, and so forth. Because there is no method of organization, it is difficult to picture the bar. The reader wonders, for instance, whether the tropical hut we are looking at is circular or rectangular and where the bar and the bartender are located in relation to flower beds, tables, and palm trees.

Describing a person calls for the same attention to ordering physical details in space. A popular romance writer, describing a favorite heroine, begins with the skirt and works up.

> At twenty-two Marianna was unmistakably lovely and just as unmistakably unhappy. The severe fashions that failed to flatter most women only emphasized her beauty. The wide hoop skirts called attention to the smallness of her waist, and the short, layered cape set off her graceful shoulders. Her hair—parted in the middle and falling in luxurious curls around her ears and neck—framed a face set with enormous blue eyes fringed by long, curling lashes. Her cheeks were only a shade lighter than her vibrantly pink, full mouth, now drooping slightly at the corners. Her expression suggested not only discontent but also distrust and disaster.

> (Jean Conrad, from *Golden Gates*)

Again the writer's pen moves like a camera. It pans the subject, then moves in for a close-up of the face. Moving from there to a discussion of the girl's expression is a natural step.

EXERCISE 4: Evaluate the organization of these descriptions of a classroom on a hot August afternoon. Try to map the organization; then discuss the paragraphs in terms of space order.

> 1.   As I sit on the middle east side of the room looking west, I see Karen and she doesn't look too happy. Beverly is writing away; I think she's onto something, maybe a new recipe or a new dress to go out in. Somebody is playing the guitar and it's echoing in the room. I wish I knew more of the people in here. Oh well, that's too bad. Too bad Jeff hurt his writing hand. Is he going to quit school? I wonder. My cup is half filled with water and Beverly is finished writing. I think she found what she is looking for. Yes, I definitely think Karen is annoyed.
>
> 2.   First of all, in front of me is a row of chairs with three people sitting in them. One guy is not writing because his arm is in a sling. Then I moved to the next row with two young women. One is writing as though she knows what to say; the other is looking around as if she will find something to say on the ceiling. I move now to the third row of chairs. Again two people are sitting in this row. They seem to be writing about something

or someone interesting. I then move my eyes to the last row which is where I am sitting. The guy next to me is staring at me. I hope he is writing something nice about me.

3. The room is hot and stuffy. The people are half dead and wishing they were somewhere else. There are only eleven students and one professor. Some of the class is not here. The room is very quiet and boring with white walls and two chalkboards. It's a sunny hot day. I wish I was at home. But I'm here, writing my little heart out.

EXERCISE 5: Plan a paragraph that describes someone you know. Begin with a prewriting activity such as freewriting or brainstorming, and be sure to focus your description with a topic sentence.

Climactic Order

Like describing a place or person or recounting an event, the presentation of ideas must also be orderly. One good method to follow is to present ideas in climactic order of increasing importance. The writer begins with the least important idea and builds toward a climax with the most important idea last. Climactic order works because of human nature. We tend to remember most vividly what we are told most recently. If a writer uses the strong points at the beginning and concludes with weak points, the reader will probably remember the weak and forget the strong points. But if the strong arguments come last, they will be remembered and, moreover, will leave an overall impression of strength.

The arguments in the following paragraph are presented in climactic order.

Because of convenience American drivers will never renounce their cars for mass transit. With a privately owned vehicle, a driver can change route in the middle of a planned trip. For instance, we were driving through Texas and discovered from a sign that we could make a thirty-mile detour to visit friends. The convenience of a car also provides a fast form of transportation. I checked the bus timetable, and I could not work out a schedule that would be convenient for me. I would have to be at the bus stop at 6:15 A.M. and make one connection in order to be at work on time. Finally, Americans need private cars to perform daily activities. After shopping for groceries, we welcome the comfort of cars to get bags filled with items home. Since it would be awkward to travel on the bus, we could not buy large quantities. This means that we would have to make more trips and stops. For these reasons merchants would have to stop selling fuel completely before American drivers give up their cars for mass transit.

The writer presents three reasons why Americans will never give up their private vehicles—convenience in traveling long distances, convenience in daily commuting, and convenience in accomplishing daily activities. The importance of the arguments increases. The first is relatively minor since long trips may not occur that frequently for most people. The second is stronger because the difficulties of bus travel would actually work a physical hardship. But the third argument is strongest because it points out duties, like weekly or monthly grocery shopping, that could not be accomplished without a privately owned vehicle.

EXERCISE 6:   Prewrite a paragraph (explore, focus, and plan) that supports your opinion on one of the following issues. Arrange your support to build toward a climax.

1. Are credit cards a blessing or a curse?
2. What should be done when terrorists take hostages?
3. Should rock music be rated like movies?
4. How open should college admissions be?
5. Should children be able to sue their parents for not raising them properly? (or their teachers for not teaching them enough?)

FOCUS ON THE SENTENCE: *Prepositional Phrases and Subject-Verb Agreement*

It is important to discover the natural pattern or structure of your materials when you plan a paragraph. It is also important to study patterns of words when you write sentences. As we saw at the beginning of this chapter, the structure as well as individual words of a sentence convey meaning. Understanding that structure can help you write a better sentence and avoid some major sentence errors.

Prepositional Phrases

A *phrase* is a group of words that fit together but do not make up a complete sentence. A phrase is both a unit of thought and a unit of sentence structure. All of the words in a phrase express a single idea (or part of an idea) and are tied together by the grammar of the sentence.

One special kind of phrase begins with a preposition and ends with a noun or a word, such as a pronoun, that takes the place of the noun.

Called a *prepositional phrase* because the key word is the preposition, this phrase is tightly structured and, therefore, easy to recognize.

Prepositional phrase = Preposition + (possible modifiers) + object of preposition

                                                                              noun
                                                                           pronoun
                                                                      noun substitute

Consider, for example, the following short paragraph. There are nine different prepositional phrases, beginning with seven different prepositions.

At noon a change came over the town square. No longer were the benches filled with chatting loungers. The clusters of children had disappeared, leaving only a forgotten red ball as a reminder of interrupted games. Dark shadows chased the sun from the trampled lawns, and a creeping dampness like a thin, invisible mist filled the air and warned of the approaching storm.

The effect and meaning of the prepositional phrases are different, but the structure remains essentially the same. No matter where we find the phrases in the sentence, they will begin with a preposition and end with an object. Sometimes there will be words in between, and sometimes there will not.

preposition	(modifiers)	object
at		noon
over	the town	square
with	chatting	loungers
of		children
as	a	reminder
of	interrupted	games
from	the trampled	lawns
like	a thin, invisible	mist
of	the approaching	storm

Other common prepositions are listed below.

about	against	beneath	by
above	along	beside	down
across	around	between	during
after	as well as	beyond	except

except for	instead of	on	through
for	into	on top of	to
in	near	out	under
in addition to	off	outside	upon

Caution: Some of these words may be used in other ways in a sentence. They are not prepositions unless they have objects.

EXERCISE 7:   Underline the prepositional phrases in the following paragraph.

Lane-hoppers are the worst kind of drivers. Not only are they unhappy drivers, but they are also very nervous in their seats. It seems that they want everyone to be as miserable as possible. They switch lanes back and forth. They cut in front of anyone and everyone, causing people to slam on their brakes and yell in anger. Once while traveling on the Interstate with my brother, I spotted one of the worst lane-hoppers I had ever seen. He was criss-crossing all over the road, making people hit their brakes and swerve to avoid him. Then an eighteen-wheeler with a woman in the cab passed me. It caught up with the lane-hopper and pushed him for six blocks. We must have laughed for an hour.

EXERCISE 8:   Combine the following sentences into a single sentence by changing one or more sentences to prepositional phrases.

Example: We built a new home. The home has solar heating panels.
We built a new home with solar heating panels.

1. The Pueblo Indians knew how to build comfortable homes. The primary building material was adobe.
2. The thick adobe walls kept the temperature even. In winter the temperature was even. In summer the temperature was even.
3. Taos Pueblo is warmer inside than outside. This is true during the winter.
4. The warm rooms are a result. Passive solar heating makes them warm.
5. Some solar heating is called passive. This heating does not have a back-up system.
6. The Pueblo Indians have learned to use the sun. It is their energy source.

7. Houses should be built facing the winter sun. The large windows should face the winter sun. The living areas should face the winter sun.
8. Adobe walls should be thick. They could resemble other walls. A cave has three walls.
9. Trees should be planted to screen the house. The summer sun should be screened.
10. Sunken rooms increase the coolness. The house is cooler. The time is summer.

EXERCISE 9:   Fill in the blanks in the sentences with prepositional phrases.

1. _____ I get up, get dressed, and get going

   _____.

2. The tumble-down house _____ is supposed to

   be haunted, but I don't believe _____.

3. Daylight Savings Time lets us take advantage

   _____ and spend more time outdoors

   _____.

4. When I drove _____, I was terrified

   _____ and also _____.

5. Reading books _____ is my favorite pastime.

Subject-Verb Agreement

In Chapter 3 you learned that the subject in a sentence is the subject of the verb. The verb gives the action or state of the subject, and the two work together to make a statement. The connection between subject and verb is strengthened by a bond called agreement. Subjects and verbs must agree in number. That is, if we have a plural subject, we must have a plural verb; if we have a singular subject, we must have a singular verb.

Nouns show number or "how many" by adding *s* or by changing the word in some way for the plural.

one—singular	*more than one—plural*
contribution	contributions
woman	women
calf	calves
syllabus	syllabi

Verbs show number primarily in the present tense and in combination with singular subjects like the pronouns *it, he,* and *she* or singular nouns. *Rule of thumb:* The signals for singular and plural verbs are almost directly the opposite of those for nouns. With nouns an *s* ending means a plural; no change means singular. With verbs an *s* ending means singular; no change means plural.

singular verb	*plural verb*
reads	read
misleads	mislead
contributes	contribute

Your subject and verb are said to agree when both are singular or both are plural.

singular subject	*singular verb*
Jonathan	surrenders.
Carla	excels.

plural subject	*plural verb*
The lions	roar.
Horses	neigh.

EXERCISE 10: Rewrite the following sentences by changing plural subjects to singular and singular subjects to plural, then altering verbs to fit the subjects. Underline subjects and verbs in the original sentences and in your revisions.

> *Example:* An eighteen-wheel truck clears a path through the traffic.
>
> Eighteen-wheel trucks clear a path through the traffic.

1. At night the freeway looks like a moving river of lights.
2. Lost in a sea of smog the travelers inch forward a few feet at a time.
3. A fog horn blows a warning to ships coming close to the reef.
4. Rocky Mountain conifers are being killed by acid rain.
5. Acid rain upsets the delicate chemical balance of the soil.
6. Noise disrupts the city dwellers' waking and sleeping hours.
7. The chemical vapors sear the plants, burning their leaves and stunting their growth.
8. In the morning an oily black cloud rolls up the valley from the factories.

9. The child's lung was damaged by breathing the dirty air.
10. In some places our wilderness wonderland is fast becoming a giant garbage dump.

More Subject and Verb Agreement

1. When a verb has more than one subject, agreement depends on the nature of the subject. If the subjects are joined by *and* and can be replaced by a plural pronoun, use a plural verb.

Jennifer Williams and Roberta Mazone are both excellent divers.
<u>They</u>   plural
                                              verb

Playing chess and playing poker exercise your mental muscles.
<u>They</u>   plural
                                              verb

But:

Bread and butter makes a meagre snack.
It   singular
                  verb

If the subjects are joined by *or* or *nor*, the verb will agree with the subject closest to it.

Either the Senator or her staff members reply to all letters.
         singular   plural plural
         subject   subject verb

Either the staff members or the Senator replies to all letters.
         plural   singular singular
         subject   subject verb

Neither the reporters nor the editor believes the politician's story.
         plural   singular singular
         subject   subject verb

Neither the editor nor the reporters believe the politician's story.
         singular   plural plural
         subject   subject verb

Note: To avoid awkwardness, you should usually place the plural noun second.

2. Some subjects may be either singular or plural, depending upon the meaning of the sentence. Collective or group nouns are singular and take singular verbs if the group acts together, but the group nouns are plural and take plural verbs if the individuals in the group act separately.

The assembly is listening intently to the speaker.
(Everyone is listening.)
The assembly are mixed in their reactions to the speaker.
(Some like the speaker; some do not.)
The committee agrees.
(The members act as one.)
The committee disagree.
(The members act individually.)

Note: When correct agreement practice sounds awkward, revise the sentence. For example, the second and fourth examples above might be rewritten with plural subjects:

The members of the assembly are mixed . . .
The members of the committee disagree.

3. Some nouns appear to be plural because of an *s* ending, but they are actually singular, referring to one thing or idea. These nouns should be matched with singular verbs.

Economics is a challenging subject.
The news horrifies the listeners.
Six inches is the length of this scrap of ribbon.

EXERCISE 11: Underline subjects and verbs in the following sentences. Correct any errors that you find in the agreement of subjects and verbs.

Example: The group ~~are reading~~ is reading Stephen King's *Carrie.*

1. Neither the players nor the coach take responsibility for losing the game.
2. Both the players and the coach take responsibility for losing the game.
3. Physics challenge my mind and threaten my grade point average.
4. Peaches and cream are my favorite ice cream flavor.
5. Steak and lobster costs too much to be included on the reception menu for our four hundred guests.

6. Pinching pennies and squeezing nickles eventually saves me dollars.
7. Our sponsor and coach is an Olympic gold medal winner.
8. Suzanne, James, Antonio, or Kim turn off the computer every night.
9. The orchestra is tuning their instruments.
10. The orchestra plays a Hindemith symphony tonight.

4. When a phrase, such as a prepositional phrase, separates the subject from the verb, neither the number of the subject nor the number of the verb changes.

The king is a log.

The king of frogs is a log.
The king of all the silly pond frogs is a log.
The king unlike his subjects is a log.

The log king sits in the pond.

The log king, as well as his subjects, sits in the pond.

Note: As well as is sometimes mistakenly used as a synonym for *and;* however, *as well as*, like *in addition to* and *together with*, is a preposition.

5. Make sure your verbs agree with their subjects, even when those subjects follow rather than precede the verbs.

There are three green frogs on the lily pad.

    plural   plural
    verb   subject

Here comes the fattest frog of them all.

    singular   singular
    verb   subject

Grumpily croak the frogs in chorus.

    plural   plural
    verb   subject

However, be careful that the word your verb agrees with is actually the subject and not a noun serving some other function in the sentence. Sometimes there will be a noun before the verb and a noun after the verb, either of which sounds as though it could be the subject.

The caterpillars are/is a nuisance.

In this case the first noun, *caterpillars,* is the subject, and you should choose the plural verb *are* to agree with it. The second noun, *nuisance,* renames the subject and serves as a predicate word that completes the sentence, rather than as a subject. (See pages 244–49) for more about predicate words.)

EXERCISE 12:   Find and underline the subjects and verbs in the following paragraph. Correct any errors you identify in subject–verb agreement.

The Frogs Who Wanted a King
(Updated, with apologies to Aesop)

In a smelly green pond near Mount Olympus, the home of the Gods, there lives sixteen frogs. As noisy a crew as ever sat on lily pads, these frogs fill the nights with their grumbling. Each of the frogs have something to complain about. Either the thirteen small frogs or one of their three fat, slime-covered leaders start the racket each evening. "We haven't enough to eat," garrumphs a leader. "We want more to eat," echo the chorus. "An ample supply of flies are our right," the leader, as well as the other frogs, grumble. "We need a king to make sure we get what we deserve." And they call out to Zeus to give them a king.

Finally the gods, who have not been able to sleep for weeks, grow tired of the noise from the pond, and they appeal to Zeus to silence the frogs. Zeus, as well as Mars and Athena, look around for something to throw at these disturbers of the peace. Athena find an old log, and Zeus with the help of Mars hurl it at the pond.

The log lands with a splash. Most of the bewildered frog population dives for the muddy bottom of the pond, but one of the leaders remain, fully expecting a message from Zeus since to the frog mind even the gods cannot refuse to answer a people so mighty as the frogs.

Seeing the size and might of the log, the leader of the frogs are overcome with admiration. "What power! What strength!" the frog bellows. "Here is majesty and presence. Here is a king and a ruler worthy of the frog people!" And soon all of the frog population is emerging from the pond to cry, "All hail, King Log!"

For several nights then all are quiet as the frogs wait for their new King Log to bring more flies, increase the number of lily pads, clean up the slime, and in general improve conditions in the pond. On Mount Olympus the gods sleep, and Zeus smile to himself, pleased with the way he frightened the frogs into silence.

On the fourth night of King Log's reign the frogs begin to notice that there is no additional flies to eat, there are just as much slime in the pond, and the living conditions generally remain the same.

"Down with King Log," grumbles the fickle frogs, and once again the night is filled with their complaints. "This mighty nation of frogs deserve a better king!"

The noises reaches Mount Olympus and awakes the gods, who had gone to bed early in preparation for their Olympic games the next day.

"The frogs in the pond is becoming a major problem," thinks Zeus, and he calls for his pet stork. The stork eats the frogs, the frogs get what they deserve, and the gods on Mount Olympus are able to sleep.

MORAL: *Let sleeping gods lie.*

EXERCISE 13: Fill in missing verbs in the following paragraph. Make sure that your subjects and verbs agree.

Successfully planning and planting a rose garden
_____ little more than an eye for beauty and the

willingness to learn. The first of several steps _____
to choose a sunny location. Problems like mildew _____
more likely to occur in shady spots near trees or under the eaves
of the house. Next _____ selecting your roses. Neither
old favorites or patented roses _____
particularly difficult to grow, but some experienced gardners like
Nancy _____ special roses for spotlight locations such
as a lamp post or beside a walkway. Preparing the soil and
arranging the watering system _____ more a science
than an art. There _____ two basic things to
remember. Roses _____ light, loamy soil with a
slightly acid composition, and either sunken beds or a bubbler
system _____ needed to ensure deep watering.
Eighteen inches _____ an appropriate depth and
diameter for your hole if you _____ planting bare-root
roses. Two inches of steer manure at the bottom, covered with a
light layer of soil, _____ the roots something to reach
for, while a measure of root fertilizer mixed into the first
watering _____ a good start.

TROUBLESHOOTING: *Subject-Verb Agreement*

Reading what you have written aloud will help you find some kinds of
errors immediately, but for others, like subject-verb agreement, you will
need first to dig deeper into sentence structure and identify subjects and
verbs. You may need to cross out prepositional phrases that might confuse
your choice of verb; then you can read the subject and verb aloud to discover whether the combination sounds right. Take, for example, the following sentence from Exercise 12.

> s   v
> *Original:* Each of the frogs have something to complain about.
> s   v
> Each have ?

s   v

Revised: <u>Each</u> <u>has</u> something to complain about.

In the original sentence the plural object in the prepositional phrase *of the frogs* makes the plural verb *have* sound correct. However, if we eliminate the prepositional phrase and read the subject and verb together, the error is immediately apparent. The subject *each* is singular, calling for the singular verb *has*.

EXERCISE 14: Troubleshoot for errors in the following paragraphs. Find and correct errors in spelling, end punctuation (fragments, run-ons, comma splices), and subject-verb agreement.

1. The gian redwoods of northern California seems out of place in our modern world. Where trees grow stunted in the smog and skyscrappers tower in all thier chrome and concrete glory. Early in the morning, drapped in swirling white mists. The forest of mammoth trees look prehistoric. Like part of another world. A world inhabited by dinasores and cave dwellers. Huge fernes grow as tall as small trees in the dim light, giant flowers—lilys, orchids, and anemones—bloom unseen, soft, green mosses draw lacey curtins across the open spaces. There is an atmospheare of unreality and a feeling of great peace. As though in this one place the ravages and relentless decay of time has stopped. Leaving, at least for a while, a timeless refuge for nature's most beautiful creations.

2. Office work has changed drasticly in the past twenty years, in 1966 an office was precided over by a secratary. She (for then a secratary was inevitibly a woman) more then her employer knew what was happening. And were responsible for making it happen! The secretary controled the pace of office work. Scheduleing appointments. Taking messages. Determineing who could and who could not see "The Boss." There was little that she did not know about the work and less that she was not

involved in. Today, however, the bespectacled private secratary with her shorthand pad and intercom are almost a thing of the past, in her place has come the compact PC with word-processing capibility, the diction machine, the office manager, and the word-processing pool. Executives dictate letters and reports into a machine or draft their own correspondence on the PC finished copies are prepared in a word processing center by technicians. Who may never meet the writer in person. Machines also answer the phones, take messages. Even survey perspective clients? And in charge of the office are the secratary's replacement and alter ego, the office manager, this person, who usally has at least a bachelor's degree in business administration, controles the pace of office work but does not make coffee. May schedule appointments but rarely takes dictation. And sometimes does not even type, moreover, today's office manager is frequently a man!

3.   A tree of life symbilizes the stages of growth. Beginning with childhood and concluding with death. To make up the symbol, there is a tree trunk, branches of varying lengths, and brightly colored birds that sit on or fly around the branches. The branches near the roots are short and leafless. Representing childhood. The branches toward the middle of the trunk, when life is vigerous and complex, spreads wide, and the birds nests among the leaves. To show the reproductive functions of that period. Later, when life is in its final stages. The branches again grow short the leaves are fewer the birds fly. No longer tyed to the tree and to life.

The subject of many Indian rugs, the tree of life make a colerful will hanging and a vivid reminder, it shows the fulness of our days rooted in life's soil. But it also shows the freedom of our spirits. Ready to fly away when we reach the end of this life. Or the top of this tree.

READING TO WRITE

In "HALO (High-Altitude—Low-Opening) Jump" on page 320 of the Readings in Part II, J. C. Pollock uses time order. He follows a parachute jump from the plane to the ground. Each step is described, and strong verbs increase the sense of motion and time.

Pollock describes more than two dozen body movements of the sky diver. For example, in paragraph five, six separate actions are described. The diver bends, rolls his shoulders, places his arms back, cups his hands, brings his head back, and stretches his legs out. Such detailed description helps us "see" the action; it also helps us understand the process.

After you read "HALO" and answer the questions in the margin, make a plan of the jump process. Does Pollock leave any gaps? Which parts of the jump does he explain best? Compare "HALO" to the Momaday article you read for Chapter 4. How does the authors' use of words differ? How does this difference affect you as a reader?

WRITING ACTIVITY WORKSHEET

Choose a process that you know especially well—a cooking specialty, a board game, a dance step, a maneuver on skis, a household chore, an art, or a craft. Limit the magnitude of the process so that you may say something significant about it in a paragraph. (Do not, for example, try to explain the entire mechanism of an engine or the entire process involved in creating a hand-woven tapestry; stick to showing how the carburetor works or how to spin the wool for the weaving.)

Once you have chosen a subject, explore your knowledge of the subject with a prewriting activity. Discover an opinion or an attitude to focus your paper. Is it difficult or easy? Is it a major motivation for your existence or a way to kill time? Do you recommend this method over others and if so, why?

ACTIVITY: Write a paragraph about a process that you know well. Focus your subject in a topic sentence, make a plan, write, and rewrite a paragraph explaining the process. Use the troubleshooting techniques you have learned in this and previous chapters as you look for errors.

CHECKLIST: As you finish each draft, check it carefully for the following:

1. Is your topic sentence clear and well focused?
2. Have you used time order effectively?
3. Are any steps in the process left out?
4. Do all of your subjects and verbs agree?
5. Are there any fragments, run-ons, or comma splices?
6. Are there any errors in spelling, any left-out words, or any reversed letters?

CHAPTER SIX
Coherence

Writing That Coheres

Something coheres when it holds or sticks together. You write coherently when you follow these guidelines:

1. Focus the subject carefully, and choose support to fit the focus.
2. Organize ideas logically, matching structure to content.
3. Use words or sentences that emphasize the relationship between things or ideas.

Paragraph 1 below shows what happens when Gregg, a student writer, does not follow these guidelines.

#1

Working and going to school can create a split personality. There's the school me—quiet, attentive, concerned about getting assignments in on time and getting a good grade. At work I am aggressive and confident. Good workers know what they are doing, and they get the job done. Good students get their assignments in on time, but they may still worry about their grades. I feel I am still learning to be a good student, so I ask a lot of questions instead of giving my opinions. Some people might think I am timid in the classroom.

The paragraph is incoherent; that is, it does not hold together. The support is disorganized. The ideas do not follow logically one from another. Gregg moves back and forth from talking about workers and students in general to talking about himself in particular. Paragraph 2, on the other hand, is coherent.

#2

Working and going to school have split my personality. The work-me is a tiger. I know what I am doing, and I get the job done well, therefore, I am aggressive and confident. Sometimes I back up my ideas with commands! "Do it this way. Don't do it that way." And always I give my opinion—asked for or not. On the other hand the school-me is a pussycat. I am just learning to be a good student, so in the classroom I am quiet and attentive. Usually I ask questions rather than give my opinions. Often I am too worried about getting my assignment in on time and getting a good grade to have formed an opinion. I guess the only cure for this split-personality is the time it will take to make the school-me also a tiger.

The writer uses subtopic sentences to organize the support. The viewpoint is consistent, staying with the writer's personal experiences. And the writer connects ideas throughout the paragraph by repeating words and by using transitional expressions.

In this chapter you will continue to study ways of focusing, organizing, and connecting ideas to improve the coherence of your writing. Some of the methods you study will become an important part of planning your paper. Others will be useful as you evaluate your work for rewriting.

FOCUS ON WRITING: *Writing Coherent Paragraphs*

Planning a Paragraph with Subtopic Sentences

You have learned to use topic sentences to focus the content of a paragraph. Occasionally you may need to use subtopic sentences to organize ideas within a paragraph. *Subtopic sentences* divide the subject of the topic sentence into parts to be developed one part at a time. In paragraph 2 above, the writer uses subtopic sentences to divide the subject of the topic sentence into two parts.

Topic sentence Working and going to school have split my personality.

Subtopic sentence The work-me is a tiger.
Subtopic sentence The school-me is a pussycat.

Subtopic sentences such as these are like road signs. They tell the writer as well as the reader when to make a turn and which direction to go in. These road signs may be particularly useful when your subject is complicated.

In the second paragraph, the writer tightens up the organization of ideas with subtopic sentences. They tell us when she will discuss her work personality and when she will discuss her school personality. Making the subtopic sentences part of the writing plan also shows the writer where she needs more support. Notice the progress as we move from the first to the final plan for the paragraph.

Plan for first draft
Topic sentence Working and going to school can create a split personality.
quiet school me
aggressive work personality
knowing the job/getting it done
turn assignments in on time
get good grades
ask questions

Revised plan with subtopic sentences
Topic sentence Working and going to school can create a split personality.
Subtopic sentence The work-me is a tiger.
aggressive
knowing the job/getting it done
Subtopic sentence The school-me is a pussycat.
turn assignments in on time
get good grades
ask questions

Revised plan with subtopic sentences and added support
Topic sentence Working and going to school have split my personality.
Subtopic sentence The work-me is a tiger.
know the job/get it done well
aggressive
confident
give commands
give my opinion

Subtopic sentence   The school-me is a pussycat.
  quiet
  attentive
  ask questions rather than give opinions
  worried about turning in assignments on
  time and getting good grades

The first revision shows clearly that Gregg needs more support for each subtopic. The subtopic sentences also help him focus more carefully on his own qualities or actions, avoiding the generalities that mar the first draft.

EXERCISE 1:   Underline topic sentences and subtopic sentences in the following paragraphs.

1.   Overcoming my phobia about airplane travel did not happen overnight. First, I had to understand why I was afraid. I had made several flights without fear before that fateful trip to Tulsa. That had been more than a turbulent flight; it had been hazardous. Caught in the edge of a hurricane, the jet had been tossed through the sky, and I had been permanently traumatized. Once a cause had been established, treatment could begin. For me even looking at an airplane on television was frightening, so I began very simply by keeping my eyes open when an airplane appeared on the screen. When I could do that without my heart beating faster, it was time to visit an airport. At first all I could do was drive through the parking lot. Then I walked into the terminal and eventually had dinner at the airport restaurant. Finally, I was ready for a real flight. It was a short one—from San Francisco to Oakland, and I took the bus back. But it was a start. I still do not like to fly, but at least I can do it when I must.

2.   Watching *Wheel of Fortune* should be educational, but for me at least it isn't. You would think that solving puzzles would help me learn new vocabulary and improve spelling skills. I solved the "Strait of Hormuz" puzzle before any of the contestants, and correctly guessed "Congressional Record" when the contestant said "Congressional Report." But yesterday I learned that I could not remember any of the things I thought I was learning. I watched a rerun of *Wheel of Fortune* and only solved one puzzle. I had forgotten how to spell "chocolate truffles" and mispronounced *cymbidium* in the puzzle "cymbidium orchid."

EXERCISE 2:   Write at least two subtopic sentences for each of the following topic sentences. Some may require more than two.

1. The color red has many meanings—some positive, some negative.
2. The express line at the supermarket attracts three different kinds of customers.
3. Changing a flat tire on a hill is not easy.
4. Driving a compact differs from driving a large car.
5. I am swearing off soft drinks.

EXERCISE 3:   Plan a revision for this incoherent paragraph, using subtopic sentences to help you reorganize the ideas. You may add details as necessary.

> The bobcat gets its name from its stubby, bobbed tail. One of the most common wildcats in North America, the bobcat may bear its kittens in tree trunks, small caves, or any dark, warm shelter. Bobcats may weigh no more than twenty pounds—the size of a large house cat. Their kittens are usually born in the late summer or early spring. Bobcats are common in most of the lower forty-eight states. They often measure about twenty-five inches in length and stand fifteen inches tall. If about the same size, bobcats are much stronger than house cats and have been known to kill small deer on occasion. They are talented hunters and feed their kittens by catching mice, squirrels, rabbits, and some birds, such as quail. Bobcats do not shun man and have even been sighted living in New York's Central Park. Adults and kittens rarely stray far from their dens.

Viewpoint

Maintaining a consistent point of view is also important for coherence. Point of view is the eyes through which we see the subject or our focus on that subject.

> You never know when disaster may strike. A California couple left their home in Yorba Linda for work in Los Angeles recently. They locked the doors carefully and turned on the burglar alarm as usual. When he returned home ten hours later, the house was gone, fallen into a fault that had opened in the earth. No one had even known there was a fault beneath the house. The couple is suing the real estate company that sold them the house.

The point of view in this paragraph begins with *you,* then shifts successively to a *couple, he, no one,* and then back to *couple.* To make the point of view consistent, the writer must choose one of these points of view and maintain it throughout the paragraph.

> An unexpected disaster struck a California couple recently. They had left their home in Yorba Linda for work in Los Angeles, locking the doors and turning on the burglar alarm as usual. When they returned home ten hours later, the house was gone, fallen into a fault that had opened up in the earth. The couple had not known there was a fault beneath their house. They are suing the real estate company that sold them the house.

In the revision the writer has focused on the couple's point of view—their actions, their interests, and their perceptions. Notice the pronouns in the revised paragraph. *They, them,* or *their* are used consistently to keep the focus on the couple.

EXERCISE 4:   Identify problems with point of view in the paragraphs. Then revise to correct those problems.

1.   The storm caught us camping in the mountains, with the top of the jeep down and our supplies on the picnic table. The campers scrambled through the downpour. George tried to pull the canvas top of the jeep over the already wet seats. I filled a soggy cardboard box with food, and the soaked camper ran for the tent. The storm beat relentlessly on the canvas tent for twelve long, wet hours while inside the campers huddled miserably, eating our damp food and worrying about how we would get out of the mountains in the morning.

2.   The reporters gathered in the rotunda of the Capitol to hear the Governor's address. No one knew what the address would be about. You could hear the scratch of a pen on paper as she waited to begin. The Governor's eyes traveled briefly over the upturned faces. The reporters leaned forward eagerly. No one was prepared as she made her opening statement, "I have called you here to announce my resignation as governor." The reporters then heard that the former Governor had accepted a position as Ambassador to Great Britain.

Transitions

Transitions are word bridges. They connect ideas by showing their relationship. Transitions between sentences help hold the ideas of individual paragraphs together. Writers make transitions by repeating words or sentence structure or by careful use of pronouns and transitional expressions.

1. You can make transitions between sentences by repeating words and using pronouns effectively.

> Professional wrestling is more hoopla and entertainment than sport. Greco-Roman wrestlers are true sportsmen. They face each other over a regulation mat, wear regulation trunks and shoes and wrestle using regulation holds like the headlock and the full nelson. In professional wrestling there are few regulations. The wrestlers dress up in costumes and call themselves outlandish names like Hulk, Bo Bo, or King Kong. They battle in a ring before thousands of fans screaming for blood, and they brutalize each other with flying kicks, knee drops, toe holds, or the claw. For professional wrestling fans the violence may be entertaining, but is wrestling a true sport?

Professional wrestling is repeated three times, keeping the paragraph's main topic clearly in our minds. Wrestlers are referred to eight times, twice by repeating the noun *wrestlers* and six times by using pronouns.

EXERCISE 5: Revise the following paragraph by using repetition and pronouns to improve coherence.

> The Lazy Susan, a deep-sea fishing trawler out of Bandon, Oregon, set to sea at dawn. The vessel's deck was filled with sightseers and hopeful anglers. The small ship's captain was at the wheel. The crew consisting of two sailors and a cabin boy, divided the time between attending to the needs of the passengers and taking care of the necessities involved in managing a boat. By eight o'clock the problems of baiting hooks and getting sea legs were over, and the tourists were having a good time. But no person had made a catch. By noon the people were getting impatient. "Paying customers were promised results," complained these seagoers. "Where are the finny tribe?" Then sharp tugs yanked two of the lines trailing in the saltwater, and disappointment was forgotten as two individuals struggled to land salmon.

2. You can make transitions between sentences by using transitional words and expressions.

> To make gourmet quality popcorn, you must begin with the finest corn, preferably Orville Redenbacher's Gourmet Original

Popping Corn. First, measure two tablespoons of vegetable oil into a saucepan on top of the stove. (For the best results you should avoid machines; they pop at too low a temperature.) Next put two kernels in the pan, cover the pan tightly, and place over low-to-medium heat. When the kernels pop, the oil is ready. Then pour a half a cup of corn into the pan, recover the pan, and shake the pan with a continuous back and forth motion until all of the kernels have popped. Now you are ready for the final steps. Empty your pan of popped corn into a large bowl. Season the corn with Orville Redenbacher's special popcorn salt. Finally, pour melted cheese over the corn and toss lightly with a fork. But do not wait too long to begin eating. Popcorn is best when it is freshly popped and hot. Enjoy your feast!

The underlined transitional words help emphasize the progress from step to step in the instructions. There is a list of transitional expressions on page 260 and more examples of their use on pages 259–61.

EXERCISE 6:   Revise the following paragraph by using transitional words and expressions to improve coherence. As you revise, you will need to connect some sentences and combine others. You may add or delete as necessary.

People today are health conscious. Most agree that some kind of daily exercise is necessary. They disagree on how to go about the daily work-out. The health spa offers a solution. The spa provides a full range of individual activities. They can lift weights using complex machinery. They require no spotters. They minimize the dangers of traditional weight lifting. They can swim, usually in an Olympic-size pool. The water is heated. They can take aerobic classes. They can work out with a group. They can enjoy the fun of dancing. Some people prefer exercising alone. They run in the park. They hike in the mountains. They pump iron in their home gyms. These people believe something. Exercising is a private matter. It is like bathing or brushing one's teeth. Some people prefer the exercise of a game. They need competition to get them moving. They are not motivated by weight loss. The possibility of losing a point makes them work their hardest. People have different ways of getting healthy. They have different ways of staying healthy. The method does not really matter. Doing some kind of exercise is important. It may lead to a healthier life. It may lead to a happier life.

3. You can make transitions between sentences by repeating certain sentence structures, making them *parallel.*

Sentence structures are parallel when they match in form and in sound and when they serve the same function. Any parts of a sentence or entire sentences may be made parallel.

Read aloud each of the parallel structures listed below. Listen as well as look for the elements that make them parallel.

Parallel words	*Parallel phrases*	*Parallel sentences*
longer	the long, hot	A cold rain drummed on
healthier	summer	the roof.
happier	the short, wet	A sharp wind pried at the
	spring	shutters.
dancing		
singing	of the people	Into the belfry flew the
	by the people	bat.
	for the people	Out of the belfry ran the
		bell ringer.
		Around the belfry leaped
		the cat.

The repeated word endings, *-er* and *-ing,* are our first clue that the words *longer, healthier,* and *happier* are parallel and that *dancing* and *singing* are parallel. The parallel words also serve the same function in a sentence.

You will live a longer, healthier, happier life.
Singing and dancing are my favorite pastimes.

The parallel phrases sound alike, are structured alike, and can fill the same slots in a sentence. The first two phrases begin with *the,* then add two words and conclude with a noun. The second set consists of prepositional phrases with different prepositions but repeated objects.

The short, wet spring and the long, hot summer make me long for the fall. (subjects)
Government of the people, by the people, and for the people shall not perish from the earth. (prepositional phrases describing *Government*)

The parallel sentences too are matched. The first two are structured exactly the same, beginning with *a* and ending with a prepositional phrase. The three parallel sentences reverse normal sentence order: they begin with a prepositional phrase and end with the subject.

Words and phrases connected by *and* should always be parallel. The matching sounds make the sentence sound smooth, and the matching structures help clarify meaning. Notice what happens when the parts are not parallel.

<u>Singing</u>, <u>dancing</u>, and <u>to play chess</u> are my favorite pastimes.

The third item in the series of subjects sounds awkward. Change it to a word with an *-ing* ending, and the awkwardness is removed.

<u>Singing</u>, <u>dancing</u>, and <u>playing chess</u> are my favorite pastimes.

Parallel sentences can be especially helpful in emphasizing the relationship between ideas.

Mo is undoubtedly not a premier basketball player.
But Mo is definitely a champion soccer player.

The market slumped because of the deficit.
The deficit rose because of lower taxes.

In the first pair of sentences, the parallel structure helps us see a contrast more clearly and therefore emphasizes that contrast. In the second pair the parallel structure underlines the relationship linking the market slump to the deficit and the deficit to the taxes.

Parallel sentences and parallel structures within sentences can work together to make a paragraph more coherent. Compare the following statements about pollution:

Pollution is not the exclusive problem of smoggy Los Angeles or New York City or any of our dirty cities. We live in a polluted world. Our air is filled with pollution, and every breath we take is polluted. The streams and lakes and underground reservoirs that supply us with water to drink are polluted. The land that we live on is filled with contaminating substances. Trees are dying in the vast western forests. They are victims of acid rain. Dead fish are floating in the ocean, killed by radioactive waste from distant industrial complexes. And in far-away places, untouched by modern civilization, little children may be dying from mercury poisoning or DDT that has entered the food chain.

[1]Pollution is not the exclusive problem of smoggy Los Angeles or of any dirty city. [2]We live in a polluted world. [3]The air we

breathe is polluted. [4]The water we drink is polluted. [5]Even the land we build our houses on and plant our crops in is polluted. [6]In the vast western forests, trees are dying, victims of acid rain. [7]In the oceans fish are dying, victims of radioactive waste from distant industrial complexes. [8]And in far-away places, untouched by modern civilization, little children may be dying, victims of mercury poisoning or DDT that has entered the food chain.

The two paragraphs say essentially the same thing. But the second one uses parallel structures to emphasize and connect ideas. For example, making sentences 3, 4, and 5 parallel helps tie together the pollution of air, water, and land and clarifies what is meant by "polluted world" in sentence 2. Sentences 6, 7, and 8, which identify victims of this pollution, are also tied together by parallel structure, emphasizing the serious and far-reaching effects of pollution.

EXERCISE 7:   Rewrite the following sentences to make some parts parallel.

1. Samson went to the mall today and purchased two records, a sweatshirt, and he also bought a pair of running shoes.
2. There are three kinds of mail carriers—the dependable ones, the sometimes dependable ones, and then there are the ones who deliver the mail to the wrong address.
3. I know I am wrong when I protest too long that I am right and I protest too loudly.
4. Wait for me on the corner, don't get on the bus, and you should never hitchhike.
5. Winning the sweepstakes, Hawaii, and to own a TransAm head my wish list.
6. Fran will not be attending the convention this year because of her asthma and because the convention is held in San Francisco—a high-risk site for asthmatics.
7. Free, remote, and it doesn't leak—these are the main advantages of the cabin.
8. Telephoning New York, London, and around the world becomes easier each year.
9. On the title page the author wrote: "None of the incidents, crimes, and what you may consider shocking scandals in this book are fictitious."
10. The names have not been changed to protect the innocent. The names have been changed for the protection of those who are guilty and also for the protection of the author.

EXERCISE 8:   Rewrite the paragraph using parallel structures and other transitions to improve coherence. Combine sentences wherever necessary.

> Salespeople at Grimm's Department Store are completely predictable. They are overeager, or they could not care less. The overeager salespeople are impossible to miss. You walk into the store. They are on you in a second. They greet you like a long-lost friend. Then the sales, clearly marked in three-foot signs, are called to your attention. They never let you out of their sight. On the other hand, missing the "undereager" salespeople is easy. They are never around. You have tried on three sweaters. You have tried on six skirts. You have tried on six dresses. Some are too big. Some are too little. The only items in your size are on the mannequins. You cannot find a salesperson to take them down. You finally find something to buy. There is no salesperson around to take your money. It's hard to say which is worse. The overeager salespeople make shopping difficult and so do the "undereager."

FOCUS ON THE SENTENCE: *More Agreement*

As you have seen, pronouns play an important role in coherence. They help you maintain a consistent point of view and make transitions. However, to be effective, these pronouns must "agree."

Pronoun Agreement

In Chapter 5 you learned that subjects must agree with, or have the same number as, verbs. Pronouns must also agree with the word or words they refer back to. Notice what happens when pronoun agreement is not observed.

> The pilot began the maneuver on their upward climb. They were at a ninety degree angle when they began to roll. He turned forty-five degrees, and broke out of the climb and dove back toward the airfield.

The shifts from singular *pilot* to plural *their* and *they* and then to singular *he* leave the reader unsure about what is happening. Who is climbing? Who turns? How many are involved in the maneuver? There are at least three possibilities: one pilot who is part of a squadron but performs this maneuver alone, an entire squadron who maneuver together, or a lone pilot. Which of these possibilities is intended in this paragraph is unclear.

To maintain agreement in a sentence or a paragraph, you should keep two things in mind.

1. What the pronoun refers to should be clearly stated and easy to identify.
2. The pronoun should agree with the word or words it refers to in three ways: number, person, and gender.

Number

If the pronoun refers to a singular word, the pronoun should also be singular. If it refers to a plural word or words, the pronoun should also be plural.

       singular   singular
The <u>parade</u> made <u>its</u> way into the fairgrounds.

       plural   plural
The <u>marchers</u> made <u>their</u> way into the fairgrounds.

When the pronoun refers to more than one word, the same guidelines you studied for subject-verb agreement apply. If the words are joined by *and,* the pronoun will usually be plural. If the words are joined by *or* or *nor,* the pronoun will agree with the closer word.

                  plural   plural
The <u>stagecoaches and balloon-covered float</u> made <u>their</u> way into the fairgrounds.

                              singular   singular
Either the stagecoaches or the balloon-covered <u>float</u> made <u>its</u> way into the fairgrounds.

                                 plural
Neither the balloon-covered float nor the <u>stagecoaches</u> made
plural
<u>their</u> way into the fairgrounds.

Note: As with subject-verb agreement, you should usually place the plural noun second to avoid awkwardness.

When the pronoun refers to a group noun such as *team* or *audience,* the number of the pronoun depends upon whether the group is acting together as one or separately as individuals.

The <u>team</u> <u>is losing</u> <u>its</u> homecoming game.
(They lose together.)
The <u>team</u> <u>are studying</u> for <u>their</u> final exams.
(They study separately.)

Note: To avoid awkwardness, revise the sentence: The students on the team are studying for their final exams.

Person

The *person* of a pronoun is found by referring to its position in a communication triangle (see Figure 6–1).

The first person is talking to the second person about the third person. Or *I* am talking to *you* about *him.* Or *we* are talking to *you* about *them.*

Nouns and pronouns such as *someone, all, any, everybody* and so forth, which are not part of this triangle, are considered to be third person.

An error in agreement of person would occur if, for example, a second-

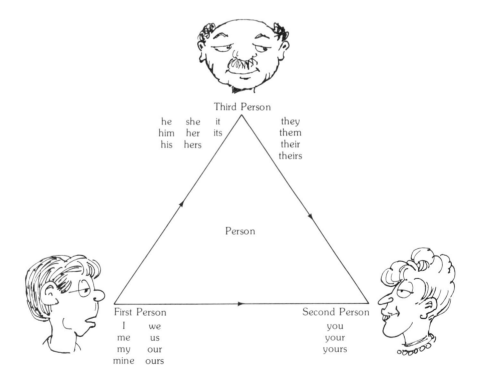

FIGURE 6–1

person pronoun is used to refer to a third-person noun or a third-person pronoun is used to refer to a first-person pronoun.

                              3rd person   2nd person

Error: The runners began the last lap by increasing your pace.

                              3rd person   3rd person

Correction: The runners began the last lap by increasing their pace.

                         1st person   3rd person

Error: I began my work as a kitchen helper in June. Her

        promotion to pastry cook came in December.

                         1st person   1st person

Correction: I began my work as a kitchen helper in June. My

        promotion to pastry cook came in December.

Gender

When the gender of a word referred to is masculine, a masculine pronoun (*he, him, his*) should refer to it. When the gender is feminine, a feminine pronoun (*she, her, hers*) should refer to it. When a singular word is neither masculine nor feminine, use *it* or *its*.

    Masculine: Giorgio combed his hair with his fingers.
    Feminine: The policewoman pinned on her badge.
    Neither: The department fired its top investigator for insubordination.

EXERCISE 9: Find and correct errors in pronoun agreement or reference in the following sentences. Make any other corrections called for.

1. A hot air balloon decorated like a fruit basket bumped his gondola against a power line.
2. The Federal Food and Drug Administration issued a statement on the safety of saccharin. They indicated that tests show carcinogens but in small amounts.
3. The novice chili eater should begin by tasting a mild salsa on tortilla chips. When the salsa no longer singes your mouth, you are ready for the real thing.
4. While Rome burned, either Nero or the senators played his fiddle.
5. With a bottle of correction fluid at hand, my secretary Curt inserted stationery in her typewriter and began typing their letter. I refused to sign them because of your errors.

6. At dawn the flag was raised over the remote outpost. They waved it proudly.
7. The famous wood carver explained that before you begin carving the wood, you must see a shape in it.
8. "I carve to free a bird or a fox from the wood," he said. "You have to see the finished product before you cut your wood."
9. Theresa, along with her twelve brothers and sisters, will celebrate their holiday by taking themselves and their skis to Vail, Colorado.
10. Alice and the Chesire Cat, probably the most famous of all the Wonderland characters, will be celebrating its partnership with an unanniversary party.

EXERCISE 10: Fill in the blanks in the following paragraph with appropriate nouns and pronouns.

A winter sun shone coldly on the lost expedition. _____ pale beams along with a light _____ of snow created a washed-out landscape where trails and landmarks were lost _____ distinctive shapes and colors blending into a white _____. The leader of the expedition, a _____ in _____ fifties, walked wearily at the head of the little _____. _____ leaned on a crooked _____ of mesquite and motioned _____ team to join _____ in searching for a _____. With map in front of _____ and the wilderness all around _____, the frightened _____ looked for some clue to _____ whereabouts. _____ food was gone; _____ courage was gone. What would _____ matter now if _____ found the Seven Cities of Gold?

EXERCISE 11: Rewrite the following paragraphs, beginning with the revision indicated in parentheses. Change verbs and pronouns as necessary for agreement.

1. The dedicated runner (change to plural) makes his morning run a ritual. First, he dresses in a designer exercise suit that cost a

week's wages. He puts a sweatband around his head, straps a famous-brand watch with stopwatch functions to his wrist, and laces up running shoes endorsed by the world's fastest man. Once these robes of his special cult have been donned, he is ready for one lap around the park and breakfast at the nearest health food bar.

2.   Trekking north to Alaska on the Alcan Highway, you (change to the tourist) come prepared. Your car is strapped with extra tires for those inevitable flats. You have crammed the trunk with emergency food, emergency water, emergency thermal underwear and blankets, and an extra-large emergency first-aid kit, complete with splints and tablets to purify water. You have bought several maps of the highway, including geological survey maps that mark springs in case you get lost. One wonders if you would have a better time if you took the bus.

3.   Street people (change to a bag lady) begin their day on a bus stop bench with all the aches and tiredness of a sleepless night. They add blankets of fresh newspapers from the nearby trash can to last night's edition in a vain attempt to keep warm. When that does not work, they heave themselves upright and go in search of a warm vent from a laundry or a warm lobby where they can stand for a few moments before they are chased away by the inevitable doorman. Their day is spent shuffling from Salvation Army post to garbage can, from rescue mission to garbage can, from bus station to garbage can. The librarian will turn a blind eye as they doze off in the comfortable library chairs, if they are lucky. If they are not lucky, they will be chased out of the library and turned away by the Salvation Army as a too-frequent visitor. If they are really lucky, they will be picked up by the police for vagrancy and spend the next night in a warm cell with a place to sleep and plenty to eat.

TROUBLESHOOTING: *Pronoun Agreement*

Like errors in subject-verb agreement, errors in pronoun agreement are not always apparent to the ear. An error may sound right because we are more accustomed to hearing the error than we are to hearing correct usage. Some special problems occur with the third-person pronouns that end in *one* or *body:*

anyone	anybody
someone	somebody
no one, none	nobody
everyone	everybody

Although some of these pronouns are habitually treated as though they were plural, all are singular; therefore, they need singular verbs and singular pronouns to refer back to them. As with subject-verb agreement you may need to eliminate intervening words and put the words that should agree close together to "hear" errors.

> *not:* Everyone of the astronauts are drinking their Tang.
>   Everyone are drinking their
> *but:* Everyone of the astronauts is drinking his or her Tang.

The use of both *his* and *her* to refer to *everyone* is necessary because the astronauts include both men and women. If you or your teacher finds this construction awkward, you can revise the sentence using a plural word as subject.

> All of the astronauts are drinking their Tang.
> The astronauts are drinking their Tang.

When pronouns throughout a paragraph do not agree, we say there are *shifts* in number, person, or gender. To identify pronoun shifts, you can make a pronoun map by circling each pronoun and drawing an arrow to the word it refers to. Then study the map for unnecessary shifts.

> Losing weight is a way of life for many people. (They) lose and gain hundreds of pounds every year, alternately starving (themselves) and feasting as a reward for the weight (they) have lost. (Some) join clubs for support. (You) never know when the urge to eat a gallon of ice cream might hit (you), and fellow club members can help you resist temptation.

The pronoun map highlights the shift between third-person *some* and second-person *you.*

> Losing weight is a way of life for many people. They lose and gain hundreds of pounds every year, alternately starving themselves and feasting as a reward for the weight they have lost. Some join clubs for support. They never know when the urge to eat a gallon of ice cream might hit them, and fellow club members can help them resist temptation.

EXERCISE 12: Identify and correct errors in pronoun agreement in the following paragraph.

The day began happily enough. Everybody in the print shop were on the job. They looked wide awake and ready to work. Suzanne began duplicating a manuscript for a local author, and George started their day with an order for stationery and business cards. Then someone remembered that they had forgotten to pull the blinds and unlock the front door. On the sidewalk stretching for half a block was a line of customers so angry you could almost see the steam coming out of their ears. The first man in line as well as the woman behind him shook their fists and held up their orders. "Your sign says we open at eight o'clock," shouted one customer. "They have made me late to my job," accused another. "None of us are leaving until you do our work," the last person in line yelled. For the rest of the morning, the print shop staff worked frenziedly, wearing out his or her shoes running from machine to machine as well as his or her patience trying to soothe everyone's ruffled feelings.

EXERCISE 13: Look for problems with pronoun agreement and shifts in Jerry's paragraph, as well as errors in subject-verb agreement, spelling, and end punctuation.

Waking up in an intensive care room can be a frightining experience. Not unlike dreaming you are being held captive by a mad scientist. The clean white walls and smell of anteseptic and alcohol remind me of a medical labratory. The presence of unfamliar beeping machinery. All with their own bouncing lighted displays attached to my body by slim electrodes can be quiet unerving. The multitude of clear plastic tubing attached to diffrent portions of your body, each of which drips. A diffrent colored substance from or into its own measured container makes one wonder what their purpose is. The coldness of the room and the hissing rush of oxygen past your face makes you feel like someone is enjoying your discomfort. My body being restrained by stiff white starched sheets give me a feeling of inprisonment. The increbile dryness and itching in your throat, along with the intense pain comming from diffrent parts of your body. It can only make you wonder. What have they done to me? Then a nurse appears, she explains what happend finally allows you to regain a sense of reality.

READING TO WRITE

Suzanne Britt Jordan's article, "That Lean and Hungry Look," begins on page 321 of the Readings in Part II. It offers some good examples of sub-topic sentences and other methods of improving coherence and pronoun use.

Consider the second paragraph:

> [1]In the first place thin people aren't fun. [2]They don't know how to goof off, at least in the best, fat sense of the word. [3]They've always got to be adoing. [4]Give them a coffee break, and they'll jog around the block. [5]Supply them with a quiet evening at home, and they'll fix the screen door and lick S & H green stamps. [6]They say things like "there aren't enough hours in the day." [7]Fat people never say that. [8]Fat people think the day is too damn long already.

The paragraph coheres or holds together. The focusing viewpoint is established in the first sentence. Then the pronouns *they* and *them* in sentences 2, 3, 4, 5, and 6 underline the viewpoint, while the content shows "how" thin people are not fun. Sentences 4 and 5 cement the relationship of ideas further with parallel structure. Both sentences begin with a verb plus *them* and repeat *and they'll* at the middle. The result of the parallels is emphasis. One can imagine the writer's voice rising and almost hear the depths of her disgust.

Study the fourth paragraph carefully. Because the content is complex, the structure of the paragraph must also be complex. In fact, Jordan uses several subtopic sentences. As you read, see if you can identify them. Notice also that in this paragraph, the topic sentence is not the first sentence in the paragraph. Which one is it?

WRITING ACTIVITY

As you have learned in this chapter, writers use many methods to achieve coherence. The more complex the subject, the more carefully writers must show relationships.

In this assignment you will pay special attention to coherence. As you plan your paragraph, think about maintaining one viewpoint throughout the paper. How will you keep your subject and your focus clearly in the reader's mind? What pronouns will you use, or what words will you repeat? Is the content complex? Would subtopic sentences help you organize it?

When you rewrite, look for gaps. Consider the use of transitional words or phrases to make connections clear. Watch for ideas that could be expressed in parallel sentences.

ACTIVITY: Write a paragraph in response to one of the following questions. When you have completed a first draft, your instructor may ask you to exchange papers with a classmate for peer criticism. (The Checklist questions provide a guide for peer responses.)

1. Are fat people more fun than thin people?
2. Which holiday is your favorite? Why?
3. What are the causes of freeway congestion (or lack of congestion) in your home city?
4. Have television commercials become more entertaining than the programs?

CHECKLIST: Check each draft of your paper carefully, paying special attention to the following:

1. Does the paragraph have a clear, well-focused topic sentence and, if appropriate, subtopic sentences?
2. Is the content well organized?

3. Do you need to add more details, facts, examples, or illustrations?
4. Is the paragraph coherent? Is the viewpoint consistent?
5. Are there errors in subject-verb or pronoun agreement?
6. Is sentence punctuation correct? Are there any fragments, run-ons, or comma splices?
7. Are there any misspelled words, left-out words, or reversed letters?

CHAPTER SEVEN
The Process
of Writing Essays

From Paragraphs to Essays

According to *Webster's New World Dictionary*, an essay is "a short literary composition of an analytical or interpretive kind, dealing with its subject from a personal point of view or in a limited way." That is, an essay may be from a few paragraphs to a few pages long; it interprets or analyzes information; and it limits and focuses a subject carefully.

Writing an essay, like writing a paragraph, is a process. It requires prewriting, writing, and rewriting. However, since an essay is longer than a paragraph, the essay-writing process calls for more information to be collected during prewriting and a more complex plan for organizing that information.

In this chapter we will look at the entire process and follow Bernardo through the different stages as he writes an essay. Later chapters will look more carefully at different parts of the process for concerns special to essay writing.

FOCUS ON WRITING: *Prewriting/Writing/Rewriting Essays*

Prewriting an Essay

Imagine a writing class on a sleepy Monday afternoon. Bernardo is seated in the back row, tipping back in his chair and occasionally glancing out the window. He is thinking of anything but the pronouns his instructor has just illustrated on the chalkboard. Visions of an afternoon playing tennis and an evening watching Home Box Office movies on the TV in the dorm are drifting lazily across the view screen of his brain. Then he hears the fatal words, "Friday, you will turn in an essay on the problems of left-handed people. Class dismissed."

What does he do? At first he may grumble a little and try to bargain, "Not Friday! How about next week? Or next year?" But when that fails, it is time for stage one of the writing process—prewriting. What does Bernardo know about the subject? Is he left-handed? Does he know any left-handed people? What does he know about the problems of being left-handed?

Bernardo is determined to do a good job on this essay, so he puts off his tennis match, goes to the Skills Center, and begins to work. He knows from his experience writing paragraphs that a good way to explore his thoughts is by freewriting. He begins with a ten-minute exercise.

> I'm not sure I can write about this subject. I don't have an opinion because I'm not lefthanded. At least I'm not now. I seem to remember wanting to use my left hand to hold a fork when I was little and having my hand slapped—or was I trying to open jars with my left hand? Anyway, where was I? Oh yes, remembering. When I was in the first grade, one of the girls in class was left handed. The teacher tied her left hand behind her back and made her do everything with her right hand. But she had a hard time so the teacher scolded her for being clumsy. That teacher was a real witch. Nobody liked her, but I guess she wasn't the only one. Come to think of it, I suppose I do have an opinion about left handedness. I don't understand why anyone would care whether people are left handed or not. Of course it is probably more convenient to be right handed. I always feel sorry for left handed people in restaurants. The place setting is a trap for them. They have to reach over their plates for their water and that invites spills. I remember Fred. He would knock over his water and stick his elbow in his gravy.

So Bernardo does have an opinion about being left-handed after all! The freewriting shows that he feels left-handed people are discriminated against. To explore this opinion further and to test it as a focus for his paper, Bernardo continues his prewriting with an idea pyramid.

Exploring the Subject with an Idea Pyramid

An idea pyramid is a good way to explore your thoughts and at the same time direct your thinking toward the kind of material you will need to support your main ideas. The pyramid begins at the top with your main idea, then branches out to subtopics and supporting details. Building the pyramid may proceed from the top down or from the bottom up. You might first think of details, then sum them up in a topic. Or you might think of the topic first and then the supporting details. Bernardo's finished pyramid includes ideas from his freewriting (see Figure 7–1).

EXERCISE 1:   Build an idea pyramid for your opinion about one of the topics listed.

1. the problems of people confined to wheelchairs
2. the needs of latch-key children
3. the work of vigilante groups such as the Guardian Angels
4. the rights of smokers or nonsmokers
5. the problems of tall or small people

Planning an Essay

Bernardo's pyramid shows him that focusing on discrimination against left-handed people will give him enough information for an essay of several hundred words. Making the pyramid also helps him make a plan of organization for his essay. Support for his main idea, discrimination against left-handed people, falls in the pyramid into several subdivisions—discrimination in the physical environment, discrimination in the English language, discrimination Bernardo has personally experienced or participated in, and discrimination in the way people are treated. Bernardo plans to write a paragraph on each of these subtopics.

But he still needs an overall plan to hold his paper together and to make his major point. To arrive at an effective plan, Bernardo tries several possibilities. He could work from his evidence to the main idea.

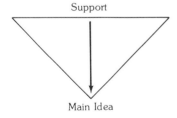

Plan 1
Discrimination in the physical environment
Discrimination in the English language
Discrimination personally experienced
Discrimination in treatment
Discrimination against left-handed people in our society

Or he could begin with the main idea and then explain the support.

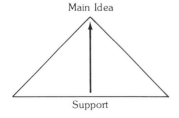

Plan 2
Discrimination against left-handed people in our society
Discrimination in the physical environment
Discrimination in the English language
Discrimination personally experienced
Discrimination in treatment

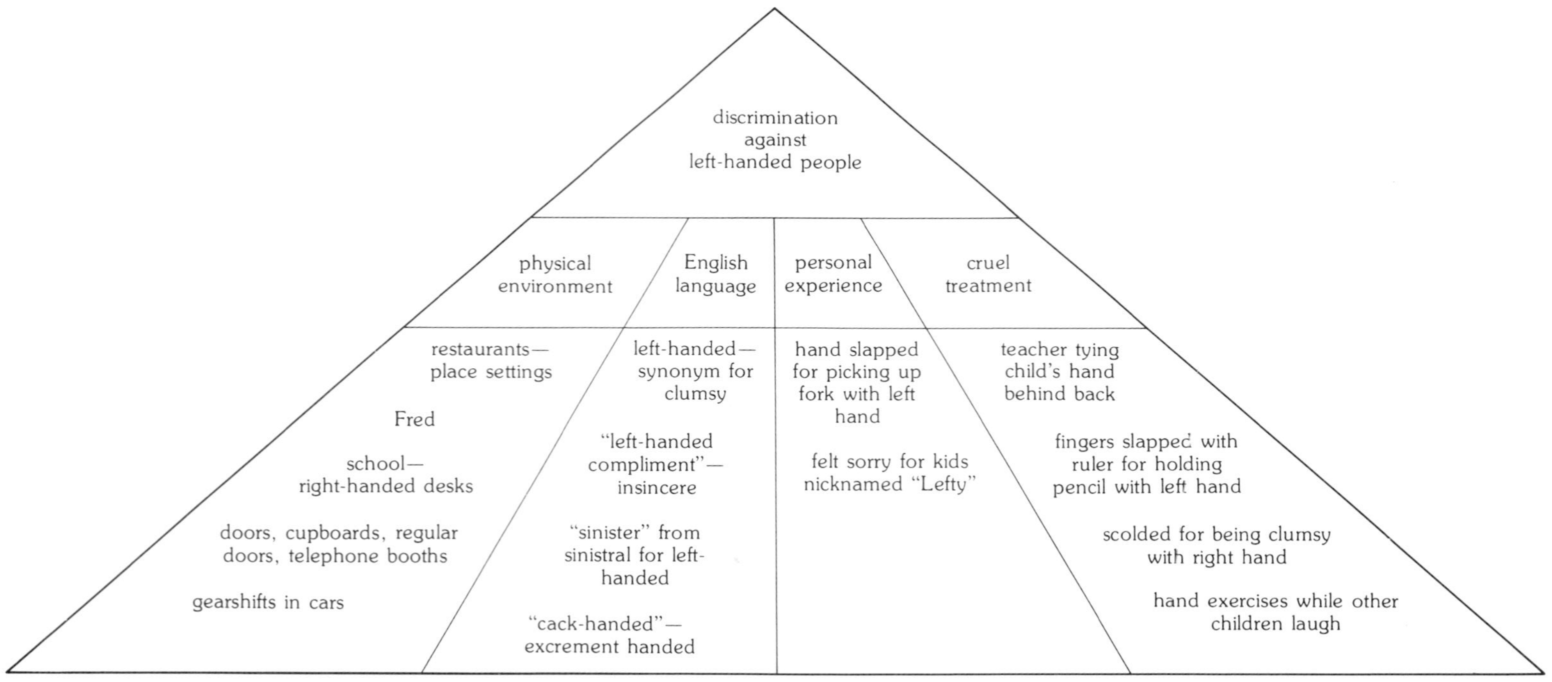

FIGURE 7-1

The figure is a triangular diagram labeled "discrimination against left-handed people," divided into branches:

physical environment
- restaurants—place settings
- Fred
- school—right-handed desks
- doors, cupboards, regular doors, telephone booths
- gearshifts in cars

English language
- left-handed—synonym for clumsy
- "left-handed compliment"—insincere
- "sinister" from sinistral for left-handed
- "cack-handed"—excrement handed

personal experience
- hand slapped for picking up fork with left hand
- felt sorry for kids nicknamed "Lefty"

cruel treatment
- teacher tying child's hand behind back
- fingers slapped with ruler for holding pencil with left hand
- scolded for being clumsy with right hand
- hand exercises while other children laugh

126

Or he could begin with the main idea, give the support, and end with a judgment or comment about the main idea.

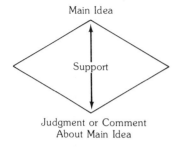

Main Idea

Support

Judgment or Comment
About Main Idea

Plan 3
Discrimination against left-handed people in our society
    Discrimination in the physical environment
    Discrimination in the English language
    Discrimination personally experienced
    Discrimination in treatment
Cruelty of discrimination against left-handed people

Bernardo chooses the third plan because it fits the material he has collected. He wants to make a general statement about discrimination and left-handedness. He has specific details, facts, and examples to support that statement. And he wants to make a personal comment on the subject. Plan 3 allows him to pull all of these things together easily and simply. (However, Bernardo realizes that a different assignment and different pre-writing materials may call for a different format.) His detailed writing plan includes some but not all of the material collected in his pyramid.

Title: Being Left-handed

Main idea: Society discriminates against left-handed people.
    Discrimination in the physical environment
        Place settings in restaurants
        Public telephones
        School desks
    Discrimination in the English language
        Sinister
        Cack-handed
    Discrimination personally experienced
        Hand slapped
        Cruel nicknames
    Discrimination in treatment
        Hand tied behind back
        Hand exercises
Comment: This discrimination is cruel and unjust.

EXERCISE 2: Use the pyramid of ideas you developed in Exercise 1 to make your own essay plan. Be ready to explain why your organization fits your material.

Writing an Essay

By Tuesday Bernardo is ready to write his first draft. He finds a quiet place in the library, takes out a piece of paper; and his mind goes blank. Fortunately, he has his essay plan. It reminds him that he had planned to begin by talking about prejudice against left-handed people, and he decides to add a definition of left-handedness.

Being Left-handed

The majority of people in our country are anti-left-handedness, therefore left-handed people are treated bad. Defining left-handedness means to use the left hand habitully or more easily than the right hand. Our country is definitely prejudiced against left-handedness.

Fifteen minutes have passed and Bernardo has finished the first paragraph. It has not turned out exactly as he had hoped, but he will not worry about that now. He goes on to the next paragraph.

Not everyone is left-handed. But the United States very rarly recognizes even few people. Eating tables are set without thought for the left-hander, public teliphones are created soley for the right-hander. Moreover, school desks are designed so that the right-handed person can take notes with perfect ease, while the left-handed sole must turn himself in nots to write anything at all! And these are just a few of the many instances of left-handed discrimination. The list is endless if one is made aware of them.

The common language is terrible. To be sinistral (the root word of which is sinister, meaning evil) is to be left-handed. To be cack-handed also means to be left-handed. Cack is Scottish word that has to do with exretement. Both of these words are dirty or evil, and both point to left-handedness. These words are commonly used in our language, and have a serious affect on peoples view of the left hand.

Bernardo's plan calls for him to discuss his personal experiences next; however, as he works, he decides it would be better to put his personal experiences last. They provide examples of cruel treatment, the subject of his next paragraph and also lead into the comment he plans to make at the end of the paper.

From the first day a child shows left-handedness concerned adults try to constantly change the child to the right hand. This effort of conversion often reaches the point of sadism. It is not uncommon to hear of a child being punished by ear pulling or the left hand is tied behind the back or severe beatings, just for showing left-handed tendencies.

I remember the cruelty of parents and other children. Getting my hand slapped for picking up my fork with my left hand stays in my mind to this day. Later I felt sorry for left-handed kids who were nicknamed "Lefty" or "Wrong Hand." But I also felt kind of smug, knowing that they were different or weird while I was okay or normal.

Not only is this cruel but also unjust. No one can help being left-handed. It's something that just happens, like having red hair or brown. Unfortunately, to be left-handed in the United States is to be subject to prejudism in everyday life. We need to wake up and become aware of the rights of the left-handed minority.

Finally, the essay is finished. Bernardo proofreads it quickly. He corrects a spelling error in the second paragraph, changes some punctuation, and takes the paper to his peer critic. By now Bernardo is tired of the subject and of writing generally; he fervently hopes that his critic thinks the paper is a masterpiece with no errors or other problems.

EXERCISE 3: Be a peer critic for Bernardo's paper. Without looking at the next section of the text, answer the questions about the paper. When you have finished, read ahead to see how your criticisms compare with those that follow.

1. Does the essay have a main idea? If so, what is it? Can you suggest any improvements for limiting or focusing the subject or for stating it?
2. Does the essay organization work well? Why or why not?
3. Is there enough support for key ideas? Does any part of the essay need more or fewer facts, examples, or details?
4. Do you find any problems with spelling, reversed letters, or left-out words?
5. Do you find any problems with punctuation, particularly fragments, run-ons, or comma splices?
6. Do you find any problems with grammar, particularly subject–verb or pronoun agreement?
7. What is the essay's major weakness?
8. What is the essay's major strength?

Rewriting an Essay

Bernardo's peer critic likes his paper but does not think it is a masterpiece—at least not yet. When she gives it back to him on Wednesday, she says the organization is good, but there is not enough support. She thinks that all of the paragraphs need more details, facts, and examples; and she points out numerous errors, particularly spelling.

At first Bernardo cannot believe what he reads. "This is all wrong," he mumbles to himself. Take *habitully.* How else could I spell it?" He grabs his dictionary and finds the spelling *habitually.* Then he looks up *affect* and finds that when used as a noun, as in his sentence, it is spelled *effect.*

Convinced that the writing process is not yet complete, Bernardo takes his paper back to his quiet table in the library and tackles the serious business of revision. To begin, he studies his paper and his peer critic's comments carefully. The more extensive changes come first, and since most of those in Bernardo's paper involve adding information, he goes back to prewriting. He finds more details in his idea pyramid and remembers others that he could add. He also decides that his first paragraph is too abrupt, and the last paragraph is too general. He thinks of an illustration to add to the first paragraph and then does some research to find out why left-handers are left-handed.

When Bernardo is satisfied with the form and the substance, he corrects all the errors in spelling, punctuation, and grammar. He uses the diagnostic chart at the end of the book for references to pages that will show him how to make corrections. Occasionally, he cannot find an answer, and he asks a tutor or an available instructor for help.

On Friday in his writing class, Bernardo turns in his recopied paper. Entitled "Against Left-handers," this revised essay is very different from the first draft he wrote on Tuesday—and decidedly better!

Against Left-handers

After a hard day in the mountains, Fred was famished, and as he and his nine friends entered the plush restaurant, he could only think of the good meal and the relaxing evening with his friends that was ahead. But the evening turned out to be far from relaxing for Fred. During the two hours they were at the restaurant Fred managed to stick his arm in his food three times and even throw his steak into the lap of the companion sitting across from him. Now, to you, Fred may sound like a really clumsy person, but that is not the problem. You see, Fred suffers from one of the many prejudices of our country; he is left-handed. By definition left-handedness means to use the left hand habitually or more easily than the right hand. Our country is definitely prejudiced against left-handedness. This can be proved by the many inconveniences left-handed people must live with day to day, the words that recognize left-handedness negatively, and the horrible way people treat left-handers.

To be left-handed is to be a minority. Only 8–10% of the world's population is known to be left-handed, and in the United States they are ignored. Eating tables are set to the advantage of the right-handed, with drinking glasses placed at the right hand corner of the table. This can be hazardous to left-handers, who must reach across their plate in order to drink from their own glass. Public telephones are manufactured solely for the right-hander, with the receiver on the left side, leaving the right hand free to dial and write with. Cars are situated so that everything is in reach of the right hand. Cutting scissors are shaped to fit the right hand perfectly, but if held with the left hand, they can cause excruciating pain. School desks are designed so that the right-handed person can take notes with perfect ease, while the left-handed soul must turn himself in knots to write anything at all. And these are just a few of the many instances of left-handed problems.

But not only are left-handers of the world discriminated against in the physical surroundings, but they are also abused by the common language. The dictionary gives "clumsy" as one of the meanings of "left-handed." A left-handed compliment is an insincere one. To be sinistral (the root word of which is "sinister," meaning evil) is to be left-handed. "Cack" is a Scottish word meaning excrement. Both of these expressions depict dirt or evil and both mean left-handedness. These words are commonly used in our language and have a serious effect on people's view of the left hand. This can easily be shown by how people react to a left-handed person.

From the first day a child shows left-handed traits, concerned adults constantly try to change the child to the right hand. Misguided parents frequently think that there is something odd about a left-handed child. Training starts early in life with constant reminders to the strange child that it is not right to use the left hand to throw things or to pick up eating utensils. As soon as the child enters kindergarten or the first grade, his left-handed woes increase astronomically. His new tormentor is called a teacher. After countless incidents of ear pulling, tying the left-hand behind the back, and frequent swats, the child is convinced that the sole purpose of this teacher's existence is torture of all left-handed deviants.

I remember my own painful experiences as a would-be left-hander. My mother gasped in shock when I reached for a fork with my left-hand, then slapped my hand so hard it stung for several minutes. Later in school I felt sorry for the left-handed kids who were nicknamed "Lefty" or "Wrong Hand." But I felt good too because it was them and not me who was different. The reactions of my teachers, parents, and friends had convinced me that being left-handed was somehow shameful.

Not only is such discrimination and abuse cruel, but it is also unjust! The use of the left or right hand is caused by the brain, depending on which of its two sides dominates. If the right side dominates, the person is left-handed. So the cause is purely physical, and it can do serious damage to the individual's balance and speaking abilities if this dominance is denied. Unfortunately, to be left-handed in the United States is to be subject to physical inconveniences, to be insulted by the English language, and often to be the victim of savage treatment by people who are trying to turn a "lefty" into a right-hander.

EXERCISE 4:   Review Bernardo's revised essay in terms of the criticisms you listed in Exercise 3. Did Bernardo correct all of the problems you identified? Did he correct some problems you did not identify? What improvements might still be made in the essay?

EXERCISE 5:   Be a peer critic for Carol's essay about a BIA school. Use the questions listed in Exercise 3, and write out your answers. If your instructor asks you to revise one of the paragraphs, be sure to explore the subject and make a plan for the paragraph before you begin rewriting.

Surrogate Parents

As I recall, it seems like only yesterday, when we were torn away from the definite security of the reservation and thrust into the mainstream of education. Three or four busloads of frightened, crying Indian youngsters going away from home for the first time. The bus travelled approximately fifty miles to the city and yet it was more like a million miles away. Being torn away from loving parents, seemed so cruel and so final, our tears were justified. At the school, namely the Indian School, we were greeted by the teachers, staff, advisors, and dormitory matrons who were to be our surrogate parents for the next six years. Through the years we were to learn to respect, obey and love them and as the final year approached to discovery what beautiful people they really were.

Departing from the reservation was a very traumatic and emotional experience. The matrons were very patient teachers, instructing the new generation about dormitory living, following rules and regulations, the penalties if they were not obeyed. We learned personal hygiene, how to make a bed the military way, and to iron clothes their way. The kitchen staff taught us the art of cooking and cleaning the dining area. We lived though History, Science, Math, and English. Above all, we discovered that our teachers were human after all.

There was little ole Miss Taul, our English teacher, very short and wiry, like a sly fox. She loved embarrassing whoever misbehaved. She forbade talking in class and one day, admonished our friend Jim, "if you do not turn around and pay attention, I will tell your mother to put lace on your shorts." Everyone burst into laughter, but with a nonchalant look she gave the impression of a cat that swallowed the canary. Than, there was the girls' advisor. Each time she put us on restriction or grounded us, she would always be quite impressed with our cooperation. We always received a shortened restriction or extra duty. I think it had something to do with her infatuation with the school principal. In summary, each faculty, staff, advisor and matron gave a little of themselves to these children. With their determination, love and devotion, they patiently helped with each step we took. They constantly stressed the importance of education and learning to stand on our own two feet. With much prodding and persistence, these frightened little children were transformed into responsible young adults. It grieves me to think, that at times we were cruel and uncaring and yet we gathered our strength and courage from them. To these beautiful, caring indiviuals, I pay my tribute.

FOCUS ON THE SENTENCE: *Modifiers or Describers*

In some ways the difference between a good and a poor writer lies in the ability to add specific details. Both a good and a poor writer may have the same main idea, but the good writer will develop that idea until we can see it, hear it, or feel it, until we understand fully what he or she wants to say.

Just as details are important to an essay, the details expressed by modifying or descriptive words and phrases are important to a sentence. While the main idea of a sentence is contained in its subject and verb, words that describe may add vital information to the message. Notice what happens to the meaning if we add describing words to this basic sentence:

The driver slammed into my car.

The drunken driver slammed wrecklessly into my new, uninsured car.

The frantic driver slammed helplessly into my car, missing a child by less than a foot.

The enormous driver of an equally enormous semi slammed into my car.

The driver of a $29,000 Mercedes slammed into my old, battered, $350 car.

The basic sentence shows the outline of an action, but the describing words add the details. We know to begin with that there has been a wreck, but we learn from the descriptive words and phrases whether to be relieved or angry about the incident, whether to laugh it off or call a lawyer, whether to yell at the driver or wait for the police.

Adjectives

Adjectives describe or modify nouns or pronouns. Adjectives tell which one, what kind, what color or size, how many, how much, how good or how bad. All of the underlined words in the example paragraph are adjectives.

A genuine Trekkie has watched every episode of the immortal *Star Trek* television show ten or twelve times and has seen each movie three times. Trekkies refer to the Captain, Bones, or Spock as old friends whose opinions are valued on such matters as the world political situation, the Star Wars weapons system, and any future space expeditions. Less visionary scientists may tell the gullible public that Halley's Comet is not a danger to the earth or the only green Martians are fungi, but these Trekkies know better. They have seen a spectacular comet torch Aurigon 4 in Star System 2 and the green inhabitants of New Mars deep in the Andromeda Galaxy.

STRUCTURE   Adjectives can fill several positions in a sentence. Most often they will come before a noun:

Evil	two
Giant	three
Green Troglodytes devoured many cities.	
Scaly	these

Sometimes they will follow a verb:

hungry
vicious
They are <u>unhappy</u>.
awkward

And sometimes they will follow a noun:

relentless   sly
Klingons—<u>heartless</u> and <u>cruel</u>—have attacked outposts.
desperate   resourceful

To find the adjectives in a sentence, first find the nouns and pronouns; then look for words that describe or modify them. In the sentences above *Evil*, *Giant*, *Green*, and *Scaly* describe the noun *Troglodytes* and *two*, *three*, *many*, and *these*, the noun *city*. *Hungry, vicious, unhappy,* and *awkward* describe the pronoun *They*, and the pairs *relentless* and *sly, heartless* and *cruel*, and *desperate* and *resourceful* describe the noun *Klingons*.

You might also identify adjectives by some typical endings.

-able/-ible	The <u>respectable</u> judge sentenced the <u>contemptible</u> mobster.
-ic	The <u>comic</u> actor began his <u>hectic</u> day at dawn.
-ful	The <u>beautiful</u> countryside was also <u>fruitful</u>.
-y	The <u>gloomy</u> agent showed us a <u>messy</u> room with a <u>drippy</u> ceiling and a <u>creaky</u> floor.
-al	<u>Situational</u> ethics means that right or wrong changes with the <u>ethical</u> situation.
-ious/-eous	The <u>obnoxious</u> waiter asked for an <u>outrageous</u> tip.
-ar	The <u>circular</u> rooms were one of the attractions of the <u>spectacular</u> resort.

Comparison

Most adjectives have three forms. They have a *basic form* to use in describing one item.

The <u>red</u> rose will win the prize.
The <u>anxious</u> salesperson overlooked a bar of soap.

A second, *comparative form* is used when comparing two items.

The <u>redder</u> rose of the two will win the prize.
The <u>more anxious</u> salesperson—either George or Suzanne—overlooked a bar of soap.

Most short words add -*er* to make the comparative form; long words add the word *more;* some words may do either (*happier, more happy*).

A third, *superlative form* is used when comparing three or more items.

The <u>reddest</u> rose of all will win the prize.
The <u>most anxious</u> salesperson of all overlooked a bar of soap.

Most short words add -*est* to make the superlative form while long words add the word *most,* and again some words may do either (*happiest, most happy*).

Some adjectives do not follow the rules. Words like *good* and *bad* have special forms for comparison.

Ice cream is a <u>good</u> dessert. Devil's food cake is <u>better</u>.
Chocolate mousse is <u>best</u>.
The casserole is <u>bad</u>. The badger stew is <u>worse</u>. The enchiladas are <u>worst</u>.

Irregular forms are listed in your dictionary under the base word.

EXERCISE 6:   Underline adjectives and circle the words they describe.

1. A black funnel cloud uprooted a hundred-year-old tree, then demolished a six-month-old office building.
2. Sunshine—bright, warm, and cheery—flooded the bare cell.
3. Happiness is red and yellow.
4. The hungry timber wolves leaped the coyote-style stick fence and stalked the chicken coop.
5. Red and gold satin balls, silver and gold garlands, and tiny reindeer decorate the tree.

EXERCISE 7:   Combine the following sentences to make a single sentence that uses adjectives.

1. Leaves cover the ground. The leaves are red, yellow, and brown. The ground is frosty.
2. Beatian Yazz worked years on the paintings. Yazz is a Navajo artist. He worked six years. The paintings depict wildlife. The paintings are famous.
3. The boss broke the switch. It was the intercom switch. The boss was angry. The boss was nervous.
4. The sea and sky blur together as the sun sets the horizon on fire. The sea is green and gold. The sky is orange. The horizon is western.

5. A tea mug should be like mine. Mine is heavy. Mine is rough textured. Mine is one of a kind.

Prepositional Phrases as Adjectives

Not only single words but also complete phrases can describe or modify nouns and pronouns. A prepositional phrase is an adjective phrase when it tells us something more about a noun or pronoun. Usually an adjective phrase will follow the word it modifies.

Pronoun adj. prep. phrase   noun   adj. prep. phrase

Each of the dancers wears a tutu of gauze and spangles.

In the sentence the phrase *of the dancers* tells "which ones" the pronoun *each* is referring to, and *of gauze and spangles* describes "what kind" of tutus.

To identify adjective prepositional phrases, first identify all of the prepositional phrases in a sentence. Then look for the words they modify. When the modified words are nouns or pronouns, the phrase is an adjective. (See pages 87–88 for a list of prepositions.)

EXERCISE 8: Underline adjective prepositional phrases and circle the words they modify.

> The computer lab at the college is always busy. Students from microcomputer courses and students from computer language classes warm the seats at each terminal for hours, running the programs for their assignments again and again. Occasionally a bored lab assistant will play computer games. One of them recently played War Games and crashed the system, causing a panic among computer instructors and students alike. Fixing the system took away two days of homework time, and panicky students with assignments due protested. Consequently, lists of computer lab *don't*s now include playing computer games.

EXERCISE 9: Combine sentences to make a single sentence that includes one or more adjective prepositional phrases.

1. When you take this course, you will need a calculator. You and I will take the course together. The calculator should have trigonometric functions.
2. All await your answer. We are awaiting it. The answer is about a pool party. The party will be at your apartment house.
3. The assistant arranged a luncheon. He is the president's

assistant. The luncheon is for members. They are members of the Press Club.

4. Six became ill after eating the main course. The six were diners. The main course included crab melt and broccoli.

5. Traffic was bumper to bumper, and the tempers were nearing the boiling point. It was freeway traffic. The drivers were becoming angry. The boiling point is 212°F.

Adverbs

Like adjectives, adverbs are words that describe or modify other words. Unlike adjectives, adverbs tell us more about verbs, adjectives, or other adverbs. They describe how, when, or where an action is done or a state of being exists, or they show the intensity of a descriptive quality.

          verb   adv.

The sun shone muddily in a smoggy sky.
(Adverb modifies the verb *shone;* it shows "how" the sun shone.)

         verb adv.   adv.

The jogger runs early and late.
(Adverbs modify the verb *runs;* they show "when" the jogger runs.)

           verb   adv.

The chess club will meet here.
(Adverb modifies the verb *will meet;* it shows "where" the club will meet.)

       adv.   adj.

The uncomfortably stiff chair is a priceless antique.
(Adverb modifies the adjective *stiff;* it shows "how" stiff the chair is.)

         adv.   adv.   adv. adv.

The meeting began very early but did not conclude until quite late.
(The adverbs *very* and *quite* modify the adverbs *early* and *late* by showing the intensity of the earliness or lateness.)

Adverbs that modify adjectives and other adverbs usually precede them, as in the example above. But adverbs that modify verbs may come in a variety of positions.

   adv.   verb

Warily the detective crept into the room.

        verb   adv.

The detective crept warily into the room.

        verb   adv.

The detective crept into the room warily.

STRUCTURE   The most common ending for adverbs is *-ly*. Adverbs are often made by adding *-ly* to adjectives.

happy + -ly = happily   sudden + -ly = suddenly
comic + -ly = comically   total + -ly = totally
capable + -ly = capably   possible + -ly = possibly

Other adverbs include words that describe time, direction, or logical re- lationships and words that negate or limit:

not, never, perhaps, now, then, soon,
often, however, therefore, moreover, here, there

EXERCISE 10:   Underline adverbs and circle the words they modify.

1. Unhappily the stock fell after I had greedily cornered the market.
2. Sometimes Sergio drives too slowly on the freeway.
3. I have not finished my gluttonously huge sundae.
4. Here are the accounts you ordered yesterday.
5. The unhappy secretary is trying desperately to finish twenty perfect and appropriately elegant invitations by noon without a word processor.

EXERCISE 11:   Combine sentences to make a single sentence that uses ad- verbs to describe verbs, adjectives, or adverbs.

1. We should visit the zoo. The visits should be often. We should visit more.
2. The orangutan grins at the startled visitors. She grins mischievously. She grins broadly. She grins suddenly.
3. A zoo keeper was bitten by a poisonous snake. It happened today. The bite was viscious. The snake was extremely poisonous.
4. Wary visitors are avoiding the reptile house. They are avoiding it now. They are careful.
5. A panther escaped and attacked a black leopard. This happened yesterday. The escape was gleeful. The attack was angry.

Prepositional Phrases as Adverbs

Prepositional phrases may serve as adverbs as well as adjectives. Like single-word adverbs, phrase adverbs may be located in different parts of a sentence.

adv.   verb   adv. prep. phrase
At dawn migrating cranes flew in a wedge formation

adv. prep. phrase
over the bosque.

All three phrases modify the verb *flew: at dawn* telling us "when" they flew; *in a wedge formation,* "how" they flew; and *over the bosque,* "where" they flew.

To test whether prepositional phrases are adverbs, try replacing them in the sentence with single-word adverbs.

Yesterday migrating cranes flew gracefully overhead.

Adverbs fit in the places occupied by the prepositional phrases in the example sentence; therefore, we can say the phrases also are adverbs. Notice what happens, however, when we use this test on phrases that are not adverbs.

The vivid red of my hat and my shimmering sequined dress without a doubt startled the bull.

Test: The vivid red now and my shimmering, sequined dress undoubtedly startled the bull.

A single-word adverb can replace the second phrase but not the first one, telling us that only the second phrase is an adverb. The first phrase is, in fact, an adjective modifying the noun *red.*

EXERCISE 12:   Underline prepositional phrases used as adverbs and circle the words they modify.

The plane took off in a raging thunderstorm. As it climbed into the sky, lightning stabbed around the wings, and the deep growl of thunder reverberated through the cabin. The Captain spoke to the passengers over the intercom. "Please remain buckled into your seats," he said. "There is no danger at this time," he added ominously, and the passengers wondered whether he meant there might be danger in a few more minutes. Then the plane broke through the clouds into a sunshiny blue sky, and the passengers put their momentary fear behind them.

EXERCISE 13:   Combine the following sentences to make a single sentence containing at least one prepositional-phrase adverb.

1. My rollerskating team practices daily. We practice at the Rollerdome. We practice for two hours.
2. The Cathedral Redwoods have lived a long time. Two thousand years is a long time. These Redwoods' home is northern California.
3. The gunfighter stalked menacingly. He stalked like a lion. The cattletown's main street was his path.
4. Trick-or-treaters, bent on tricks rather than treats, were hidden. The shadows hid them. The porch made the shadows.
5. The cow jumped while the dish ran away. The moon was the cow's hurdle. The spoon accompanied the dish.

EXERCISE 14: In the following nonsense sentences, underline and label words and phrases used as adjectives and as adverbs. Circle the words modified.

1. A tupstic vitter slumphed over the liddle and under the nep.
2. The riddip of buppy puds hrums cruppily through the kimption.
3. Crampton, dupple and vimpible, prahed with a mocket into the hippity hib.
4. Vettily, our tinsy tuppit twipped tippily around the chwait.
5. The dwollop with the sopter will stun be fwinking into the fwiddle.

EXERCISE 15: Add adjectives and adverbs (both words and phrases) in the spaces provided.

In the early light _____ the bird watchers

crept _____ into the meadow. The winter

morning was _____ and a

_____ layer of frost decorated the grass. The

sky _____ glowed _____,

while a _____ twilight hung over the

_____ mountains. The watchers found their

stations, hidden behind a screen _____.

Shivering with excitement, they crouched

_____. Most had brought a pair

_____, and they trained these

_____. For _____ minutes
they waited _____. Their cramped limbs
ached, and their _____ fingers and toes were
growing _____. Then just when they could
wait _____ longer, the birds came—
_____, white whooping cranes, their heads
held _____ and their
_____ legs stepping _____.

TROUBLESHOOTING: *Adjectives and Adverbs*

Several kinds of errors are common in using adjectives and adverbs.
    1. Occasionally a writer may use an adjective where an adverb is needed or an adverb where an adjective is needed.

> This chicken pot pie tastes <u>real</u> good.
> Go <u>slow</u> and <u>careful</u>.
> The queen felt <u>badly</u> about beheading her gardeners.

The errors may not sound immediately apparent to your ears because they are made so frequently that we may be accustomed to hearing them. However, in the first two sentences, adjectives are used where adverbs are needed. *Real* modifies *good,* an adjective; therefore, we should use an adverb such as *very* that shows intensity:

> The chicken pot pie tastes <u>very</u> good.

Slow and *careful* are adjectives; they cannot modify a verb like *go.* The adverbs *slowly* and *carefully* are the correct choices:

> Go <u>slowly</u> and <u>carefully</u>.

And in the final sentence it is not *feeling* which is bad but rather *the queen,* and we should use the adjective *bad:*

> The queen felt <u>bad</u> about beheading her gardeners.

2. Sometimes writers will confuse the forms used to compare adjectives and adverbs. The comparative form might mistakenly be used when com-

paring three or more items or the superlative form when comparing two items.

> *Incorrect*: Of the two golfers Geraldine is the <u>best</u>.
> *Correct*: Of the two golfers Geraldine is the <u>better</u>.
> *Incorrect*: Monte Vista Fire Station is one of the <u>better</u> restaurants in town.
> *Correct:* Monte Vista Fire Station is one of the <u>best</u> restaurants in town.

3. Errors also occur when writers compare adjectives or adverbs illogically. For example, if something is *perfect* or *unique*, it cannot be compared since it is impossible to be more than perfect or more unique than being one of a kind.

> *Incorrect:* This sweater is my <u>most favorite</u> garment.
> *Correct:* This sweater is my <u>favorite</u> garment.

EXERCISE 16: Troubleshoot for errors in the use of adjectives or adverbs in the following sentences. Underline and correct the errors.

1. In the contest between my Bavarian Cream Confection and Aunt Minnie's Hawaiian Pineapple Delight, Aunt Minnie won the blue ribbon for best pie.

2. I had been waiting a real long time, and I was tired of playing it smart. I was ready for action, stupidly or wisely.

3. Shopping at the better stores allows you to pay higher prices for cheaper merchandise.

4. This exercise machine is the most unique one on the market. It is more ideal for firming muscles and trimming weight than the competing model.

5. On the *Wheel of Fortune* you must think fast or you lose quick.

EXERCISE 17: Troubleshoot for errors in the use of adjectives or adverbs, agreement, or sentence punctuation in the following paragraph. Mark the errors; then rewrite the paragraph, correcting them.

My favorite books have been read until the covers of each is torn and the pages are dogeared. I have read Tolkien's *Lord of the*

Rings at least ten times, I have read Patricia McKillip's *Riddlemaster of Hed* almost as often. I still get excited when Bilbo Baggins disappears at his party; I feel the bewilderment they must feel. His place suddenly empty. Although I know the answer to the riddle of the High One. I still become intrigued as she weaves her spell. Sometimes I think I read too quick, or writers write too slow, that's why I keep reading and re-reading the same books. But probably I would do the same. Even if I had a dozen more favorites.

READING TO WRITE

Many of the readings in Part II provide good examples of the use of modifiers and descriptive words. Two of the best, particularly for adjective use, are Dick Schaap's "The Greatest Team I Ever Saw" (pages 323–327) and Diane Ackerman's "Where a New World Began" (pages 327–329).

Schaap uses the superlative adjective *greatest* in his title, and throughout his article he piles superlative upon superlative: *most efficient passer, most feared and respected and successful coach, the greatest team.* As you read the article, see how many superlative adjectives you can find. Evaluate their effect. Does Schaap support his enthusiastic praise adequately, or do you feel he is exaggerating?

Ackerman is a poet, and she uses words carefully and intensely. Her descriptive words and phrases give shape, color, and motion to her pictures. The Ellis Island buildings are not only described as "studded with windows," but the shapes of the windows are also described—squares, port holes, and half moons. Immigrants are pictured as wearing "tags around their necks" and filing "through mazes like cattle." Generalities and opinions are kept to a minimum—no more than one per paragraph, while some paragraphs have none. Yet the effect of the many details and examples leads us as readers to form opinions of our own. As you read, imagine what it would have been like to be an immigrant.

WRITING ACTIVITY

Up to this point, the writing assignments in this text have called for paragraphs. In this assignment you will be writing a complete essay. Be careful to work your way through the writing process step by step. Use an idea pyramid as part of exploring your subject and planning your essay, and use adjectives and adverbs to give your ideas depth and detail.

> *Prewriting*: Explore and focus your topic. Make a writing plan.
> *Writing*: Draft the essay.
> *Rewriting*: Evaluate, revise, and correct the draft.

ACTIVITY: Write a complete essay on one of the following topics. Your instructor may ask you to hand in all of the steps in your writing process, so be sure to keep all of your activities and drafts.

1. An injustice that you have observed or experienced
2. The greatest (or worst) group that you have been part of
3. A public or historical site that has emotional associations for a group of people

CHECKLIST: Check each draft of your essay for the following:

1. Does the essay have a main idea?
2. Does the essay organization work well?
3. Is there enough support for key ideas?
4. Are there any errors in adjective or adverb use?
5. Are there any errors in subject–verb or pronoun agreement?
6. Are there any fragments, run-ons, or comma splices?
7. Are there any misspelled words, left-out words, or reversed letters?

CHAPTER EIGHT
Beginning the Essay

The Audience: Who Are You Writing For?

All writing is done for an audience—the readers, who will learn from, enjoy, or be persuaded to change their opinions by what you have written. Occasionally you may be your own audience. When you write some personal entries in your journal or express private feelings in a poem, you are usually writing for yourself, with no thought of others' reading what you have written. But most of the time your audience is other people. You write letters to friends or to people you must do business with. You write memoranda to co-workers and reports for supervisors. And you write essays for the educated audience of instructors and classmates in your college courses.

Who you are writing for—your audience—has a significant impact on what you will write and how you will write it. Your audience affects the tone of your writing, influencing whether it will be serious or humorous, personal or businesslike. It affects your grammar and your choice of words, examples, and details. Consider the following accounts of an office worker's first day on the job.

The black hands of the office clock pointed primly to 8:05 as Cynthia slipped through the door. The receptionist, a gray-haired woman whose habit of peering at newcomers over the top of her glasses thoroughly unnerved most people, did not glance at the clock, but Cynthia was sure the woman knew the hour and knew too that the new member of the word-processing pool was late on her first day of work.

Ms. Barnes arrived at 8:05. She was taken to see Mr. Liu, the business manager. It is he who will supervise her work during the training and probation period. Between 8:10 and 8:30 Ms. Barnes filled out a W-4 form and personal data questionnaire. Between 8:30 and 9:00 she met with the company psychologist to begin a personnel profile. At 9:03 she reported to the office manager, Janene Strong, who gave her a mailing list and a sales letter for production on the word processor. She completed the work by 12:15 and then went to lunch.

Today was a disaster! Am totally wasted. First off, I had a flat on the freeway and was late to work. And wouldn't you know it? The fish-eyed receptionist caught me, and I'm sure she lost no time turning me in. Old Man Liu sent me to the company shrink and then the O.M. cracked the whip all a.m.

The first paragraph might have been written for an audience of novel readers. It starts like a story, and the details are highly visual. The tone is sympathetic, encouraging the reader to side with Cynthia and to identify her as the heroine. The second paragraph is more objective. Its audience might be the company official who hired Ms. Barnes. Her activities, including her lateness, are reported without evaluative comments. The language is restrained, and the grammar, formal (*It is he* rather than *It's him*). Office procedures and tasks rather than personalities are emphasized. The final paragraph, on the other hand, is both informal and unrestrained. Composed perhaps for a diary or a personal letter, it includes slang, abbreviations unacceptable in formal writing, and partial sentences.

The following chart lists a number of audiences and their effects on some of the basic elements of your writing. Another major factor affecting these elements, your purpose, or why you are writing, will be discussed in Chapter 9.

Effects of Audience on Writing

Audience	*Tone*	*Vocabulary*	*Grammar*	*Conventions*	*Examples*
1. Well-educated public	Serious to humorous	Standard Avoid slang, most colloquial expressions, and most jargon.	Semiformal Avoid object pronouns after linking verbs, but rhetorical fragments are often acceptable.	Semiformal Avoid most contractions and abbreviations. You may use *I* and *you*. Emphasize the active voice of verbs.	I earned an A on the biology examination. It is I who made the mistake.

Audience	Tone	Vocabulary	Grammar	Conventions	Examples
2. Supervisor/ others in authority	Respectful	Formal Avoid slang and colloquial expressions.	Formal Avoid object pronouns after linking verbs. Write complete sentences.	Formal Avoid contractions and abbreviations. Limit the use of *I* and *you* to maintain an objective stance. You may use the passive voice of verbs.	My performance on the biology examination was superior, earning a letter grade of A. It is I who erred.
3. Older friends and relatives	Friendly but respectful	Informal Avoid slang and jargon, but use colloquial expressions if your audience does.	Informal You may use object pronouns after linking verbs, and rhetorical fragments are acceptable.	Informal You may use contractions, abbreviations, *I* and *you*. Emphasize the active voice of verbs.	I got an A on the biology exam. It's me that's wrong.
4. Younger friends and relatives, yourself	Casual	Popular Slang, jargon, and colloquial expressions are acceptable.	Popular Pronoun case and sentence completeness are not emphasized.	Popular Emphasize *I* and *you*. You may use contractions and abbreviations.	I pulled an A on the bio exam. It's l'l ol' me that messed up.

FOCUS ON WRITING: *The Introductory Paragraph: Gaining an Audience*

The first paragraph of your essay does more than introduce the subject to your audience. It sets the tone for your paper, establishing whether you are writing humorously or seriously, and sets the limits of your treatment of the subject. It can convince the audience that your essay is worth reading; in effect, it may win an audience for your essay by making them want to read further.

To accomplish so much in one short paragraph requires careful planning and organization. The process involves composing a thesis statement and providing a context that leads into the thesis. A thesis statement is much like the topic sentences you wrote in earlier chapters; it gives the main idea of your essay. However, leading into the thesis with a context requires a kind of paragraph different from that you are used to writing. Among the ways to introduce a paper, the funnel-shaped introduction is especially effective. It captures your audience and "funnels" them into the paper.

Thesis Statement

The introductory paragraph may seem upside down in more ways than one. Not only does its most important sentence, the thesis statement, often come last, but also that important, final sentence should be written first. The reason is simple: since the rest of the paragraph prepares the reader for the thesis, the thesis must be written before the writer can select appropriate preparatory material. In other words, we must identify the gate before we can build a road to it. Although the thesis statement is the first sentence to be written, it is by no means the easiest; in fact, the thesis may be the most difficult sentence in the entire essay to write, primarily because it must accomplish so much. In the thesis the writer must limit the subject, focus it, and in some cases, provide a framework for the rest of the essay.

Limiting the Subject

An essay may seem as impossible as a book to write, when the writer is faced with an empty page. However, an essay of a few pages or a few hundred words is actually quite short—too short to discuss a big subject such as Civil War history or architecture. On the other hand, you can discuss a small part of one of those subjects in a few pages. For example, you could write about the firing on Fort Sumter or the gargoyles on the new cathedral in Washington, D.C.

Limiting or narrowing down a subject involves a question-and-answer process. Writers must first examine its scope and implications. Have entire books been written about this subject? Is what the writers know and believe about the subject what people generally know and believe about it? Must treatment of the subject cover centuries and the experiences of many people? Might the essay begin with a phrase such as "since the dawn of time," "people have always," "it is well known"? If the answer to any of these questions is "yes," the subject is probably too broad to be dealt with meaningfully in a short essay.

To limit the subject, the writer should make it more specific, tying it, if possible, to a specific time or place or person by asking some of the following questions: who, what, when, where, why, which one, or which kind. For example, the broad topic "hunting" might be narrowed down in this way:

Hunting
Who?
Author hunting

What?

Author hunting turkey

When?

Author hunting turkey in November of '88

Where?

Author hunting turkey in November of '88 in Wisconsin forest

Why?

Author hunts Thanksgiving turkey in November of '88 in Wisconsin forest.

One hunt, in one place, at one time can be discussed well in an essay. Notice too that the more specific the topic becomes, the more information it takes to describe it.

Another general topic that we can practice limiting is "restaurant." This time the ordering of the questions may be different, but the general effect of moving from the general to the specific is the same.

Restaurants?

Which kind?

Fast-food restaurant

Which one?

Long John Silvers

Where?

Long John Silvers on Central, near San Mateo

What about it?

Long John Silvers on Central, near San Mateo was mobbed.

By whom?

Highland High students mobbed Long John Silvers on Central, near San Mateo.

Why?

Highland High students mobbed Long John Silvers on Central, near San Mateo for fish specials.

EXERCISE 1: Choose and limit five of the following broad topics. Write out the different steps in the narrowing-down process.

transportation	sports	animals	education
grades	vacations	energy	dancing
music	people	discipline	children
dating	lifestyles	presents	plants
food	politicians	films	laughter

Focusing the Subject

Finding and limiting a subject are only half the battle; the writer must still focus the discussion. Even a subject limited to one person, one time, one place, and one purpose is too complex for a short essay if it is unfocused. For example, the Thanksgiving turkey hunt mentioned earlier could be discussed in terms of hunting safety, the pleasures of hunting, the miseries of hunting, hunting methods, hunting equipment, and so forth.

To focus a subject means to identify one particular way of looking at it—a position which will be maintained throughout the essay. This focus may be an attitude or opinion of the writer about the subject or simply a special perspective to be developed. You can discover your focus in your prewriting materials by reading them carefully and asking yourself: How does it all add up? What do I really feel or think or see? What approach is the most interesting? Depending upon the prewriting materials, the turkey-hunt topic might be focused in any of these ways:

> My hunt for a Thanksgiving turkey was a disaster.
> My hunt for a Thanksgiving turkey was idyllic, like an episode from the *Leatherstocking Tales* of James Fenimore Cooper.
> When I hunted for our Thanksgiving turkey, I violated every safety rule in the book and suffered the consequences.

Notice that it is not necessary to mention all of the elements of the limited subject in the thesis; all will probably be worked into the introduction.

EXERCISE 3: Examine the following statements. Identify the limited subject and the focus. Are the subjects sufficiently limited? Are they tightly focused? Why or why not?

1. Both women and men drivers are crazy when behind the wheel.
2. War has always been a big factor in solving world problems.
3. One of the worst times of my life was receiving news of my father's death.
4. As a teenager I learned many lessons that have helped me as a young adult.
5. One of the better places to get drunk is in a bar.
6. The worst time in my life was on a hunting trip I took last spring.
7. I'm in love with my Karmann Ghia.
8. My younger brother and I are two good examples of how a majority of teenagers lack responsibility.

9. I am going into the nursing program here at City College for my registered nursing license.
10. My kitchen gives off a very homey feeling to my friends, and strangers get the feeling of belonging there.

Sometimes you will include no more than a limited subject and a focus in your thesis statements. That is, you will name the narrowed-down subject and the focusing attitude, opinion, or perspective but not the individual topics to be covered in the body of the essay. Since you leave open what steps you will follow in discussing central ideas, we say that these are "open" thesis statements. Other times, however, you may feel the need for stronger guidelines; you may want to name explicitly what topics you will cover in your discussion and write a "closed" thesis statement.

Providing the Frame: Closing the Thesis

A closed thesis statement gives a limited subject, a focus, and several reasons for the writer's opinion or several major divisions of the focused subject or even simply several ideas related to the focused subject. Since the writer must compose several paragraphs after the introduction, dividing the thesis idea into parts can determine the subjects for those paragraphs and, therefore, organize the remainder of the essay.

The example essay in Chapter 7 gives us a good example of a closed thesis statement. You will notice that because of the complexity of Bernardo's subject, he has broken his thesis statement into two sentences.

> Our country is definitely prejudiced against left-handedness. This can be proved by the many inconveniences left-handed people must live with day to day, the words that recognize left-handedness negatively, and the horrible way people treat left-handers.

The second sentence provides a miniature outline for the rest of the essay. Bernardo's second paragraph is about the inconveniences left-handed people must live with, his third paragraph is about the negative words, and his fourth and fifth paragraphs are about the cruel treatment of left-handers.

EXERCISE 3: Discuss the following closed thesis statements in terms of limited subject, focus, and divisions. Would any be more effective as an open thesis statement?

1. The problems of living in a tourist-oriented community are some of the worst that I have encountered yet. Housing is poor, jobs are hard to get, and the cost of living is outlandish.
2. As I babysit, I begin to have doubts about myself, marriage, family life, and children.

3. In-depth teaching and religious training are advantages of sending children to a private elementary school.
4. My day in Santa Fe visiting the capitol, the shops, the plaza, the museums, and the churches was very enjoyable.
5. Exercise is very important to our bodies because it burns up calories, firms the muscles, relieves tension, and helps us to relax.
6. The kinds of students I noticed at Sam Houston High School were the overachiever, the mediocre, the timid, and the reluctant.
7. My favorite place at City College is the Learning Center because the director Ms. Pitts is friendly and understanding, the exercises help me develop my reading and English skills, I have met many friends there, and I can go there just to relax.
8. I am going into the nursing program because I like to spend my time giving help to people who need it, I like the reward you get from nursing, and nursing will always be necessary as long as life goes on.
9. Memories can be a real bummer; they can sadden, cause emotional stress, create tension, and even kill.
10. I will always remember the Talk of the Town, a restaurant in Ladonia, Texas, because of the way it looks, the people that come there, and the food that is prepared there.

EXERCISE 4: Practice writing open and closed thesis statements for essays covering the following subjects.

1. The writer wants to talk about different kinds of hitchhikers seen on the freeway.
2. The essay will describe the author's favorite place, a small town or recreation spot.
3. The writer will give examples of memories that are personally depressing or cheering.
4. The writer wishes to convince the reader that women in the service should (or should not) be allowed to serve in combat.
5. The essay will discuss noise pollution in a college dormitory.
6. The essay will argue for banning some advertisements aimed at children.
7. The writer will explain why the earthquakes have not frightened more Californians into moving.
8. The writer wants to show the reader how to make the most of a day off.
9. The essay will discuss the dangers of radioactive waste.
10. The writer will explain the need for everyone to be computer literate.

EXERCISE 5: Discover a subject and focus in the prewriting activities. Then write an open or a closed thesis statement for each one.

1.

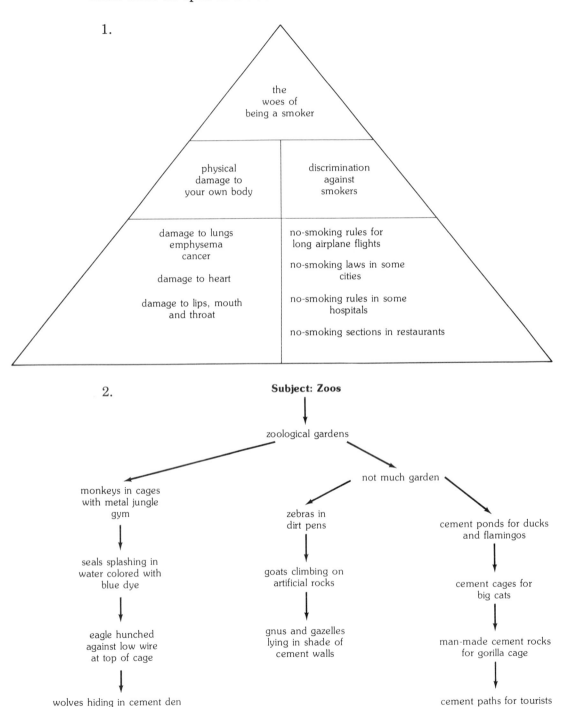

3. *Freewriting:* Writing a paper about trees is not going to be easy. I don't know much about trees having grown up in the city and not ... I guess there were plenty of trees even in my neighborhood. There were some in the park on the corner— maples I think because they turned red in the fall. The restaurants and bistros in the historic district had cement containers with lots of little trees like umbrellas in front ... I remember a favorite tree in our schoolyard. It was an oak I know that because our teacher taught us how to tell from the shape of the leaves. We would climb that tree at recess or sit under it to eat lunch. There were names carved into the tree and some hearts with initials. Now what? What are trees good for? I remember hearing that trees help clean the air. If that's true, every city should start planting trees right away. They should dig up parking lots and put in forests. The tops of buildings should be covered with trees in large round pots. If it will help with pollution, we could dig up the middle lanes of every street and plant trees, trees, trees.

Leading into the Thesis

Now that we have the "gate" to our essay, the thesis statement, we need a road to the gate. Providing a context for what will follow and winning an audience for the essay are two important purposes of the sentences that lead into the thesis statement. To accomplish these things, you must give us something more than vague, generalizing sentences. You might explain why the thesis idea is important to you or to the readers; give some background or a definition; provide an interesting story, quotation, or images; or appeal to the reader's sense of humor. Many introductions will use more than one of these lead-in or interest-catching devices. For example, Bernardo's introduction on page 130 combines a story about his left-handed friend Fred and a definition of left-handedness. The introduction to Jeanette's descriptive essay "At the Mall" uses lively language and a dramatic quotation to interest us in a moment that was important to her.

I awoke early Saturday morning with nothing to do for the rest of the day. I had cleaned the house and washed the laundry. Every book in the house had been read twice and all the records were scratched. Feeling bored, I had sat down to watch TV when a commercial blared at me, "Jeans, jeans, and more jeans at Jean Nicole's half-price sale today only!" I decided going to the Mall for jeans would pick me up, but the noise, the crowds, and the outrageous prices only increased my depression.

EXERCISE 6:   Discuss the following introductory paragraphs. Evaluate the lead-ins for interest and appropriateness. Evaluate the thesis statements for subject and focus.

1.   Having a few years of driving experience under my belt, I've realized that both women and men drivers are crazy when behind the wheel. There are many different kinds of crazy drivers, but I'll only mention a few; there are the road-hogs, the curb-huggers, the lane-hoppers, the poke-alongs, and the lead-feet.

2.   It is a warm, hot summer night and I could be doing so much more on a Saturday evening. Instead I am cooped up in a house, babysitting for the next door neighbors and wondering what my friends are doing. I'm thinking about all the exciting things that are going on outside and around. I wonder how that party turned out. I sure wish I could be there. It is of no great surprise to me that as I sit here thinking, I feel a streak of depression fall upon me. As I babysit, I begin to have doubts about myself, marriage, family life, and children.

3.   As a senior in high school, I began to look back at my high school years. I noticed one thing in particular. I had always had all my classes with the same people. The college-bound students were always put in the advanced math and science courses. I became very familiar with my fellow classmates' study habits. I noticed four main categories: the over-achiever, the mediocre student, the student who didn't care, and the student who was forced to go to school.

4.   I am quite an outdoors person. I enjoy hunting, fishing, and camping. The worst time of my life was on a hunting trip I took last spring. I got trapped in the mountains by a snowstorm, I almost froze to death, and I did not get a bird.

5.   There is a very big need in the medical field today. In every state there is a large demand for registered nurses. Most hospitals are understaffed because the need for a registered nurse is not met. I am going into the nursing program for my registered nursing license because I like to spend my time giving help to people who need it, I like the reward you get from nursing, and nursing will always be necessary as long as life goes on.

EXERCISE 7:   Write introductory paragraphs for three of the thesis statements you wrote in Exercise 4.

FOCUS ON THE SENTENCE: *Verbs II and Verbals*

One of the main functions of the introductory paragraph and the thesis is to focus the subject. One of the main functions of verbs, as you have seen, is to serve as a focal point of the sentence. Verbs show what action is happening or what condition is taking place. They show the time of the action or the condition, and to a large extent, they determine whether the sentence is complete or will need more words to finish the thought.

In this section you will be improving your acquaintance with verbs by studying the principal parts of verbs, nine verb tenses, and some *verbals* (parts or forms of verbs that serve other functions in a sentence).

Principal Parts of Verbs

The basic building blocks for all the functions of a verb are its principal parts. Each verb has five basic parts, some of which are used alone and some of which are used with other words to form the various tenses or to serve other functions (see Table 8–1).

The *base* is the beginning point—the form of the verb from which the other parts are made. You will find the base form as a major entry in your dictionary. The *present* form has two versions, one to be used with plural words like *we* and one to be used with most singular words like *Cynthia: We jump. Cynthia jumps. We smile. Cynthia smiles.*

Both the *past* and the *past participle* of many verbs are formed by adding *-ed* or *-d* to the base. The past form can be used alone, but the past participle will be used with helping verbs to form various past tenses. The *present participle* is formed by adding *-ing* to the base. With helping verbs the present participle makes up tenses that show continuous, or ongoing, action.

Most verbs form their principal parts in the manner just described; therefore, they are called *regular verbs* (see Table 8–1). Some, however, have special ways of forming the principal parts.

TABLE 8–1

Base	*Present*	*Past*	*Past Participle*	*Present Participle*
jump	jump jumps	jumped	jumped	jumping
smile	smile smiles	smiled	smiled	smiling
open	open opens	opened	opened	opening

Irregular Verbs

Irregular verbs may form one or all of the principal parts differently. Instead of simply adding -*s*, -*ed*, or -*ing*, they may change internally or use a completely different word. The two irregular verbs you use most often are *be* and *have* (see Table 8-2).

TABLE 8-2

Base	Present	Past	Past Participle	Present Participle
be	is are am	were was	been	being
have	has have	had	had	having

We use these words so often that you may find it useful to practice saying and using each part until you are completely comfortable with each one. The principal parts of some other common irregular verbs are listed below, but you can find many of the principal parts of any verb in your dictionary under its base form. Most dictionaries will give the past and the past participle separate listings only when they are different. Some verbs will have more than one acceptable form (see Table 8-3).

TABLE 8-3   Principal Parts of Irregular Verbs

Base	Present	Past	Past Participle	Present Participle
awake	awake awakes	awoke/ awaked	awoken/ awaked	awaking
become	become becomes	became	become	becoming
begin	begin begins	began	begun	beginning
bite	bite bites	bit	bit/bitten	biting
blow	blow blows	blew	blown	blowing
break	break breaks	broke	broken	breaking
bring	bring brings	brought	brought	bringing
build	build builds	built	built	building
burst	burst bursts	burst	burst	bursting
catch	catch catches	caught	caught	catching
choose	choose chooses	chose	chosen	choosing
cling	cling clings	clung	clung	clinging
come	come comes	came	come	coming

TABLE 8-3 **Principal Parts of Irregular Verbs (Continued)**

Base	Present	Past	Past Participle	Present Participle
do	do does	did	done	doing
dig	dig digs	dug	dug	digging
draw	draw draws	drew	drawn	drawing
drink	drink drinks	drank	drunk	drinking
drive	drive drives	drove	driven	driving
eat	eat eats	ate	eaten	eating
fall	fall falls	fell	fallen	falling
feed	feed feeds	fed	fed	feeding
find	find finds	found	found	finding
fly	fly flies	flew	flown	flying
forget	forgot forgets	forgot	forgotten	forgetting
forgive	forgive forgives	forgave	forgiven	forgiving
freeze	freeze freezes	froze	frozen	freezing
give	give gives	gave	given	giving
go	go goes	went	gone	going
grow	grow grows	grew	grown	growing
hear	hear hears	heard	heard	hearing
lay	lay lays	laid	laid	laying
lie	lie lies	lay	lain	lying
read	read reads	read	read	reading
ride	ride rides	rode	ridden/rode	riding
ring	ring rings	rang	rung	ringing
rise	rise rises	rose	risen	rising
run	run runs	ran	run	running
see	see sees	saw	seen	seeing
set	set sets	set	set	setting
shake	shake shakes	shook	shaken	shaking
shoot	shoot shoots	shot	shot	shooting
shrink	shrink shrinks	shrank/ shrunk	shrunk/ shrunken	shrinking

(continued)

TABLE 8-3   **Principal Parts of Irregular Verbs (Continued)**

Base	Present	Past	Past Participle	Present Participle
sit	sit sits	sat	sat	sitting
sing	sing sings	sang	sung	singing
sink	sink sinks	sank	sunk	sinking
speak	speak speaks	spoke	spoken	speaking
spin	spin spins	spun	spun	spinning
spring	spring springs	sprang/ sprung	sprung	springing
stand	stand stands	stood	stood	standing
steal	steal steals	stole	stolen	stealing
strike	strike strikes	struck	struck	striking
swear	swear swears	swore	sworn	swearing
swim	swim swims	swam	swum	swimming
swing	swing swings	swung	swung	swinging
take	take takes	took	taken	taking
teach	teach teaches	taught	taught	teaching
tear	tear tears	tore	torn	tearing
think	think thinks	thought	thought	thinking
throw	throw throws	threw	thrown	throwing
wake	wake wakes	woke/ waked	waked/woken/ woke	waking
wear	wear wears	wore	worn	wearing
win	win wins	won	won	winning
wind	wind winds	wound	wound	winding
wring	wring wrings	wrung	wrung	wringing
write	write writes	wrote	written	writing

EXERCISE 8:   Fill in the blanks in the paragraphs with the form of the verb listed in parentheses. Refer to the list of verbs whenever necessary. If the word is not on the list, it forms its principal parts regularly.

San Francisco, always a colorful city to visit, has ＿＿＿＿＿＿

(have, past participle) an equally colorful history. ＿＿＿＿＿＿

(build, past participle) like many California cities on the site of an old Spanish mission, it _____ (mushroom, past) into existence almost overnight. In 1848 a few hundred people _____ (live, past) at Yerba Buena Cove on San Francisco Bay. Then gold was _____ (discover, past participle) at Sutter's Mill on the Sacramento River. Within months a tent city had _____ (spring, past participle) up, and Yerba Buena Cove had _____ (become, past participle) one of the busiest harbors in the world. A forest of ships' masts _____ (fill, past) the skyline, and more ships _____ (arrive, past) daily, _____ (bring, present participle) hopeful adventurers through the Golden Gate to _____ (seek, base) their fortunes in the California gold fields.

While some of the forty-niners _____ (dig, past) for gold at Sutter's Mill, others _____ (find, past) their fortunes in San Francisco itself. Within a few short years, the tent city had _____ (grow, past participle) into a modern metropolis with a _____ (thrive, present participle) financial district, _____ (pave, past participle) streets, and residential neighborhoods. Often _____ (call, past participle) the wickedest city in the world, San Francisco in the 1850s _____ (be, past) a mixture of respectable prosperity and disreputable, boom-town exploitation of that prosperity. Casinos and bawdy houses _____ (stand, past) side by side with courthouses and churches. Murders _____ (be, past) so common that vigilante committees were _____ (form, past participle), and war _____ (break, past) out between outlaws and vigilantes.

Fire _____ (pose, past) a major threat to life in

early San Francisco. Large buildings had _____ (be, past participle) _____ (build, past participle) quickly of wood. Some _____ (have, past) canvas walls. Even the streets were _____ (pave, past participle) with flammable material—timber from the nearby Redwood forests. Fires _____ (devastate, past) the city again and again between 1850 and 1855. _____ (fight, present participle) fires _____ (become, past) such a common pastime that many fire companies _____ (do, past) double duty as gentlemen's clubs and were _____ (house, past participle) in elaborately decorated structures. Upstairs there would _____ (be, base) a library and pool tables; downstairs, the fire engine.

Tenses

The tense of a verb reflects the time at which either an action happens or a condition takes place. There are nine major tenses, or times, that we will consider here, and all of them are either principal parts of the verbs or can be made by adding helping verbs to principal parts.

Simple Tenses

There are three simple tenses—present, past, and future. The present and past tenses are themselves listed here as principal parts of the verbs. Therefore, if you would like to talk about something done yesterday or something broken today, you need only consult Table 8-3 for the appropriate form.

The villain <u>did</u> the dastardly deed yesterday.
The dishwasher <u>breaks</u> at least one plate and one bowl each day.

To form the future tense of a verb, add *will* to the base.

The challenger <u>will be</u> late for the duel.
The duelers <u>will stand</u> twenty paces apart.

EXERCISE 9: Underline and identify the tenses of the verbs in the paragraph.

Until today my life was in a rut. Everyday I get up at dawn, shower, and eat breakfast. I am at my desk from eight until noon when I eat my brownbag lunch in the park on the corner. I work without a coffeebreak all afternoon and drive home at five. Today, though, I bounced out of the rut. I overslept, was late to work, and missed lunch. By midafternoon I was faint with hunger and took a coffeebreak to gobble Mars Bars and Fritos at the vending machine in the hall. My boss caught me stuffing in my third candybar and gave me a scolding and a booklet on nutrition. To make matters worse, when I sped home, late again, at five-thirty, I ran a stop sign and got a ticket. I hope that by tomorrow I will be back in my same old, safe-and-sane rut.

Perfect Tenses

There are three additional past tenses, called *perfect* tenses, not because they are faultless or the best, but because they indicate perfected, or completed, actions or conditions. These tenses are formed by adding a helping verb to the past participle of the verb. The helping verb is a form of the verb *have*; which form to use is determined by the first word in the name of the tense.

1. **PRESENT PERFECT**   The present perfect tense shows an action or condition that began in the past and continued into the present. For example, if you began the novel *The Blessing Way* last night and just now finished it, you could use the present perfect tense to show what you did.

I <u>have</u> just now <u>finished</u> the novel *The Blessing Way.*

To form the tense, add the present tense of the helping verb *have* to the past participle of your main verb. Since there are different forms of the present tense (*has, have*) to use with singular and plural subjects, make sure the helping verb agrees with the subject.

The poet <u>has written</u> an ode to the kitchen sink.
Few poets <u>have written</u> odes to the kitchen sink.
One historian <u>has depicted</u> San Francisco as a cultural mecca.
Other historians <u>have depicted</u> San Francisco as a moralist's nightmare.

2. *PAST* PERFECT   The past perfect tense shows an action or condition that began and ended at some time in the past before some other past action or condition occurred. For example, if yesterday you first took your poodle for a manicure and shampoo and then went home to do your own nails and hair, you would use the past perfect tense for the first action and the past tense for the second action.

> After the groomer at the Pampered Pet had manicured Fifi's nails and had shampooed her coat, I manicured my own nails and shampooed my own hair at home.

To form the past perfect tense, add *had* (the past tense of have) to the past participle of the main verb.

> We had swabbed the deck before the gale struck.
> The detective had shot before the knife pinned his arm.

3. *FUTURE* PERFECT   When something will be completed by some definite future time, use the future perfect tense. For example, if you set a deadline of noon tomorrow for wallpapering the den, you can write in this tense.

> I will have wallpapered the den by noon tomorrow.

To form the future perfect tense, add *will have* (the future tense of *have*) to the past participle of the main verb.

> The broken clock will have chimed fifty times by the end of the hour.
> I will have broken my resolution a dozen times before the end of New Year's Day.

EXERCISE 10:   Underline and identify the tenses of the verbs in the sentences.

1. The cow will have jumped over the moon by ten o'clock.
2. Then the little dog will laugh to see such sport, and the dish will run away with the spoon.
3. Mary had had a little lamb before she lost it at school.
4. London Bridge has not fallen down.
5. An American bought London Bridge and shipped it to Arizona where it serves as a tourist attraction for a little town in the desert.

6. Little Miss Muffet had already sat on her tuffet when along came the spider and sat down beside her.
7. Being nimble and quick will have helped Jack to jump over the candlestick.
8. Jack and Jill had gone up the hill to fetch a pail of water, but Jack fell down and broke his crown.
9. If Peter Piper picked a peck of pickled peppers, where is the peck of pickled peppers that Peter Piper picked?
10. Pussy cat, pussy cat, where have you been?

Progressive Tenses

The progressive tenses show continuous or ongoing action. All use the present participle of the main verb and add to it an appropriate form of the helping verb *be*.

1. *PRESENT* **PROGRESSIVE**   The present progressive tense indicates that an action or condition is going on at the present time.

> I <u>am washing</u> my car now.
> The meteorologists <u>are predicting</u> rain today.

To form the present progressive tense, add the present tense form of the verb *be* that matches your subject to the present participle of the verb.

> I <u>am writing</u> a letter, while you <u>are typing</u> a grocery list.
> We <u>are finishing</u> our discussion, but they <u>are beginning</u> a new argument.
> The dog <u>is scratching</u> at the door, but the cat <u>is sitting</u> quietly in the window.

2. *PAST* **PROGRESSIVE**   The past progressive tense shows that an action or condition was going on during some time in the past.

> Yesterday at this time, I <u>was dozing</u> on the couch.
> Yesterday, the meteorologists <u>were predicting</u> a storm.

To form the past progressive tense, add *was* or *were*, depending upon whether your subject is singular or plural, to the present participle of the verb.

> The sun <u>was shining</u>; the birds <u>were singing</u>; the flowers <u>were blooming</u>.

3. *FUTURE* PROGRESSIVE   The future progressive tense points toward an action or condition that will be happening in the future.

Tomorrow, I <u>will be dancing</u> the hula in Hawaii.
Soon the sun <u>will be shining</u>.

To form the future progressive tense, add *will be* (the future tense of *be*) to the present participle of the verb.

On my Hawaiian vacation, I <u>will be staying</u> on Waikiki Beach.
The *Wheel of Fortune* television show <u>will be sponsoring</u> my visit.

EXERCISE 11:   Underline and identify the tenses of the verbs in the paragraphs.

> An uneasy quiet had stilled the forest when we woke on that fateful morning in May, 1980. No birds were singing in the trees. The squirrels had ended their relentless thefts of our camp stores and were hiding in their holes in the ground. As we crawled out of our sleeping bags and looked nervously around, we heard the screams of a pair of eagles high overhead. They were circling their nest in the top of a jagged dead pine. Their cries carried a message of anger as well as fear.
>
> "They sound like they are scolding the mountain," I told my companion.
>
> We looked across the misty blue of Spirit Lake to the lush, green slopes of Mt. St. Helens. Its peak was hiding behind a cap of smoke, but the mountain still looked peaceful and serene in the thin morning light. Later we wished we had taken more pictures of the beautiful volcano before its awesome eruption devastated the countryside.

Meaning and Tenses

The right tense to use is the one that best fits your meaning. Use common sense. If you are writing about an event that happened in the past, you will probably not need to use too many present tense or future tense verbs.

If you are writing about something happening right now, you will probably not need to use too many of the perfect tenses.

You may find it helpful in choosing which tenses to use, to map out the events you are writing about using a *time line*. A time line lets you list events in the order in which they happened and then helps you choose appropriate tenses (see Figure 8–1).

Space the events you wish to write about along the time line, adding exact times wherever possible. Write the events to the left. Then choose a reference point, and as you write, move back and forth along the time line, referring to the tenses on the right as a reminder of your options.

It <u>is</u> two o'clock in the afternoon and I <u>am drawing</u> a cartoon depicting a battle between my cat Mitzy and my new pincushion

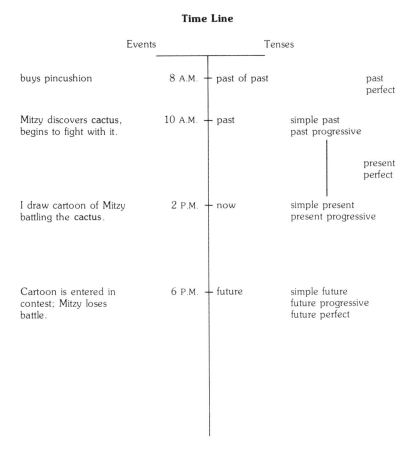

Time Line

Events		Tenses
buys pincushion	8 A.M. — past of past	past perfect
Mitzy discovers cactus, begins to fight with it.	10 A.M. — past	simple past / past progressive
		present perfect
I draw cartoon of Mitzy battling the cactus.	2 P.M. — now	simple present / present progressive
Cartoon is entered in contest; Mitzy loses battle.	6 P.M. — future	simple future / future progressive / future perfect

FIGURE 8–1

cactus. Mitzy <u>discovered</u> the cactus only two hours after I <u>had bought</u> it at Rowland's Nursery. She <u>was</u> curious. She <u>touched</u> it carefully, and, I <u>am</u> sure to her way of thinking, the cactus <u>bit</u> her. Then <u>began</u> the battle that <u>has been going</u> on for nearly four hours. Mitzy <u>has attacked</u> the cactus from behind the sofa, from across the dining room table, and from under the rocking chair, but she <u>has</u> not <u>managed</u> to defeat it yet. The cactus needles <u>are stinging</u> as sharply as ever. I fear Mitzy <u>will</u> not <u>win</u> this battle, but I hope I <u>will win</u> the Pets in Action cartoon contest. The contest <u>will close</u> at six o'clock, but I <u>will have submitted</u> my entry by then.

The times involved in the events described in this paragraph are somewhat complicated because they occur at several different points along the time line. The writer kept from confusing the tenses by starting with the present as a reference point and then moving back and forth along the time line, choosing different tenses to match the times and events.

EXERCISE 12: Rewrite the following sentences in the tense indicated in parentheses.

1. The Gobots are coming. (present perfect)
2. At noon the spaceship landed on Mars. (future progressive)
3. Ollie has won $2,500 worth of prizes, but she is quickly losing the grand prize. (past perfect, past)
4. David paints surrealistic pictures on bus stations walls. (past)
5. He uses spray cans of red, blue, green, and yellow paint. (past progressive)
6. The custodians will wash away David's painting before the commuters see it tomorrow morning. (future perfect, present perfect)
7. But David will be painting the walls again tomorrow night. (future)
8. Koko the Gorilla talks to her pet kitten. (present progressive)
9. The gorilla is learning approximately 350 words. (present perfect)
10. Carbon dioxide in the atmosphere is increasing the earth's temperature. (present)
11. The Circle K advertised a sale on potato chips. (past perfect)
12. I buy groceries on Monday instead of Saturday to avoid the rush. (past)
13. Gerald Tafoya grew a giant sunflower in his back yard. (present progressive)

14. Gerald won the annual Jolly Green Giant contest for the largest sunflower. (future)
15. I read an adventure novel every night this week. (future progressive)

EXERCISE 13: Rewrite the following paragraphs changing the tenses. Begin with the change noted in parentheses; then change other tenses as appropriate for meaning.

1. Sam awakes (past) at dawn when he vacations in the mountains. He showers in the tiny shower stall of his nineteen-foot travel trailer. He brushes his teeth at the miniature sink and cooks a breakfast steak and two eggs on a stove no larger than his lap. Sam eats outside, sitting on a fallen log and watching the sun as it rises in a misty blue sky. Then he washes his plate and utensils in a munchkin-size sink and sets out on his morning's adventure.

2. The night disc jockey's life at KRVC was (present) not easy. She arrived at the station at midnight and usually found records out of their jackets, soft drink cans stacked by the turntables, and groupies wandering in and out of the broadcast studio. It took as a rule until one o'clock to clean up the mess and to clear out unwanted visitors. But it took until dawn and the end of her shift to straighten out the traffic log and put all the records back in their places.

EXERCISE 14: Plan and write a paragraph about a series of events that happened to you. Choose a reference point and then write carefully, using appropriate tenses for each verb. You may find it helpful to draw a time line to help you visualize the sequence of events.

Verbals

When is a verb not a verb? When one of the principal parts of a verb serves some other function in a sentence, we call it a *verbal*. The base form, the past participle, and the present participle may serve as modifiers or even as nouns.

THE VERBAL NOUN (GERUND) Present participles, the *-ing* verbals, are frequently used as nouns in a sentence. They are easy to recognize because they fill the slots in a sentence where we are accustomed to seeing nouns or pronouns.

Subject: George means a lot to Susan.
          Running means a lot to Susan.

Predicate Word: The city council has banned <u>parties</u> in the park.
The city council has banned <u>running</u> in the park.

THE VERBAL ADJECTIVE Both present and past participles may be used to describe nouns or pronouns. Again, they are easy to recognize because they fill the slots in the sentence usually filled by single-word or phrase adjectives.

adj.   adj.
<u>Red and shaky</u>, I stumbled to the platform.

     adj.   adj.
<u>Embarrassed and shaking</u>, I stumbled to the platform.

The speaker, <u>red and shaky</u>, stumbled to the platform.
The speaker, <u>embarrassed and shaking</u>, stumbled to the platform.

THE "TO" VERBAL (INFINITIVE) When you add *to* to the base of a verb, you form a verbal that may be used as a noun or a modifier.

<u>Flight</u> is the eagle's joy and salvation.
<u>To fly</u> is the eagle's joy and salvation. (serves as noun, subject of verb *is*)

The teams battled <u>desperately</u>.
The teams battled <u>to win</u>. (serves as adverb describing verb *battled*)

The decision <u>for victory</u> was made in the locker room.
The decision <u>to win</u> was made in the locker room. (serves as adjective, telling which decision)

VERBAL PHRASE Often a verbal will be followed by other words which add to or complete the thought. The verbal and all of its modifying or completing words makes up a verbal phrase. The entire phrase will serve as a noun, adjective, or adverb, just as a prepositional phrase serves as an adjective or an adverb.

<u>Running a roulette wheel</u> can be demanding work. (verbal phrase as subject)
<u>Broken in a dozen places</u>, the vase could not be glued together. (verbal phrase as adjective, describing *vase*)
The teams battled <u>to win the championship match</u>. (verbal phrase as adverb, modifying *battled*)

EXERCISE 15: Replace the underlined words or phrases in the following sentences with verbals or verbal phrases.

1. <u>Ms. Smythe</u> will require dedication and hard work from all employees.
2. My <u>culinary</u> skills go no further than <u>peanut butter and jelly sandwiches</u>.
3. <u>Sad and weary</u>, the climbers started back down the mountain.
4. On Tuesday we voted <u>on the school bond issue</u>.
5. The fight <u>against calories</u> is being waged in the spas and lost at McDonald's, Wendy's, and Burger King.

EXERCISE 16: Combine the following sentences to make a single sentence that includes a verbal or a verbal phrase.

1. My soufflé stunned our dinner guests. My soufflé had fallen.
2. Garfield made two New Year's resolutions. He will eat less lasagna. He will not kick Odie.
3. The golfer sliced into the woods. He was squinting in the sun.
4. Suzanne dreams big dreams. She wants to write mysteries. The mysteries will be best sellers.
5. The television picture is giving me a headache. It quivers. It blurs.
6. The person owns the greenhouse. Ask him. He knows the price of violets.
7. The Gobots are fighting the Transformers. The winner rules the electronic toy market.
8. Will-o'-the-wisps lead the travelers into the swamp. The will-o'-the-wisps beckon. The travelers are confused.
9. The real estate agent unloaded the house on strangers. The strangers were unsuspecting. The agent was chuckling to herself. The house was haunted.
10. A dry wind swept across the desert. The wind was filled with dust. The wind tore up tumbleweeds. The wind battered the yuccas.

TROUBLESHOOTING: *Verb Tenses and Verbals*

Three major problems associated with the use of verb tenses and verbals are shifting tenses, verbal fragments, and dangling or misplaced modifiers.

    1. When you change tenses without a reason for doing so, the error

is called shifting tenses. If you begin writing in the past tense, you should continue in the past tense unless the meaning requires a change. The same principle applies if you begin in the present tense: change tenses only when a change is logical.

> The driver drove slowly and carefully onto the busy expressway. To his left the traffic was barreling along at sixty miles per hour. Behind him cars are picking up speed so that they can merge with the traffic.

The tenses in the first two sentences are consistently past, with the past tense *drove* in the first sentence fitting logically with the past progressive *was barreling* in the second sentence. However, in the third sentence there is a shift to present tense first with *are picking* and then with *can merge.* We can correct the problem in one of two ways: we can rewrite the sentences using only past tenses, or we can rewrite using only present tenses.

> *Past tense:*   The driver drove slowly and carefully onto the busy expressway. To his left the traffic was barreling along at sixty miles per hour. Behind him cars were picking up speed so that they could merge with the traffic.
>
> *Present tense:*   The driver drives slowly and carefully onto the busy expressway. To his left the traffic is barreling along at sixty miles per hour. Behind him cars are picking up speed so that they can merge with the traffic.

EXERCISE 17:   Rewrite the following paragraphs, finding and correcting any problems with shifting tenses.

1.   At noon on a hot, sultry day a wagon train rumbled through the gates of the fort. The wagon master is none other than Buffalo Jones, as infamous a frontiersman as Billy the Kid or Jesse James. He has sixteen notches on his gun, and there are ten notches on his rifle.

2.   I have been typing all day. The white letters on the green screen of my word processor blurred and ran together before my eyes. My fingers keep hitting the wrong keys, and I was wondering how many more letters and memos the boss can write in one morning.

3.   Archeologists arrived at the site on a Monday. By Tuesday they begin roping off the area of the dig. They hoped to find

evidence that the canyon has been the home of the Anasazi, ancestors of today's Pueblo Indians throughout New Mexico.

2. A second common error occurs if you punctuate a verbal phrase as a complete sentence.

> The mosquito flew quickly and stealthily. Distracting me with its sudden attacks and equally sudden retreats.

Although the second group of words ends with a period, it lacks both the subject and the helping verb needed to make it a complete sentence. To correct the error, you might either attach it to the complete sentence (so that the phrase describes the actions or the mosquito) or add the missing elements.

> The mosquito flew quickly and stealthily, distracting me with its sudden attacks and equally sudden retreats.

> The mosquito flew quickly and stealthily. Its noise was distracting me with its sudden attacks and equally sudden retreats.

Be careful, however, not to add a subject only and forget the helping verb. The result is still a fragment.

> *Not:* The mosquito flew quickly and stealthily. Its noise, distracting me with its sudden attacks and equally sudden retreats.

The present participle *distracting* cannot serve as the verb in a sentence without a helping verb such as *was.*

EXERCISE 18: Rewrite the paragraphs to correct verbal fragments.

> 1. Dolls' costumes in the nineteenth century were sometimes as elaborate and extravagant as those of the nobility. Gowned in satin or velvet court dresses. Studded with gems and sown with pearls. Dolls were even presented at the Queen's Drawing Room. Their formal debut, mimicking the debutantes whose entry into society began with their first appearance at court.
>
> 2. Managing air traffic in a thousand-watt radio station. This was Antonio's first job after graduation. Arranging the commercial spots to make sure that no competitors' commercials aired together. Inserting public service announcements throughout the

day, not just late at night. He even retyped the radio log. Allowing the announcers room. To log in each spot and program as they are broadcast.

3.   Timber-cruising in the Oregon forests requires a knowledge of lumber and the strength of ten. The timber-cruiser's job may seem deceptively simple. Estimating the number of board feet of lumber that can be logged in a particular forest. But doing that job! That's another matter entirely. The timber-cruiser must hike through miles of the densest fir or pine. Climbing up hills where there are no trails except the ones the forest animals make. Climbing down into canyons thick with brush and steep with sharp inclines. If the cruiser is good, an entire forest may be surveyed in less than a month. The survey resulting in an accurate bid for timber rights or a work schedule for loggers.

3.   A verbal phrase used as a modifier may also present problems if it is not placed close to the word it modifies.

The balloonist scraped a telephone wire flying overhead.

The sentence creates the absurd picture of a telephone wire instead of the balloonist doing the flying. Because the modifier is in the wrong place in the sentence, the error is called a *misplaced modifier*. To correct it, simply move the modifier.

Flying overhead, the balloonist scraped a telephone wire.

If the word the modifier describes is not in the sentence, the error is called a *dangling modifier;* the modifier is left dangling without any word to attach itself to. To correct this error, add a word for the modifier to describe or rewrite the sentence.

Singing in the shower, it was a beautiful morning. (Who is singing?)
Singing in the shower, I knew it was a beautiful morning. (I am singing.)
In spite of George's singing in the shower, it was a beautiful morning.

EXERCISE 19:   Rewrite the sentences to eliminate misplaced or dangling modifiers.

1.   Sirens blaring and red lights flashing, I watched as the fire engine stopped outside our house, bewildered.

2. Astonished by the clamor, it took me several minutes to answer the door.
3. To make a sandpainting, it is important to begin with true colors and materials, grinding sand from turquoise or pipestone rather than dying sandstone particles blue or red.
4. This morning I saw cliff dwellings hiking in the canyons.
5. Long abandoned but never forgotten, the Pueblo tribes hold the homes of their ancestors in reverence.
6. Fighting viciously over every crumb, I watched the finches battle the sparrows at the bird feeder.
7. Excited and peering out the window, the jet taxied down the runway, taking me on my first trip to Bermuda.
8. While coming home late last night, three burglars were seen climbing out of my bedroom window.
9. Masked and loaded down with booty, I saw them hide behind the junipers.
10. Afraid to move, I sat in my car shivering and wondering what to do next.
11. To get the courage to scream, the car had to be locked and the windows rolled up.

READING TO WRITE

Erwin Bauer's "Devils in Fur Coats?" (pages 329–31 in the readings) provides a good example of the funnel-shaped introductory paragraph we have been studying in this chapter. Bauer begins broadly with general statements about North American wildlife and their abuse by hunters and trappers. Then he narrows his subject to one kind of wild animal, the grizzly bear. Leading into this subject with the negative context of other animals that have been mistreated prepares us for Bauer's sympathetic focus. The grizzly, he suggests, is feared and colorful but, most importantly, it is misunderstood.

Bauer's writing can also supply you with examples of another kind. Throughout this text you have been looking at the readings for ways to select or organize ideas. You can also use the readings to provide models to improve your writing of individual sentences.

Modeling sentences takes place in two distinct steps.

1. You must understand the plan or shape of the sentence you are modeling. Take, for example, this sentence from "Mowgli's Brothers" by Rudyard Kipling.
   The man's cub is ours—to kill if we choose.

Notice the relationship between *man's* and *cub,* the position of the dash after a complete sentence idea, the groups of words that start with *to* and *if.* Then listen for the way the words and groups of words fit together—the way *the man's cub* makes one word cluster, *to kill* another, and *if we choose* another. Identify words that act as hinges or glue for the pattern—*the, is, to, if.*

2. Then write your own sentence or sentences, following the pattern as closely as you can.

   The computer's access code is lost—to find if you can.
   The woman's hat is hers—to trim as she pleases.
   The yarn's message is clear—to expose how humans exaggerate.

Bauer's sentences can also supply models for effective writing and specifically for writing with verbals such as you have been studying in this chapter. While Bauer does not use verbals extensively in his writing, when he does use them, they add to the dramatic effect. Consider, for example, the following pair of sentences. The first uses no verbals; the second shows Bauer's use of the "to" verbal.

   Potentially, the grizzly is the most dangerous and formidable creature.
   Potentially, the grizzly is the most dangerous and formidable creature to walk on four feet.

The verbal in the second sentence adds picture and motion to the abstractions *dangerous* and *formidable.* Something large may be awesome, but set it moving, and we run!

EXERCISE 20: Practice using verbals in sentences modelled on the following (from Bauer's article).

1. Potentially, the grizzly is the most dangerous and formidable creature to walk on four feet.
2. He can run with startling speed, and an actual charge must be a chilling, fearsome thing.
3. A grizzly has a bolder, more confident and rolling gait.
4. The animal proceeded to maul and mutilate Glass beyond recognition, breaking bones and tearing most of his scalp away.
5. Unattended, and after lying in a coma for days, Glass survived.

WRITING ACTIVITY

Human beings have usually been poor neighbors to the other creatures who share this planet. In this assignment you will focus on some of the misunderstandings between people and animals.

Pay special attention to your introductory paragraph. You may wish to lead into your thesis with some background information, as Bauer does in "Devils in Fur Coats?" Or you might use an illustration, a quotation, or description. If you find, as you prewrite, that your support calls for a complex plan, you may wish to use a closed thesis statement to help you control your materials.

ACTIVITY: Identify a misunderstood creature and write an essay to explain or to correct the misunderstanding. Be sure to follow through on all parts of the writing process: prewriting, writing, and rewriting. Your instructor may ask you to turn in all your activities, plans, and drafts, so do not throw anything away— including the comments of your peer critic if you are asked to exchange essays.

Some possible topics follow. You may choose one of these or find a topic of your own.

1. Wolves
2. Snakes
3. Tarantulas
4. Hawks
5. Mountain lions
6. Ants

CHECKLIST: As you complete each draft of your essay, check it carefully for the following.

1. Does the essay have an effective introduction with a clear thesis statement?
2. Does the organization of the essay work well?
3. Is there enough support for key ideas?
4. Are there any misplaced or dangling modifiers?

5. Are verb tenses consistent and well chosen?
6. Are there any errors in adjective or adverb use?
7. Are there any errors in subject-verb or pronoun agreement?
8. Are there any comma splices, run-ons, or fragments, including verbal fragments?
9. Are there any misspelled words, left-out words, or reversed letters?

CHAPTER NINE
The Purpose
of the Essay

Why Are You Writing?

In Chapter 8 you discovered the impact your audience has upon your writing. Who you are writing for can affect what you say and how you say it. Your audience affects the words you choose, your sentence structure, and even your grammar. Another important audience-related factor influencing your writing is purpose—why you are writing. Are you writing to persuade your audience to share an opinion, to communicate facts, to amuse, to contrast, to teach, to describe?

Consider the following accounts of a hot-air balloon launch:

The balloon port blossomed as hundreds of hot air balloons prepared to launch. Gaudy envelopes in rainbow colors filled slowly with hot air and then lifted off, one after the other, into a blue, sunlit sky.

There are three major things to remember when you ride for the first time in a hot-air balloon. Wear warm clothes. Do not look down. And never leave the gondola!

The morning's launch went smoothly. Two hundred and fifty balloons lifted off in twelve-mile-per-hour winds. Only one minor accident occurred when George Patterson's gondola grazed a telephone line near Cutter's Field. There were no injuries.

In the first paragraph the writer's purpose is to describe the scene; in the second, to give tongue-in-cheek advice to a participant (what first-time rider would dream of leaving the gondola of a balloon in flight?); and in the third, to report on the event. The differences in purpose affect the content and also the writer's point of view—that is, whether the writer will assume the stance of a detached observer or enter the scene as a participant. In the first paragraph the writer is an observer, drawing a picture with words. In the second the writer gets closer to the action to give advice on behavior and addresses a participant as *you.* And in the third paragraph the writer is again an observer, but this time the writer emphasizes facts rather than pictures.

EXERCISE 1:   Study the following paragraphs. Try to determine the writer's purpose and the ways that purpose has affected the paragraph.

1.   The air show at Lackland Air Base began at dawn. A crowd of eighty thousand overflowed the stands into the fields surrounding the airfield. A partly cloudy sky obscured visibility for many of the Blue Angels' routines throughout the two-hour show.

2.   The tornado snaked out of the darkened sky. A menacing, undulating tunnel, it ripped off roofs and tore up trees, miraculously leaving a house standing here or a car upright there.

3.   June 15 was one of those perfect days when nothing can go wrong and everything does. I was sitting on my porch swing, breathing in the pleasing smells of freshly mown grass and blooming honeysuckle and congratulating myself on the splendid spectacle my roses were making of themselves. I had just reached that delightful state when the mind is at rest, the body is saturated with physical sensations, and sleep is not far away. Then it happened.

4.   The best way to wash dishes is the old-fashioned way. Forget machines that send water cascading gently over and around the dishes. Your dishes will be cleaner if you scrub them in a sinkful of suds with a washcloth and an SOS pad and rinse them with a teakettle of boiling water.

5.   There are two ways to wash dishes. The old-fashioned way requires a sinkful of hot suds, a washcloth, an SOS pad, and a teakettle of boiling water. Each dish is dipped into the suds, subjected to a thorough scrubbing, and rinsed with boiling water. The modern, machine method, on the other hand, eliminates the elbow grease as well as the greasy smears and spots on the dishes. The dishes are placed in a machine which sends hot, soapy water cascading gently over and around them.

FOCUS ON WRITING: *Finding a Purpose*

Purpose is your reason for writing. It provides direction and limits. Often you will find your purpose in your instructor's assignment.

> Define the *greenhouse effect.*
> Discuss the meaning for you of the color green.

Both assignments ask for meanings, but the first one asks for an *objective* response—that is, for facts without personal comments or interpretation. The second assignment asks for a *subjective* response; the writer is encouraged to give personal views.

> The *greenhouse effect* refers to the Earth's ability to maintain a warm temperature. The atmosphere produces this effect by reabsorbing heat emitted from the Earth. According to some scientists, the effect may cause a significant rise in the Earth's temperature as the amount of carbon dioxide in the atmosphere increases. Drastic changes in world climate could result.

> Green has always been my favorite color. Green makes me feel good because it reminds me of things I enjoy, like green grass, green beans, and green money. Green is also my lucky color. Finding a green four-leaf clover guarantees me good fortune. When I catch a green-clad leprechaun from the Emerald Isle, the pot of gold at the end of the rainbow will be mine. Green is a soothing color too. It makes me feel calm and cool, as though I am walking in a peaceful mountain meadow. I always wear green for an important test or interview. Its soothing effect calms my nerves, its pleasant associations help me feel good about myself, and its magic charm just might bring me luck.

EXERCISE 2:   Listed below are writing assignments from a variety of subject areas. Study each one, identify its purpose, and decide whether the assignment calls for an objective or a subjective response.

1. Discuss the effects of cigarette smoking on human health.
2. Do you support or oppose the smoking ban on airline flights?
3. Explain the plight of the blue whale.
4. Should there be a ban on killing blue whales?
5. Write an essay about the most unforgettable character you have met.

6. Daniel Boone is one of the most unforgettable characters in American history. Write an essay about the man and the legend.
7. Henry David Thoreau's *Walden* contains a number of economic and social ideas. Identify and explain those ideas.
8. Did you enjoy reading Thoreau's *Walden?* Why or why not?
9. President Lincoln's signing the Emancipation Proclamation in September, 1862, was a memorable event. What made it memorable?
10. Write about a memorable event in your life. What made it memorable?

EXERCISE 3:   Discuss the following excerpts from student papers in terms of the purpose listed. Is the writing successful? How might it be improved?

1. *Purpose:* Short essay exam question explaining the scientific principles of electricity

   The word *electricity* has special meanings to everyone. To me electricity is more than the mysterious juice that lights my lamps and turns on my TV. It is the charged atmosphere when a person I like a lot enters the room. It is the tingly feeling I get when I'm excited or happy or in love.

2. *Purpose:* Sales pitch for a brand of soap

   According to *Webster's New World Dictionary,* soap is "a substance used with water to produce suds for washing or cleaning." Soap is usually made by alkali acting on fats or oils. In pioneer days people used soapbark or even the flowers of wild lilac bushes as a substitute soap.

3. *Purpose:* Appeal to the Dean of Students for a new soccer program

   Here's the dope. Soccer is where it's at. The U.S. is behind the times. This planet is into soccer.

4. *Purpose:* Discussion of the plight of the bald eagle

   Not only are bald eagles the victims of poachers, but they are also the victims of too much civilization. In areas where eagles once nested, vacation homes have been built. Garbage dumps that once fed hundreds of eagles have been replaced by landfills and sanitary processing. In the process the eagle has been left without a home and without food.

5. *Purpose:* Explanation of how to pop popcorn

   I once planted patches of sweet corn and popcorn side by side. The two kinds of corn crossed, and soon I had corn that wouldn't pop and did not taste good roasted or boiled.

Sometimes your assignment will not specify a purpose. For example, your instructor might ask you to write an essay on a topic of your own choice. In that case, finding a purpose will become part of prewriting. For example, Maria found a purpose while she brainstormed about a flock of finches at a birdfeeder.

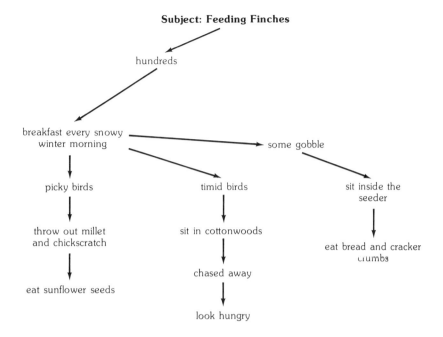

Subject: Feeding Finches

hundreds

breakfast every snowy winter morning

some gobble

picky birds

timid birds

sit inside the seeder

throw out millet and chickscratch

sit in cottonwoods

eat bread and cracker crumbs

eat sunflower seeds

chased away

look hungry

Maria's brainstorm showed that not all of the finches ate the same food in the same way. In fact, she noticed several different types of behaviors. Identifying and explaining those behaviors became the purpose of her short essay.

Breakfast at the Birdfeeder

On snowy, winter mornings I get up early and hurry outside to fill the birdfeeders. Then I sit down at my window with a cup of coffee and enjoy watching my breakfast guests. This morning flocks of gray and red finches arrive first. As I watch them, I notice several different kinds of eating behaviors.

First, there are the picky eaters. They search through the seeds for their favorites, flinging aside the hardy millet and chickscratch. When they find a special treat, like a sunflower seed, they fly away with it to the top of the apple tree. There they crack the shell and greedily eat the oily, gray seed inside. These finches are the fattest birds at the feeder and are probably part of the flock that dines with us each morning and evening.

Next to the picky eaters, grabbing every discarded seed, are the gobblers. These hungry birds eat everything, including the bread and cracker crumbs that I spread out on the snow. They crowd their way into the feeder and stand tummy deep in the seeds, shoveling it in. Their boldness tells me they are not

strangers to our birdfeeder, but they probably have not eaten
here for awhile.

The birds I worry about are the timid eaters. They fly onto
the feeder and just manage to sneak a bite when they are chased
away. Then they sit forlornly in the branches of the cottonwood
tree, waiting for another opening. These finches look
undernourished and have probably not visited our feeder before.

While I have been watching the picky eaters, the gobblers,
and the timid eaters, the seed in the feeder has gone down. I
leave my window to refill the feeder, making sure no birds go
hungry on this snowy day.

EXERCISE 4:   Find a purpose for an essay in each prewriting activity.

1.

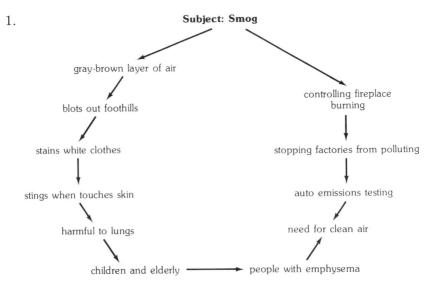

2. *Freewriting:* Writing about vacations would be easy if I had
   been anywhere exciting. I could talk about going to Hawaii only
   I haven't been there yet. Or a trip to Europe would be exciting if
   I had been there. In a way, though, it doesn't matter where you
   go on vacation as long as you go. I once went three years
   without a vacation, and I was a nervous wreck. Vacations only
   work if you get away. Staying home and cleaning out the garage
   won't do it. For a vacation really to be a vacation you have to go
   somewhere and do something you don't usually do. Vacations
   can be an important mental health tool. You get out from under,
   away from it all, out of the rut, rat race, or saltmines.

EXERCISE 5:   The two essays that follow are responses to the assignment:
Write about a place that has special meaning to you. Evaluate their suc-

cess in fulfulling the assignment. What purpose do you think the writers found in the assignment? Explain. How is that purpose reflected in each essay? As you read, look also for problems with each essay's organization, introductory paragraph, or thesis, and for errors in spelling, punctuation, agreement, and so forth.

Essay 1

As a child I spent alot of time traveling. I have lived and visited, Iceland, Germany, France, Spain, and every state in the U.S., including Alaska. There is an island at the end of the Alaskan Alution Chain called Adak. The Alution chain is a string of islands streaching south from Alaskas Mainland. Adak is the third island from the end of this Chain. While living on the island of Adak, I learned much about it. The beaches are composed of sand and alot of rock. The land is different and unusual to the eyes of an easterner. The weather in Adak can also be very unpredectable.

If asked what the most beautiful part of Adak was, I would say the beaches. Naturally Adak being an island, it is surrounded by the sea. For the most part the beaches are rocky, but there are also miles of pure black sand caused by erupting volcanos. on the eastern side of the island there are 80 to 90 foot, towering cliffs of solid volcanic rock. As the sun sets in the evening the rushing tide crashes huge 6 and 7 foot waves against the giant cliffs. On parts of the there are natural rock jetties that stretch as far as one half mile out to sea. When the tide is in the jetties are completely covered by the sea. When the tide is out, they are uncovered, and all the shell life that dwell among the rocks are exposed.

As you travel away from the beaches, the black and rocks begin to disappear. The land turns into rolling hills of high tundra grass. Tundra grass is much like field grass, only it is light broun in color and usually grows to four foot high. There are also small fresh water lakes on the island of Adak. There Are streans flowing from, and to these small lakes. These streams often disappear underground only to reappear some hundred yards away. While exploring the land one must be careful not to fall into these underground streans, for the water is very cold and swift. There are no trees to speak of on the island of Adak. There are about 30 swarf pine trees that are jokingly called; Adak international forest.

While on Adak one must be prepaird to weather violent

storms. Adak is known as the storn center of the world. In the time a person can walk a mile, he may go through snow, 60 mile winds, rain, and sunshine. If a person is out in the wilderness, he must be prepared for a storm at anytime. If not, one could die very quickly from exposure to the freezing wind. Most of the summer months are mild. Tempatures are between 40° and 60°, but it is not uncommon to have a storm that will drop three to four feet of snow in mid July.

Having spent 2 years on the island of Adak, I have learned much about it. With the beaiful beaches and rolling hills it is worth the disadvantages of the bad weather.

Essay 2

Since becoming an adult, summer vacations have become an unaffordable luxury, but as a child every summer vacation was a Huckleberry Finn adventure. Every summer was spent at "the lake" a place called Jackfish Lake in Saskatchewan, Canada.

Our home was twenty miles from the lake. At the beginning of summer holidays we would load up the car with all the necessities for two weeks (including the pet guinea pig "Susie") and head for our cottage at the lake. There was no store or laundry facilities near the cottage, so we would return home to furiously was clothes and hurriedly buy groceries every other Saturday.

My three sisters and I planned a new adventure everyday. We had very few neighboors, so had to make up the games we played. Dad had built our cottage, so there were lot of odds and ends of lumber, tiles, shingles, pipes and what nots to create with. Designing huts becmae a daily contest. Many misadventures including caved in walls, smashed fingers, and bruised knees only gave new energy to the contestants. I think mother always prayed that summer only last two weeks. We kept her mending basket full.

There was an old dairy farm on the hill behind the cottage. The farmhouse was made of logs with a manure and mud mortar between the logs. The old "gentleman" still lived there. My two sisters and I would love to help him mix up mortar when the walls needed repair (much to Mother's dismay). He would give us warm milk, fresh from the cow, and oatmeal cookies as a reward for our assistance.

Observing that logs and manure plaster made great walls,

my sisters and I thought it would also make a fantastic raft. We proceeded to create one, amazingly it could float! Unfortunately the longer we kept it in the water, the more the manure mortar dissolved. Before long, we were standing in chest deep water—or rather manure soup—with logs floating away in all directions.

The vegetation of the area was varied and beautiful. We collected cactus roses of yellow and salmon, sucked nectar of wild honeysuckles, and tried to make dandelion wine (after all Mother did it, why couldn't we). We feasted on gooseberries—green ones that curled up our tongues and red ones that always had worms—and conned Mother into baking Saskatoon berry pie for breakfast.

We swam every morning and took a bar of soap with us for a "swim-bath" every night. We were as brown as berries, with hair like straw, sand in our toes and possessed an unending zest for the next sunrise. The queens of Jackfish Lake!

FOCUS ON THE SENTENCE: *Meaningful Mechanics I*

Your purpose for writing an essay will affect the point of view, content, and language of the essay. Your purpose for writing a sentence will affect not only the structure and words of the sentence but also the way you punctuate and capitalize. Punctuation and capitalization are part of the mechanics—the nuts and bolts—of writing. Nouns, verbs, and other words may provide the timber, but capitals, periods, commas, and other punctuation marks help rivet the whole together to make a solid structure.

When you capitalize, you show that a noun has special meaning, or you signal the beginning of a new idea. When you punctuate, you separate thoughts, show that an idea is complete, signal that something follows, or distinguish one word from another. Punctuation also shows whether the purpose of your sentence is to make a statement, show surprise, or ask a question. Each mark and each letter mean something, and leaving out even one comma may change the meaning drastically.

At dawn the army will attack Georgia.
At dawn the army will attack, Georgia.

The first sentence sounds like an order to attack the state of Georgia. The second is a statement to someone named Georgia; where the army will attack is not explained.

The Meaning of End Punctuation (. ? ! ;)

The primary meaning of end punctuation is completion; but each mark also tells us something more about a sentence.

Periods (.) signal the end of sentences that make statements or requests or give commands:

> The agent has filled out the claim forms in triplicate.
> The club should have the leaky roof fixed.
> Please try to finish the proposal today.   ⎱ (understood
> Fix the leaky roof before the furniture is ruined. ⎰ subjects *you*)

Question marks (?) signal the end of sentences that ask questions:

> Who are you? Why are you here? Where are you going? When will you be back?

And exclamation points (!) signal the end of sentences that express surprise or strong emotion:

> I don't believe it!
> The ship is dead in the water!

Semicolons (;) also may signal the end of one sentence and the beginning of another when they are used to separate two closely related ideas.

> The morning paper came; your dog ate it.
> The time may be right to buy a new car; however, I do not have the money.

Periods, question marks, and exclamation points also have some secondary meanings.

Periods mark the end of some abbreviations:

> Oct.   Mr.
> 12:00 p.m.   Ms.
> U.S.A.   Dr.

A question mark in parentheses shows uncertainty about a date or a fact.

> Jean Conrad began writing *Golden Gates* in 1985(?) and finished the novel in 1986.

An exclamation point after a single word is the written equivalent of shouting the word.

Ouch! That hurt.

The Meaning of Capitals

Capitals are used in six major ways:

1. A sentence begins with a capital letter. In this way, capital letters act as partners of end punctuation.
   Yellow shafts of sunlight are cutting through the clouds. A rainbow is arching across the valley.
   "Please finish your milk," the pet owner pleaded with his cat. "You need it to grow strong claws and sharp teeth."

2. The pronoun *I* is capitalized wherever it occurs in a sentence.
   I broke a fingernail at breakfast, and I cut myself on my knife at lunch; now I am afraid to eat dinner.

3. Proper nouns—the names of specific people, places, things, times, or ideas—are capitalized.
   Christopher Columbus thought the West Indies were the Orient.
   During the Renaissance the British, the Spanish, the Portuguese, and the Dutch explored and conquered vast territories in North America and South America.
   Is Beauty Truth?

4. Words and abbreviations made from proper nouns are also capitalized.
   John F. Kennedy → JFK
   George Bernard Shaw → Shavian drama
   the United States of America → USA or American imports

5. Titles are usually capitalized before but not after names.
   Land Commissioner Baca →   but Baca, the land commissioner
   Professor Wayne Moellenberg → but Wayne Moellenberg, professor

6. Titles of books, magazines, newspapers, articles, plays, poems, songs, and artwork are capitalized. You will capitalize the first and last words and all other words except short conjunctions and prepositions and *a, an,* and *the.*

The Maltese Falcon	*Between Midnight and Dawn*
The Chicago Sun	"On the Street Where You Live"
Whistler's Mother	"Bees Are Black with Gilt Surcingles"
Man and Superman	

EXERCISE 6: Add capitals and end punctuation wherever needed in the following paragraphs.

1. on the morning of oct 19, 1985, mr gregory polinski drove to his office as usual he was wearing his usual work clothes and carrying a lunch pail with his name printed on it what happened to mr polinski no one seems to know he was last seen turning from parkway onto grande if you have any information about this man's whereabouts, please call lt duffy at missing persons

2. what does it take to get you going in the morning do you spring out of bed to face the world or do you crawl back under the covers and hide your days would start with energy and vitality if you started them right with exercise exercise is the solution to blue mondays and sluggish tuesdays get started now it will make a difference

3. i started out at dawn to climb mt ashland the elders—jack, char, and jason—were with me as we drove down the siskiyou highway past callahan's lodge and the mt ashland ski resort and found an old logging road to take us to the foot of the mountain my jeep waggoner bounced along the washboard road on four-wheel drive all around us were thick stands of ponderosa pine and colorado blue spruce at the side of the road we could see masses of wildflowers including buttercups, redbells, and indian paintbrush

it was nearly eight o'clock when we found the little-used trail leading to the summit of the mountain "let's go" i urged my party on, but jack was hungry "let's eat first," he told me "then we'll be ready to start" so then we ate and walked around a bit to get the kinks out of our legs

finally at noon we started up the mountain, singing mountain songs from *the sound of music* to start and then marine corps marching songs and, finally, when our imaginations gave out, "the ants go marching one by one" to the tune of "when johnny comes marching home again"

The Meaning of the Apostrophe (')

When you use an apostrophe in a word, the apostrophe will mean one of two things: (1) the word is a contraction or (2) the word is possessive.

1. *Contractions* may actually be more than one word. Two words are contracted when they are pushed together, squeezing out one or more letters in the process.

> Dudley <u>is not</u> a great shooter from the field.
> Dudley <u>isn't</u> a great shooter from the field.
> He <u>will</u> be getting a free throw from the foul line.
> <u>He'll</u> be getting a free throw from the foul line.

The apostrophe shows where the letter or letters have been left out.

If you are not certain whether a word is a contraction and, therefore, needs an apostrophe, try substituting the words that you think may have been contracted.

> *<u>Ill</u> be sitting on the fifty-yard line.*
> *Substitution:* <u>I will</u> be sitting on the fifty-yard line.
> *Use apostrophe:* <u>I'll</u> be sitting on the fifty-yard line.

> <u>Yall</u> come.
> *Substitution:* <u>You all</u> come.
> *Use apostrophe:* <u>Y'all</u> come.

> <u>Hell</u> froze over.
> *Substitution:* <u>He will</u> froze over.
> ***Do not*** *use apostrophe:* <u>Hell</u> froze over.

Single words or dates may also be contracted by leaving out one or more letters or numbers.

> The year '88 was hot and dry. (The apostrophe shows the *19* has been left out.)

Some writers use apostrophes to show letters left out in pronouncing words, but this usage is not accepted as a standard writing practice.

EXERCISE 7: Add apostrophes as needed to show contractions.

1. Ive been reading all night but havent finished *War and Peace.*
2. Theres been a rumor going around that were flying to Acapulco tonight.

3. When youve played the roulette wheel, well try blackjack.
4. Bens losing quarters to a one-arm bandit while Im winning dollars at the crap table.
5. The Furies wont spend their vacation in Las Vegas this year; theyll go to Atlantic City instead.
6. Its easy to see youre having a good time.
7. Lets finish this discussion after weve eaten dinner.
8. Isnt the sky blue and arent the grass and the trees green?
9. I dont know whether theyre planning to celebrate with a champagne breakfast.
10. The teams discouraged because our players were defeated in their first conference game.

2. The *possessive* form of words shows ownership; that is, it shows to whom or to what something (or someone) belongs. Both nouns and pronouns can be made possessive, usually by adding an apostrophe and -*s*.

Janene's ship has come in.
(Whose ship? *Janene's*.)
The parole board rejected Gene's appeal.
(Whose appeal? *Gene's*.)
The riot resulted from the prisoners' grievances.
(Whose grievances? The *prisoners'*.)
Someone's guitar playing is rusty.
(Whose guitar playing? *Someone's*.)

Notice that possessive nouns and possessive pronouns describe other nouns or pronouns and sometimes occupy the same places in a sentence as adjectives.

Suzanne's car is now Roger's.
Her car is now his.
The green car is now blue.

a. You can form the possessive of most nouns and pronouns that do not end in -*s* by adding an apostrophe and -*s*.

The horse's mane was braided with ribbons.
The bankrupt company owes me a month's salary.
I found someone's book.
The men's feet were blistered.

b. You can form the possessive of most singular nouns that end in -*s* by adding an apostrophe and -*s*.

The boss's management style is aggressive.
Chris's spine was injured in the fall.

However, if the extra -*s* is difficult to pronounce, you should simply add an apostrophe.

Joe Valesquez' book received rave reviews.
Ms. Rubens' lawn is filled with crab grass and dandelions.

c. You can form the possessive case of plural nouns that end in -*s* by adding an apostrophe.

The trombone players' instruments sound brassy.
Pour milk over the kittens' dry food.
Will Simeon be at the Ortegas' party?
The roughnecks' complaints of safety violations at the rig were supported by the accident.

d. You can form the possessive of a word group representing one idea by adding an apostrophe and -*s*.

The attorney general's office is filing suit.
Your sister-in-law's car broke down on the freeway.
No one else's mailbox was vandalized.

e. You can form the possessive of a phrase made up of several names by adding an apostrophe and -*s* to the last word if ownership is shared or to each word if ownership is individual.

Liu and Nguyen's Chinese restaurant opens Saturday.
The great dane tore up Ellen and Gilbert's prize daffodil bed.
Chris's, Teresa's, and Jason's birthdays fall in the same month.
Muriel's and Roberta's accounts of the event do not match.

EXERCISE 8:   Fill in the blanks in the paragraph by making the words in parentheses possessive.

The _____ (captain) voice sounded calm

as he announced an emergency landing, but one

_____ (passenger) screams cut his words short.

The _____ (stewardess) face was grim and the

_____ (steward) face was white, but they

explained emergency-landing procedures calmly. Another

passenger helped with _____ (Mrs.

Douglas) seat belt, and an off-duty pilot tried to calm

_____ (everyone) fears by describing the

_____ (crew) actions step by step. Outside the

_____ (passengers) windows, they could see

the lights of emergency vehicles flashing on the runway.

_____ (No one) courage was very high; even

the off-duty pilot sounded nervous as he explained, "We are

relatively safe here in the cabin. The _____

(captain and co-pilot) location is the most hazardous in a crash."

My _____ (seat mate) crying softly seemed

less appropriate than _____ (someone else)

hysterical sobs. I was surprised at what went through my own

mind: worries about _____ (Doris)

birthday party (Who would give it if I were not there?);

the _____ (canaries) red color food (Would

anyone remember to put it in their seed?); and the

_____ (Lopezes) bridge party (Who would take

my place?). Then suddenly we were on the ground, and

_____ (everyone) tears of relief were mixed

with laughter. Once again the _____ (hero

of the day) calm voice came over the intercom, "We have

landed safely at L. A. International. Aside from the

_____ (co-pilot) fainting, the landing was

without incident."

There are several words that do not require an apostrophe to show
possession. The personal pronouns have special possessive forms; the

words themselves change instead of adding punctuation to show possession.

Personal pronouns	Possessive forms
I	my, mine
you	your, yours
he	his
she	her, hers
it	its
we	our, ours
they	their, theirs
who	whose

Notice that several of the pronouns have two possessive forms. The first one is for use before nouns; the second, for use alone, after verbs.

<u>My</u> horror was only exceeded by <u>his</u> delight.
The pleasure is all <u>yours</u>.
<u>Whose</u> kite is tangled in <u>my</u> television antennae?
<u>Our</u> boss has noticed <u>your</u> long hours at <u>your</u> desk.
<u>Their</u> party became a riot when <u>her</u> relatives arrived.
The dog who buried <u>its</u> bone among <u>their</u> radishes and carrots is not <u>mine</u>.

EXERCISE 9:   Fill in the blanks in the paragraphs by making the pronouns in parentheses possessive.

1. _____ (You) report on the workers' safety problems

gets to the heart of _____ (they) concerns.

_____ (I) advice at this point is to give

_____ (you) data to the union representatives and

allow _____ (they) lawyers to pursue the matter

further. _____ (Who) toes we step on is irrelevant.

2.   A finch has built _____ (it) nest in the tree beside

Sue's window. Every morning _____ (she) sleep is

interrupted by _____ (it) joyous song; and all day the

hungry twitterings of _____ (it) babies call her to the

window to watch _____ (they) feeding time.

3. _____ (We) telephone lines were out today. The company president could not make _____ (she) conference call to the New York office and _____ (she) personal secretary could not complete _____ (he) arrangements for the administrators' annual retreat.

EXERCISE 10:   Fill in apostrophes as needed to show possession in the following sentences.

1. The Jorgensens new baby has eyes like his mothers and a nose like his fathers.

2. My grandfathers, my dads, and my brothers new cars reflect their different values as well as their different tastes.

3. Grandfathers car is a Lincoln Continental, reflecting his generations love affair with big, fast cars.

4. Dad bought another Volkswagen bus to conserve the worlds energy supplies, to balance our familys budget, and to provide plenty of room for camping gear on next summers vacation.

5. My brothers new Mercedes matches his status-hungry life style, but unfortunately it cost two years salary.

6. The strikers placards were hand painted by their families.

7. Your father-in-laws call seems to have upset your routine.

8. Doriss friends support her during crises, but mine worry only about their own problems.

9. The medias reaction to the terrorists threats was to send reporters to interview the organizations leader.

10. The scientists study indicates that womens ability to cope with high-stress jobs equals mens and that both groups show high incidence of heart disease and ulcers.

EXERCISE 11:   Using possessives, combine the following sentences to make a single sentence.

1. A new flower shop opened in Coronado Mall. The shop belongs to Lupe. The shop belongs to Hans.
2. The reporter questioned the findings. He questioned the findings in an article.
3. The car was wrecked on the freeway. The car belonged to the Smiths. The car was wrecked by the son of the couple.
4. The nest is built on a cliff. The nest belongs to an eagle.
5. Samson stole a newspaper. The newspaper belonged to a neighbor. Samson is a dog. He belongs to me.

Occasionally you will see an apostrophe and -*s* used when symbols, letters, numbers, dates, abbreviations, or words are discussed as things.

> There are too many *however*'s in my paragraph.
> The *1960*'s was a turbulent time on campuses.
> My *i*'s look like *e*'s.
> The many *&*'s in the manuscript are distracting.
> The *7*'s made by this typewriter are too light, and the *4*'s are too heavy.

In these sentences the apostrophe and -*s* mean plural. Notice also that the item made plural is italicized, but the apostrophes and -*s* are not.

EXERCISE 12:   Add apostrophes in the following paragraphs to show contractions, possession, or special plurals.

1.   The sergeants orders were for all of us to clean out our lockers. Drews locker was spotless, but mine rated two *bad*s and three *unbelievable*s. As a result Im on report; Ill also be given two weeks assignment to the camp kitchen.

2.   Hopes run high among citizens for prosperity in the *1990*s, but economists forecasts recall the inflation of the *1970*s and warn us to curb our appetites and save at least a weeks wages each month. Most workers can now expect to change their careers at least once; therefore, jobs should not be our only security. Its money in the bank that we need for the future.

3.   The detectives assistant reconstructed the victims last day by questioning their neighbors. Mrs. Browning, whose apartment is next door, said, "Theyre always up early, and I saw them get their paper at around six oclock." Mrs. Martins apartment is below the Tates. She said, "Id heard them fighting the night before so I didnt think much about it when I heard some yelling." And George Trambly, who couldnt recall having seen them, added, "Theyre usually up n about. Thats why I called the police."

4.   The weathermens forecasts usually conflict. KOBs Bill Eisenhood says, "Its going to rain." KOATs Howard Morgan insists, "Were due for snow in the higher elevations." And KGGMs Mark Smith claims, "Itll be partly cloudy with some smog in the valley."

5.   Citizens groups are arguing over how the mayor should spend the taxpayers money. One groups focus is upon beautifying our citys streets. Another groups major concern is a place to park their cars at city hall. And still other groups are involved in their own neighborhoods special needs. Before the *i*s are dotted and the *t*s are crossed on any funding authorizations, the mayors office should determine what the city as a whole wants and needs.

TROUBLESHOOTING: *Sentence Sense and Common Sense*

When you are searching your papers for errors in mechanics, use your sentence sense and also your common sense. Ask yourself questions about the sentence you are punctuating. What kind of sentence is this? What kind of end punctuation does its meaning call for? What is the purpose of this word or phrase? How can I show this purpose with punctuation or capitalization?

Once you understand the sentence you are writing and the reasons for punctuating it, use your common sense. Consider, for example, the following sentences.

> The coach shouted, "Are you ready?".
> Please bring camping gear: sleeping bags, tents, mess kit, etc..

Common sense will tell you that the extra end punctuation, the periods, serve no useful purpose. We do not need them to know that the sentences have ended; in fact, doubled-up end punctuation rarely adds important information to what the reader already knows about a sentence.

Similarly, when you are not sure where to put a question mark, use common sense.

> Did you state, "Dolphins are more intelligent than people"?
> The skeptic asked, "Are dolphins really more intelligent than people?"

If you think about which part of each sentence asks a question and which part makes a statement, you will have no problem placing the question mark. In the first example it is the sentence overall that asks a question; the quotation is a statement. Therefore, the question mark goes outside the quotation marks. In the second example the sentence overall is a statement while the quotation is a question, and the question mark goes inside the quotation marks. Notice that in both cases the questions begin with verbs.

Apostrophes are especially troublesome to many writers; therefore, we will pay special attention to problems with apostrophe usage in this section.

Because the plural and possessive forms of most nouns sound alike, sometimes people are tempted to put in an apostrophe wherever there is an -*s* or to leave out apostrophes entirely.

> Two teddy bears were sitting in a giant teddy bear's lap in the teddy bears' section of the toy store.

If you read this sentence aloud, the words *bears, bear's,* and *bears'* are pronounced exactly alike, but their meanings are very different. *Bears* is a plural noun used as subject of the verb *were sitting. Bear's* is a singular possessive noun that tells us whose lap is meant. And *bears'* is a plural possessive noun telling whose section of the store we are referring to.

To decide both whether an apostrophe is needed and where to put it, first consider the words within the structure of the sentence. Try replacing the words with adjectives to see whether they are possessive.

> Two fat were sitting in a giant fat lap in the fat section of the toy store.

The adjective *fat* can modify *lap* and *section* with some success, so you know that the second and third uses of the noun *bear* are possessive. But the first substitution does not make sense because *bears* is the subject of the verb. Next, think carefully about the meaning of the sentence to decide whether you want a singular or a plural possessive noun. Look for clues in the sentence structure that will help. In the example the word *a* in the phrase *in a giant teddy bear's lap* tells us we are talking about one teddy bear. Logic tells us that the section of the toy store has more than one teddy bear; in fact, three are mentioned in the sentence. Therefore, the final use of the noun must be plural possessive.

EXERCISE 13:   Add or delete apostrophes in the following sentences.

1. The girl's tree house contains one girls' chemistry set and two girl's insect collections.

2. Typesetters' walked off the job today after the speakers' at the typesetter's convention recommended demonstrations' and strikes' to force managements' cooperation.

3. A hundred angry red ants' charged to revenge an ants' death at the hands of black ants' who were disturbing the red ants' herds of aphids'.

4. The clubs members have voted to donate the proceeds of the clubs annual dance to two other clubs that are having financial problems.

5. The teddy bears picnic begins when all of the teddy bears have arrived and the chief teddy bears special speakers podium is in place.

A second major problem with apostrophe usage results from confusing other words that sound alike. Specifically, some contractions sound like and even look somewhat like possessive personal pronouns.

Contractions	*Possessive pronouns*
you're (you are)	your
it's (it is or it has)	its
they're (they are)	their
who's (who is or who has)	whose

When you are not sure whether to use a contraction or a pronoun, try inserting the uncontracted pronoun and verb as you read the sentence. If the sentence still makes sense, use the contraction. If it does not make sense, use the possessive pronoun.

> (It's/Its) _____ been a turbulent, unproductive meeting.
> *It has* been a turbulent, unproductive meeting.
> *It's* been a turbulent, unproductive meeting.
> (You're/Your) _____ hat is creative but ugly.
> *You are* hat is creative but ugly.
> *Your* hat is creative but ugly.

EXERCISE 14:   Insert the appropriate form of the words in parentheses in each sentence.

1. _____ (You're/Your) early with _____ (you're/your) report, but _____ (you're/your) accounts still need some work before _____ (they're/their) ready for the business office to give _____ (it's/its) stamp of approval.

2. The skydivers began _____ (they're/their) demonstration at noon, and by 12:30 _____ (they're/their) team captain was having trouble with his shute. _____ (It's/Its) rip cord was jammed, and _____ (it's/its) backup would not open the shute. _____ (It's/Its) safe to say this would not be _____ (you're/your) everyday, routine jump.

3. _____ (It's/Its) twilight, and next door the Murphys are watering _____ (they're/their) lawn while across the street _____ (you're/your) family is sitting down to dinner.

4. _____ (Who's/Whose) turn is it to do the dishes? _____ (Who's/Whose) going to walk the dog? And _____ (who's/whose) not finished the evening paper?

5. _____ (They're/Their) playing _____

(you're/your) song. Once _____ (it's/its) words were on everyone's lips; now _____ (it's/its) a "golden oldie."

READING TO WRITE

"The Donora Smog Episode" (pages 332–34) provides a strong example of writing with a purpose. The writers analyze an incident in order to give a strong warning about the dangers of smog. Support in the article is objective and extremely detailed. It includes facts and descriptive details.

> Donora is an industrial town of about 14,000 people, located on the inside of a sharp horseshoe bend of the Monongahela, about 48 km (30 miles) south of Pittsburgh, Pennsylvania.

> . . . Streams of sooty gas from locomotives did not even rise, but hung motionless in the air. The visibility was so poor that even natives of the area became lost. Such dense fog is much worse than mere darkness, which can be pierced by a flashlight beam. During such episodes, a driver cannot see the side of the road, nor even the white line that marks the center.

A key paragraph to achieving the article's purpose is paragraph 5. The writers emphasize the danger by listing the deaths.

> The first death came to a retired steelworker named Ivan Ceh at 1:30 Saturday morning; the second occurred an hour later. by 10 A.M. nine bodies lay at one undertaker's, one at a second undertaker's, and another, the eleventh death so far, at a third.

Why mention the undertakers? While those details do not tell us anything specific about the people who died, they do bring the deaths closer to us emotionally, making them more real.

The "two sequels to the Donora episode," mentioned in the sixth paragraph, explain more about the article's purpose. What are the two sequels? What do they tell us about the purpose?

WRITING ACTIVITY

Writing with a purpose calls for paying special attention during prewriting to why you are writing. Make finding a purpose an integral part of your writing process. After you explore your topic and before you write a thesis and make a plan, put your purpose into words. For example, your purpose in an essay about smog might be explained in this way: "In this essay I will try to convince the readers to share my concern about pollution caused by automobiles and convince them to vote for auto emissions testing. I will approach the topic objectively and use facts and descriptive details for support."

ACTIVITY: Identify a health hazard or public nuisance that deserves people's concern. Then write an essay in which you explain the causes for concern and urge some action. Some possible topics follow. You might choose one of these or a topic of your own.

1. Smoking in the workplace
2. Unsanitary practices at food or salad bars
3. Noise pollution
4. Preservatives in foods
5. Handling of money by food preparers in fast-food restaurants.

CHECKLIST: Check each draft of your paper carefully for the following:

1. Is the purpose of the essay clear? Do the approach, language, and content respond appropriately to that purpose?
2. Does the essay have an effective introduction with a clear thesis statement?
3. Does the organization of the essay work well?
4. Is there enough support for key ideas?
5. Are there any errors in capitalization, apostrophe use, or end punctuation?
6. Are there any misplaced or dangling modifiers or errors in adjective and adverb use?
7. Are verb tenses consistent and well chosen?
8. Are there any errors in subject–verb or pronoun agreement?
9. Are there any comma splices, run-ons, or fragments?
10. Are there any misspelled words, left-out words, or reversed letters?

CHAPTER TEN
Developing and Organizing the Essay

Discovering Details

The writing process takes time, and the more skilled you become, the more time it takes. In fact, the more you learn about exploring a subject, finding a purpose, focusing the subject, planning and developing your essay, the longer you must spend on prewriting. And the more you learn about ways to revise essays and to troubleshoot for errors, the longer it will take you to rewrite. Taking the time to work through all of the parts of the writing process will increase your skill and also improve the quality of your product—the finished essay. And nowhere is taking time more important than when you are developing and organizing your essay.

Haste results in vague and general writing. Filtered through a hasty pen, flesh and blood become bare bones and water. The time the marching band's trombone player slipped on a wad of bubblegum may be diluted to three general words, "a funny incident," or a vivid picture of a summer morning on Uncle Jim's ranch may become simply "a nice day in the country."

Discovering details that give life to general statements or events begins with prewriting. As you prewrite, compose a mental picture of the subject. Then translate what you saw in your mind into a word picture on the page. For example, the following writers discovered details to rewrite and fill out the same, bare-bones sentence: Studying is hard.

Studying late at night with the lamp glowing over a page
covered with tiny black lines all merging together at the right-
hand side of the page is gruesome.

Studying includes straining to keep your eyes open at 4 a.m. to
cram for a physics test, forcing yourself to keep your mind off
that good-looking hunk in your English class so you can write
that blasted research paper, writing 12 pages of notes on a 6-
page chapter, and cursing under your breath because you have
to read 10 chapters in your biology text before tomorrow.

The first writer translated just one mental picture—a black and white
snapshot of a student studying late at night. The second writer gives us
a series of quick flashes—cramming at 4:00 a.m., writing a research paper,
taking notes, and reading a biology text.

The same writers discovered lively details to fill out the sentence:
Cats are cute.

Cuddly little balls of fur, climbing up and falling head over heels
down, sneaking up to attack a vicious piece of string or just
curling up and sleeping—that's a cat.

Kittens have silky fur that stands on end, pug noses, huge
questioning eyes, and legs that wobble when they walk.

EXERCISE 1: Rewrite the following bare-bones sentences, using details
that provide life and color; that is, rewrite the sentences as word snapshots.

1. Studying is hard.
2. Cats are cute.
3. Books are boring.
4. I have a good car.
5. Harry is a nice guy.
6. Pies taste good.
7. Tea is refreshing.
8. I write with a pencil.
9. The weather is bad.
10. It's hard to get up in the morning.

Writing word snapshots is a good beginning. Now let's take a little
more time to go a step further and think and write in technicolor, 3-D, and
motion. Start with a skeletal account of an action. Then imagine it is actually happening, and brainstorm the details. Finally, translate your imag-
inings into sentences for a word movie.

BARE-BONES ACTION: The dog ran down the street, trying to catch the cat. It was a hot day and the dog was tired afterwards. The cat sat in the tree looking down at him.

BRAINSTORM:

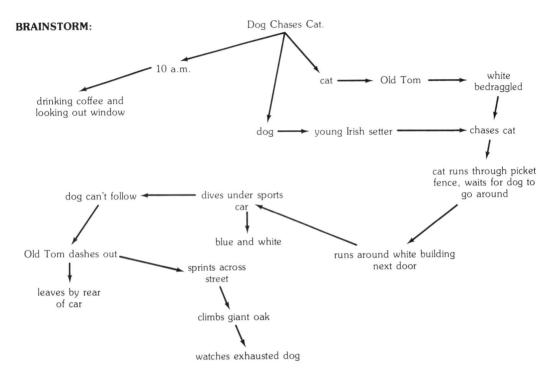

WORD MOVIE: This morning as I sat drinking my 10 a.m. coffee, I saw out the window a large red dog chasing an old, bedraggled white cat. I could plainly see that the old tom had been through this several times before; he knew all the tricks. First, he went through a picket fence which the dashing young Irish had some trouble getting through. Old Tom sat patiently waiting for Irish to find the end of the fence, and then the chase was on. After once around the big, white building next door, Old Tom dove under a car. It was one of those small foreign jobs, so Irish couldn't follow. After a short break to recover his wind, Old Tom dashed out at the rear of the little blue and white car and sprinted for the great oak across the street. Irish loped along as best he could considering he had been doing most of the work while Tom sat and watched. You could plainly see that Irish would soon give up his quest due to the heat of the day and Old Tom's experience at dodging young fools.

EXERCISE 2:   Brainstorm; then write a word movie using one of the following bare-bones paragraphs as a take-off point.

1.   After each meal I collect the dishes and put them in the sink. I fill the sink with water, add soap and start scrubbing. I rinse the dishes with water and put them on a dish rack to dry.

2.   I look outside. The grass is very high. I take out the lawn mower. It will not start. Forget it. I go in and watch television.

3.   This morning I got up late. I hurried to get ready. There was no time for breakfast. I forgot my books. The freeway was jammed. I was late for class.

4.   Shopping on Friday is hectic. I can't find a parking place. There are no baskets. There are too many people in the store. Everything has been bought. I have to stand in a long line at the check-out counter.

FOCUS ON WRITING: *The Middle Paragraphs of the Essay*

While the first paragraph of the essay introduces the subject, the paragraphs that follow develop it. Developing the subject means using details, facts, examples, or illustrations (as you learned in Chapter 4) to give ideas substance.

What materials you choose and how you organize them depends upon your subject and also your purpose. For example, if your subject is a Ford Tempo and your purpose is to sell it to someone who is thinking about buying a Dodge Colt, you would develop your ideas by contrasting the two vehicles. If your subject is a group of people and your purpose is to make comments on some activity or behavior, you might organize your observations by dividing the group into types.

In the pages that follow, you will look at various ways of developing and organizing your ideas. You might use one method in an essay overall or use different methods for different paragraphs. How many methods you can use effectively depends upon the length of your essay and the complexity of your subject.

Developing by Using Patterns

When you study a group of things or people, you will notice patterns. For example, as you sit in a classroom, look at the shoes your classmates are wearing. The assortment might include tennis shoes, work boots, high-heeled sandals, cowboy boots, loafers, running shoes, low-heeled slip-ons, and thongs. You might observe a pattern on the basis of heels (high heels, low heels, and no heels) or on the basis of how the shoes are held on the foot (slip-ons, laced shoes, and buckled shoes).

These patterns give you a way to organize your information and also a way to focus your search for additional materials. For example, three sets of the shoes you observed fit the general type "no heels": tennis shoes, running shoes, thongs. If you expand your search outside the classroom, you might notice that moccasins, slippers, and some sandals also do not have heels.

Rizzi uses a pattern he discovered while observing passengers to organize the middle paragraphs of his essay, "On an Airplane." He identified three types of passengers, and he writes a paragraph describing each one. Some of the details in those paragraphs were part of Rizzi's original observations; others were discovered as the essay plan called for additional development.

On an Airplane

Lately I have had to go on a plane pretty often because my wife lives here in the States and my parents live in Europe. Sometimes I feel like a ping-pong ball. I don't particularly like to fly, so during the flights I developed an interest in watching the way people act on an airplane, maybe because I was trying to avoid looking out of the window. I think people start acting in a peculiar way when they sit in a plane and even when they go into an airport. Airplane passengers, I think, can be divided into three main categories: the "I hate to fly" group, the over-active group and the cool, expert travelers.

The people who belong to the "I hate to fly" group are easy to spot, especially during landing and taking off. They usually sit very straight, holding tightly to the arms of their chair. Their eyes are wide open and fixed on the back of the next seat. After the plane takes off, they usually stare at the wing, even if that position will certainly cause a terrible stiff neck. When the airplane reaches the normal flying altitude, they look a little more relaxed, but they will assume their "alert" position at the first unusual noise or vibration. My wife certainly belongs to this group. When she sees the "no smoking" sign on, she immediately thinks that there is a fuel spill inside the plane. If the "fasten the seat belts" sign appears, she is sure that the plane is already crashing. People in this group are usually plainly dressed; in fact, they think if they have to die, they want to be presentable at least. I wouldn't suggest to anyone to sit by one of them because when they aren't questioning you about strange noises or vibrations, they will tell you all their problems. If they are flying, they always have problems. In fact, they wouldn't be on a plane unless there were an emergency, such as an old sick relative or their son arrested for smoking marijuana.

The over-active group includes many different people. Among this group we can find the photographers, for example. They are easily recognizable, even when they are still in the airport. They usually start taking pictures of the check-in line, of the luggage and the sign of a Japanese airline just because it is written in Japanese. If they find a window that looks out on the runway, they start taking a picture of an airplane landing when it is still a little white spot in the sky; by the time it gets close enough for a full view, they are usually out of film. Once on the airplane they take hundreds of pictures of each other with or without the stewardess. If an over-active passenger doesn't have a camera, he probably will pull out a guitar and organize a little band. If he doesn't have any musical instruments, he probably gets completely drunk and starts doing imitations or telling jokes about plane crashes. I don't suggest that anyone sit by a passenger of this group unless he wants to get involved in high-altitude parties or participate in a little chorus.

The cool, expert traveler is harder to spot, but if your eye is trained enough, you'll immediately notice his typical behavior. He dresses casually and carries one bag with the name of an exotic airline, but never a lot of packages or cameras; in fact, he doesn't want to be mistaken for a tourist. When the stewardess passes with the newspapers, he will probably ask for the *Wall Street Journal* and *Le Figaro*, even if he doesn't speak French. When he can get ahold of a stewardess for a few minutes, he usually tells her that he saw her somewhere before, maybe on the flight from Tokyo to Bangkok. Of course, he has never been to Tokyo or Bangkok. In his bag he usually carries all the ultimate flying accessories: a pen with a built-in alarm clock, a passport holder with a calculator on one side, and a miniature magnetic chess set. Among this group, in fact, there are some of the best customers of the duty-free shops in airports. Before landing he usually goes to the bathroom with his miniature electric shaver, which also can be used, with the right attachment, as a toothbrush. He is probably the best passenger you can sit by; in fact, he will probably only make a few statements about how the stewardesses used to be more pretty, even if he has never flown before, or at the worst he will pull out his miniature chess set, but you can always say that you forgot your glasses.

Whenever I fly, I usually try to find three empty seats so I can go to sleep, but I've been in each of these groups also. The first time I flew, I could have certainly been placed among the "I hate to fly" group. My second flight I was the cool, expert traveler. I have been the over-active passenger also; I remember once using up an entire roll of film on clouds, which certainly looked good from the plane, but once developed, the pictures looked like dirty pieces of paper. Another time when I didn't have a camera, I had a couple of drinks too many, which resulted in my getting completely airsick for the rest of the flight. For me flying is now interesting and, if I could take a parachute with me, it would be almost a pleasure.

EXERCISE 3:   Observe a group of people involved in some activity. Look for patterns in the way they look or act and try to divide the group into types. Take notes on specific details and behavior that could be used in developing an essay.

EXERCISE 4:   Plan an essay based on the materials you gathered in Exercise 3.

Developing by Using Comparison

Comparing things, people, or ideas presents several problems. To begin with, the items must have something in common that can be compared, that is, a basis for comparison such as having the same function or name or birthdate. You could not, for example, compare peanuts to peacocks or apple dumplings to applewood. But you could compare the plumage of a peacock to that of a peahen or the merits of apple dumplings to those of apple pie for dessert.

EXERCISE 5:   Evaluate the basis of comparison for the following items. Revise items, as necessary, to make them comparable. Be ready to explain your decisions.

1. applesauce and applejack
2. Scotchtape and Scotchguard
3. coffee and tea
4. guardhouse and lighthouse
5. paper and pencil
6. paperclips and staples
7. ice cream and milk
8. computer and abacus
9. scissors and hammer
10. pen and pencil

Comparing will show differences or likenesses or both. A short, simple comparison may be organized in two parts as in the following paragraph. Notice that each item is introduced by a subtopic sentence.

Living in the country and living on the moon seem much alike to me. If I lived on the moon, I would be out of touch with civilization. Corner laundries, Circle K's, and Pizza Huts would be far away. If I ran out of bean dip, I would have to wait for the next supply ship to come in, and if I wanted a pizza, I would have to make my own. Similarly, living in the country is different from life on earth as I know and love it. Stores, restaurants, and theaters are miles away over sometimes impassible roads. Oh, there are hot and cold running water and indoor plumbing, but the *real* conveniences of modern life—express mail delivery, drive-through car washes, and McDonald's carry-out breakfasts—are unknown in the country.

Longer, more complicated comparisons can be organized point by point. Each area of comparison can be covered in a separate paragraph. Sarina's essay contrasts the cookbook she uses with her great grandmother's cookbook in terms of the ingredients called for, the units of measurement, the methods used, and the recipes listed.

Cooking Now and Then

I used to pride myself on being an old-fashioned, from-scratch cook. Then I discovered my great grandmother's 1859 cookbook and discovered what old-fashioned cooking really means. Comparing her cookbook, *The Young Housekeeper's Friend*, to mine, *Creative Cooking for Everyday Living*, illustrates some of the differences.

The ingredients Great-grandmother used in 1859 and those I use today are completely different. Under puddings, for example, her cookbook suggests rosewater or saleratus as flavoring and rye meal, pounded potatoes, sago, or farina as basic ingredients. My cookbook calls for vanilla extract, cinnamon, flour, and occasionally cornstarch.

The units of measurement were completely different in 1859. *The Young Housekeeper's Friend* talks about gills of cream and milk, a "little" nutmeg, a "large spoonful" of sugar, and a "small spoonful" of cinnamon. Mine uses cups, tablespoons, and teaspoons.

The methods are different too. To make a sponge cake, Great-grandmother is told to "beat steadily with a smart stroke half an hour"; I am told to beat on the high setting of my mixer one or two minutes. To fix fried chicken for dinner, she is told first how to kill the chicken, drain the blood, pluck and singe its feathers. I am told how to choose a fresh frozen chicken at the supermarket.

The menus have also changed drastically. Great-grandmother's cookbook recommends bread crusts, boiled in milk and sprinkled with salt, as a good breakfast dish. Boiled calf's head is a dinner entree, and moss blanc-mange (made with real moss!), a favorite dessert. My cookbook suggests French toast for breakfast, frozen pizza dressed up with extra cheese for dinner, and ordinary blancmange with chocolate rather than moss for dessert.

If I had to cook using my great-grandmother's cookbook, I think my family would starve. But then if I served the food her cookbook suggests, they would probably rather starve than eat anyway.

EXERCISE 6: Prewrite and plan an essay that compares something old with something new, something popular in the country with something popular in the city, or something that works with something that does not work. Be sure the things you choose are comparable.

Developing by Using Meaning

When you explain what something is or what it means, you are defining it. But developing an idea by using meaning goes beyond simple dictionary definitions. Meaning may be objective and scientific, like the meaning of *greenhouse effect* explained on page 181 of Chapter 9 or subjective and personal like the meanings of *green* discussed on the same page.

Si-yu's paragraph about the Fourth of July uses examples of several meanings to develop the main idea stated in the topic sentence. Subtopic sentences introduce each meaning and organize the material.

The Fourth of July means different things to different people. To Sam Ralston, a rancher in Australia, it is an important birthday—his own. Sam was born on a wintry July day in 1944 while a cold south wind blew a blizzard across the out-back. Among some British citizens the date is remembered reluctantly as the anniversary of an uprising. On that day a radical group of colonists committed treason and rebelled against the throne. To U.S. citizens the Fourth is Independence Day. It is the anniversary of the signing of the Declaration of Independence and the birthday of the nation. Americans celebrate this major holiday with parades, fireworks, and picnics in the park.

EXERCISE 7:   Discuss the use of meanings to develop the following paragraphs. How would you improve the development or the organization of the paragraphs?

1.   Happiness is not a warm puppy. *Happiness,* according to *Webster's New World Dictionary,* is a noun. It refers to contentment, gladness, or a feeling of great pleasure. The word comes from a Middle English word *hap,* which means convenient or suitable.

2.   Democracy is a form of government that we enjoy here in the United States. To me it means standing up for my rights and being counted. Because I believe in democracy, I am a democrat. *Demo* has to do with the people.

3.   TV means "television," which means "pictures from a distance." Another name for it is the "boob tube." The British call it the "telly." It has also been called "a vast wasteland."

Developing by Using Reasons

To develop your ideas with reasons, begin with a thorough analysis of the condition or situation you are writing about. The key question to guide your study is "why?" Why did this or that happen? or why did it not happen? Once you have identified reasons, you are ready to look for examples to illustrate them. What happened because of this? What specific effects can you identify?

The short essay that follows was written in response to an essay exam question. Mosen explains why geologists now believe that volcanoes in the Pacific Northwest may erupt soon. Notice the abbreviated introduction and conclusion.

For years scientists assumed that many volcanoes in the Pacific Northwest were extinct. Now many geologists believe that several volcanoes may erupt before the end of the century.

First, temperature readings at various peaks indicate danger. Mt. Shasta, Mt. Hood, and the Three Sisters are all registering high temperatures. In fact, Hood and Shasta exceed the temperature of Mt. St. Helens before its 1980 eruption.

Second, several of the volcanoes have begun emitting steam for the first time in this century. Even Wizard Island in the collapsed caldera of ancient Mt. Mazama has been "smoking" once again.

Rumblings and earthquakes are increasing up and down the chain. Some observers estimate that a tree falls every fifteen minutes in one active volcanic area near Crater Lake. The phenomenon suggests significant activity beneath the earth, and seismic readings at all the major peaks have supported this finding.

Finally, Mt. St. Helens continues to be active. The volcano has gone through several cycles of dome-building and eruption since 1980. Scientists record constant earthquake activity and have noted movements of magma.

The ending of the peaks' dormant stage points to a new phase in the volcanic life of the Northwest mountain ranges. A new phase of building like the geologic upheavals that originally created the peaks may be underway.

EXERCISE 8:   List several reasons why in response to each question. You may need to do some research in an encyclopedia or other reference book.

1. Why is the sky blue?
2. Why did the Boston Tea Party occur?
3. Why are you going to school?
4. Why should people who smoke stop?
5. Why are there 365 days in the year?

EXERCISE 9:   Prewrite and plan an essay based on one of the questions in Exercise 8. Look for examples to illustrate your reasons and facts to explain them.

Developing by Explaining How

Explaining how to do something or how something works calls for step-by-step or part-by-part analysis of the process involved. In other words, you must examine each part or step, and then show how one step follows another or how all the parts work together.

At the simplest level, an explanation of how is a set of instructions. Every day we give and we take instructions. We explain to our friends how to find our homes, we show a child how to tie his or her shoe, or we teach a co-worker how to operate the copy machine. We follow instructions to cook a frozen dinner, put together a new toy, or fill out our income tax. To a large extent, the quality of those instructions determines the quality of our product. Miss a step or an ingredient, and your friend winds up at an eastside warehouse instead of at your home, or the frozen dinner is burned.

Whether you are speaking or writing instructions, the essential elements are the same:

1. Explain clearly what you are instructing the audience to do.
2. List any tools or materials that will be needed.
3. Explore the process, part by part and step by step, making sure that no step or part is left out.
4. Add enough details so that the audience can visualize what you are talking about.

A set of instructions for weed pulling, for example, might look something like this:

> Pulling weeds is simple, if you have the know-how, the tools, and the energy. Before you start, you will need a hoe, a rake, a shovel, heavy-duty gloves and strong fingers as well as a good, working knowledge of which of the plants in your garden are flowers and which are weeds. Once your tools are assembled and you have identified your targets, you are ready to begin. First, soak the ground to loosen up the soil around the weeds' roots. Then using gloves to ensure you do not blister your hands and a shovel to ensure that you get all of the roots, pull the largest weeds. Next use a hoe and rake to tackle the medium-sized weeds. Dig and pull in a small area; then rake the weeds into a pile to be bagged and burned later. Finally, use your strong fingers to pull the smallest weeds and those that have grown up close to your flowers.

If you compare these instructions with the student essay "How to Kill Weeds," you will see a major difference. The instructions give the bare facts in a simple, straight-forward manner. The essay, on the other hand, not only outlines the process but also interprets it. The writer explains the meaning of the activity as well as the procedures. In fact, the extreme measures taken by the writer leave the readers wondering whether something has been lost in the process. What happens to the garden if the gardener concentrates on killing weeds and not on raising flowers?

How to Kill Weeds

The battlefield is the garden; and you—the caring gardener—are its sole protector, the guardian whose mission is to seek out and destroy the insidious destroyer of gardens—weeds. Gardeners discover early on in their hobby that rose tending and tomato cultivating are merely minor features of gardening. The true test lies in developing those skills necessary to kill weeds. Anyone can water a plant, but it takes true tenacity, vigilance, and intelligence to weed-kill. This calling, which occurs to but a few real gardeners, involves searching out these loathesome weeds, identifying them properly, and annihilating them totally.

The search can be an exciting adventure. Weeds can be small like dandelions or tall like the Chinese elm; they can spread out like clover, or cling to rose bushes, crawling up the stems like morning glories. The not-too-bright weeds can be found in obvious out-in-the-open places, while the cunning ones remain hidden among flowers and vegetables. The most clever ones actually pretend to be flowers. They disguise themselves so well that only the gardener with a weed-killer instinct can tell the difference.

Proper identification is a must. Many a zealous gardener has returned from what he or she thought was a successful mission only to be told that 200 zinnias, 151½ violets, countless number of innocent marigolds, and one prize rose bush had been wiped out in an attack. But if one is going to reach the heights of gardening skill, such incidents cannot be dwelled upon. Survival in a garden is possible only for the fittest and those which are missed by a hack of a hoe or a cut of the shovel.

By far the most enjoyable part of gardening is the utter destruction of weeds. Because the roots of many weeds go so deep and branch out so widely, they must be watered prior to pulling. Water softens the soil and deceives the weeds into thinking that they are being cared for. After enough soaking, you have a choice of weapons with which to carry out your mission: a sharp hoe, a huge shovel, and a strong rake. I prefer the shovel in the preliminary stage to dig around the weed. Once you've exposed the roots, get a good grip on the central root and pull. If it resists, twist, pull, and yank hard. If it still resists, hack at it awhile with a hoe or a shovel. Even if you're exhausted, don't give up. Keep hacking and cutting until the roots yield or break. If they yield to a good pull, you've won. If they break, they'll return next year even stronger, but then so will you.

It has been written by many a wise person that proper attitude and training can reap great rewards in any endeavor. These hints shared with you from years of experience should make your weed-killing hours adventuresome. Indeed, with the right frame of mind and the proper training and tools, killing weeds can be most enjoyable.

Whether you write instructions or a more in-depth analysis will depend upon the assignment, your audience, and your purpose in writing.

EXERCISE 10:   Write a paragraph of instructions for one of the following simple processes. When you have finished, exchange papers and read each other's instructions; look for missing steps or unclear directions. In some cases you may wish to test the instructions by following them.

1. sharpening a pencil
2. washing dishes
3. folding a fitted sheet
4. cutting down a tree
5. changing a flat tire
6. catching a bus
7. eating spaghetti
8. painting a shelf
9. threading a needle
10. making a tuna fish sandwich

EXERCISE 11:   Prewrite and plan an essay that expands and develops the paragraph of instructions you wrote for exercise 10. Be sure to interpret as well as describe.

Organizing by Using an Outline

When your essay is short or the content simple, an idea map like the one illustrated on page 127 works well for planning. However, as your essays become longer and the content more complex, your instructor may want you to use a more formal outline. A good outline should be about one page long. It should include all major ideas but very few sentences: It is not a first draft of the paper, but a way to organize ideas. An outline also acts as a reminder of important supporting information you may want to use as you write.

Since your major organizational problems come in the middle of the paper, the simplest kind of outline focuses on those paragraphs. The outline begins with your title and thesis statement, then uses a Roman numeral (I, II, III, IV, V), to mark each paragraph. Capital letters (A, B, C, D) mark major subdivisions such as subtopic sentences. Arabic numbers (1, 2, 3, 4) and lower-case letters (a, b, c, d) list support, such as details, facts, or examples under the subdivisions.

An outline of Rizzi's essay, "On an Airplane," would look like this:

Title: On an Airplane

Thesis Statement: I think people start acting in a peculiar way when they sit in a plane and even when they go into an airport. Airplane passengers, I think, can be divided into three main categories: the "I hate to fly" group, the over-active group and the cool, expert travelers.

I. "I hate to fly" group
   A. Stiffness
      1. Sit like zombies
      2. Stare at wing
   B. My wife's reaction to noises and announcements
   C. Clothes chosen for their own funerals
   D. Emergency travelers
II. The over-active group
   A. Picture-takers
      1. Shots of airport
      2. Shots of airplane landing
      3. Shots with stewardess
   B. Guitar-players
   C. Drunks
III. The cool, expert travelers
   A. Experienced-traveler uniform
      1. Casual clothes
      2. Carry-on bag with name of an exotic airline
      3. No packages or cameras
   B. Name-dropping
      1. *Wall Street Journal* and *Le Figaro*
      2. Flight from Tokyo to Bangkok
      3. Ultimate flying accessories
         a. Pen with built-in alarm clock
         b. Passport holder with calculator
         c. Miniature magnetic chess set
         d. Miniature electric shaver with toothbrush attachment
IV. Personal experiences in each group
   A. First flight—"I hate to fly" group
   B. Second flight—cool, expert traveler
   C. Over-active passenger
      1. Took pictures of clouds
      2. Drank too much and became airsick
   D. Now—sleep through flight

Outlining can be useful during two stages in your writing process. First, an outline helps during the planning stage to limit your subject and focus your ideas. A too-large subject will be immediately apparent if your outline threatens to stretch to page after page, and the one-page format will help you detect problems with wandering from subject to subject (or focus to focus) by allowing you to see the entire plan at once. Second, outlining can help during the evaluation stage of the process. Making a careful outline of what has been written will help spotlight problems such as paragraphs that lack development or topics that do not follow from the thesis.

EXERCISE 12: Write outlines for the essays you prewrote in Exercises 9 and 11 of this chapter. Does using the outline format help you make a better plan? Why or why not?

EXERCISE 13: Outline the student essay printed on pages 185–86 of Chapter 9. Does the outline help you identify problems you did not notice before? Does it help you suggest ways to correct problems you may or may not have noticed?

FOCUS ON THE SENTENCE: *Compounding and Sentence Variety*

Ideas are developed by adding supporting information. Sentences can also be developed by adding words or groups of words. How those additions are made shows their importance and also their relationship to the rest of the sentence. In this section you will be studying ways to add or combine ideas to make different sentence structures and different sentence types.

Compounding

You have already seen that it is possible to have more than one subject for one verb and more than one verb for one subject. It is also possible to have more than one noun following a verb or more than one modifier serving the same function in a sentence.

> Billionaire Walton has purchased another store and another factory. (Both *store* and *factory* were purchased.)
> The short, cold winter in the high desert is soon forgotten. (Both *short* and *cold* describe *winter*.)
> The fox ran through the cornfield, under the fence, and through the barn. (All three prepositional phrases describe where the fox ran.)

When you use words or phrases that serve the same function in a sentence, you are *compounding*. Compounding means adding one on top of the other. Generally, compounding is a good way to avoid repetition and to increase the meaningful content of your sentences.

My canary Cherub is a master singer. My canary Buttercup is a master singer. My canary Dandelion is a master singer.	My canaries Cherub, Buttercup, and Dandelion are master singers.

By combining the three sentences on the left, we have deleted twelve words and created a single sentence with more meaning than any one of the original sentences. Moreover, the new sentence "sounds" better— smoother and less awkward—than the originals.

Usually parts of a compound will be joined by a conjunction, or joining word, such as *and* or *or*. Compound adjectives (as in the second example at the beginning of our discussion) may use only a comma. When there are more than two words or phrases in the compound, commas will be used to separate the items, and a conjunction will join the last two. A compound made up of three or more words or phrases is called a *series*.

Any of the basic sentence elements that you have been studying may be compounded.

1. *Compound subjects:* The planet and the comets orbit the sun.
2. *Compound verbs:* The infant cooed, gurgled, and burped.
3. *Compound adjectives and prepositional phrases:* The President read a short and elegant speech. "Government of the people, by the people, and for the people shall not perish from the earth."
4. *Compound adverbs:* The Cheshire cat disappeared quickly and completely.
5. *Compound objects of prepositions:* Fly above the trees and the clouds.

EXERCISE 14: Combine the following sentences to make single sentences with compound elements.

1. There were mice in the attic. There were mice in the basement. There were mice in the garage. There were mice in the storeroom.
2. Carlos ate two tacos. Carlos ate three enchiladas. Carlos ate six sopaipillas. Carlos ate a bowl of green chili stew. Carlos ate everything in half an hour.
3. The child painted the sunset. The art student painted the sunset. The impressionist painted the sunset. The Navajo sandpainter painted the sunset. The results were very different.
4. Through a tornado Dorothy flew. Over the rainbow Dorothy flew. She flew to Oz.

5. Poinsettas prefer a sunlit window. African violets prefer a sunlit window. Poinsettas prefer warm air. African violets prefer warm air.

6. The terrorists mailed a bomb. They mailed it to the embassy. The terrorists mailed an extortion letter. They mailed it to the State Department.

7. The green tiger growled. It growled ferociously. It growled hungrily.

8. The pampered spruce grew tall. The pampered spruce grew straight. The pampered spruce grew green.

9. A bristlecone pine grows on a shelf. The pine is gnarled. The pine is ancient. The shelf is bare. The shelf is bleak. The shelf is rocky. The shelf is in the Sierra Nevada Mountains.

10. The blooms of the American beauty rose are red. The blooms of the common blaze rose are red. The blooms of the starfire rose are red.

11. Recordings lose the excitement of a live concert. They lose the excitement on the radio. They lose the excitement on the home stereo.

12. The party-goers rocked all night. The party-goers rolled all night. The party-goers danced all night. The party-goers ate all night.

13. Houston is growing rapidly. Atlanta is growing rapidly. Albuquerque is growing rapidly. Phoenix is growing rapidly. All are Sun Belt cities.

14. Rain washes the air. Rain washes the leaves. Rain waters the flowers. Rain waters the grass.

15. Wind is a sign of spring. Dust is a sign of spring. These are the signs of spring in the desert.

Sentence Variety

Using a variety of sentence types is something you do to a certain extent automatically. Your ear tells you when too many sentences of the same length or type make writing sound monotonous or awkward.

Read the following paragraphs aloud:

A dust devil swept across the mesa. It kicked up sand. It pulled up tumbleweeds. A rickety bus came behind it. The old frame groaned. The driver urged it along the rutted road. The road was dirt. The passengers held onto their seats. They wished for the ride to be over.

A dust devil swept across the mesa, and it kicked up sand, and it pulled up tumbleweeds. A rickety bus came behind it, but the old frame groaned. The driver urged it along the rutted road, and that road was also dirt. The passengers held onto their seats, and wished for the ride to be over.

Both paragraphs are awkward. The first one sounds choppy; the second is jerky, like moving up and down on a teeter-totter. If you were asked to rewrite the paragraph to make it "sound" better, you might write something like this.

A dust devil swept across the mesa, kicking up sand and pulling up tumbleweeds. Behind it came a rickety bus. The old frame groaned as the driver urged it along the rutted, dirt road, and the passengers held onto their seats, wishing for the ride to be over.

This rewritten paragraph differs from the earlier versions in three major ways:

1. **THE SENTENCES ARE DIFFERENT LENGTHS.** All of the nine sentences in the first paragraph are short, and the four sentences in the second paragraph are, for the most part, between fourteen and seventeen words long. However, in the third paragraph there are three sentences—the first medium-length, the second short, and the third long.

2. **THE SENTENCES FOLLOW DIFFERENT PATTERNS.** In the first two paragraphs, each sentence follows basic sentence structure—subject + verb + predicate word. (See Chapter 11, p. 244, for more about predicate words.) In the third paragraph, modifiers vary the shapes of the sentences, and the second sentence reverses the normal order to predicate word + verb + subject.

3. **THE SENTENCES REPRESENT A VARIETY OF TYPES.** The first paragraph is made up exclusively of simple sentences and the second of compound sentences, but the third paragraph contains two simple sentences and one compound-complex sentence.

In this section, you will study the different types and practice writing a variety of sentences.

Simple Sentence

The sentences you have been studying to this point have been simple sentences. A simple sentence is a basic sentence. It makes one complete statement or expresses one complete thought.

You may add modifiers without changing the simple sentence structure.

subj.   verb
Snow in giant white flakes falls softly over the frozen lake.

                 subj.   verb   pred. word
The cold, wet snow blanketed the rocky ground.

You may also compound or add to any or all of the parts without altering the simple sentence.

         subj.   comp. verb   pred. word
Snow falls and blankets the ground.

And you may change the order of the major parts without changing the type of sentence.

         verb   subj.
Softly falls the snow.

EXERCISE 15: Combine each set of sentences to make a single simple sentence.

1. The station manager arranged a meeting. He and the Federal Communications commission are meeting. He arranged the meeting nervously.
2. The sun rose. It turned the desert gold. It turned the desert pink. The desert had been colorless.
3. Yvonne has opened a boutique. Angie is her partner. The location is the mall.
4. The new assistant manager broke the electric pencil sharpener. She disabled the word processor. She jammed the copy machine. The jam was hopeless.
5. The entrance was blocked. It was the entrance to an Air Force base. There were trucks in the way. There was earth-moving equipment in the way.

Compound Sentence

Compound sentences are formed the same way as compound nouns or verbs; however, instead of adding words or phrases, you add simple sentences.

The starting point is the simple sentence. Join two or more simple sentences with *and, but, or, nor, for, so, yet,* or a semicolon (;), and the result is a compound sentence. These words are called *coordinating conjunctions* because they join or coordinate (like matching a shirt and slacks) ideas of equal importance.

> The rocket exploded, and the tower collapsed.
> The car is comfortable, but a motorcycle is inexpensive.
> I might buy a house in the country, or I might rent an apartment in the city.
> The subscription had to be cancelled, for we could not tolerate the newspaper's racist editorials.
> The loan officer could not reach my partner, so she called me.
> Snails seem inedible to me, yet many people consider them a delicacy.
> The apartment building on the corner hired a guard; ours should hire a guard also.

Your compound sentences will be effective if you make certain your ideas are equally important and the conjunction accurately describes their relationship.

> *Ineffective:* We ate at a restaurant, but it was on the roof.
> *Effective:* We ate at a rooftop restaurant, but our friends dined underground.

You should also avoid writing a compound sentence when a compound subject, verb, or other sentence element would sound better or be more economical.

> *Ineffective:* In my watercolor class, I painted a bowl of flowers first; then I tackled a sunset, and finally I painted a live model.
> *Effective:* In my watercolor class, I painted first a bowl of flowers, then a sunset, and finally a live model.

When there are more than two simple sentences in your compound, you have written a series.

> Arnold reads an occasional western novel, Dawn speeds through one science fiction epic a week, and Vickie devours romances—as many as one a night.

Note: The punctuation of a series of sentences is like that of a series of subjects or verbs: each item is separated by commas, and when a conjunction joins the final two items, the comma comes before the conjunction. However, when only two subjects or verbs (or any two sentence elements) are joined by a conjunction, no comma is used; when two sentences are joined by a conjunction in a compound sentence, a comma is used before the conjunction. (See pages 267–70 for more about punctuating series and compound sentences.)

EXERCISE 16: Identify the compound sentences in the following paragraph. Be careful not to mistake a compound subject or a compound of any other sentence part for a compound sentence.

[1]The blue whale is a fascinating animal and one of the earth's most intelligent creatures. [2]The largest animal ever to live on this planet, the blue whale is a hundred feet long, and it weighs a hundred tons. [3]It has no teeth, but it strains plankton and krill through plates in its mouth called baleen. [4]The blue whale lives and reproduces in the icy waters of the Antarctic Ocean. [5]For years this dangerous ocean protected the blue whale from its only enemy—man; however, for a hundred years now whalers have been systematically destroying the species. [6]In 1900 there were around 200,000 blue whales; now there are only a few thousand. [7]This majestic, but slow-breeding animal faces extinction.

EXERCISE 17: Combine the following sentences to make a single compound sentence. Use a comma and a coordinating conjunction (*and, but, or, nor, for, so, yet*) or a semicolon to join the sentences. You may need to make other compounds as well or to change some sentence ideas to modifiers.

1. In medieval cosmology the earth was the center of the universe. The sun orbited the earth. The moon orbited the earth. The stars orbited the earth.
2. On Earth Superman has super powers. On Krypton he would have been an average citizen.
3. Rocky Marciano might be called the champions' champion. He never lost a professional fight. He fought forty-nine times.
4. Larry Holmes nearly equaled Marciano's record. He lost his forty-ninth fight. He lost it to Michael Spinks.
5. The world's largest tree is a redwood. The world's oldest tree is a bristlecone pine. The world's most massive tree is a Sequoia.
6. In an emergency the body pumps adrenalin into the bloodstream. The adrenalin prepares the body for survival. It prepares the body for a fight. It prepares the body for flight.

7. Distress is negative. It decreases the body's ability to cope with crises. Eustress is positive. It triggers coping mechanisms.
8. The pollution index must be high today. I cannot see the pollution indicator. I cannot see through the smog.
9. The Olympics once featured hand-to-hand combat. Occasionally the wrestlers would dislocate limbs. Sometimes the wrestlers would kill their opponents.
10. Once, feeding the chipmunks was a favorite pastime. Tourists did this at Crater Lake National Park. Now the rangers caution us not to come near the animals. They may be infected with bubonic plague.

Complex Sentence

Like a compound sentence, a complex sentence can be formed by joining two simple sentences. However, instead of using a coordinating conjunction to show that the two sentences are equal, you use words like *although, because, since, if,* and *when.* These are called *subordinating conjunctions* because they show that one idea is less important than or subordinate to the other.

Our dreams of a championship ended <u>when</u> Sal fumbled the ball.

The word *when* shows that Sal's fumbling the ball is less important than what the fumble caused—the end of our dreams. Notice that *when Sal fumbled the ball* might also be placed at the beginning of the sentence; if so, it will be followed by a comma.

<u>When</u> Sal fumbled the ball, our dreams of a championship ended.

Subordinating conjunctions should be chosen carefully to show the relationship to the two ideas they connect (see Table 10–1). You would not, for example, use *where,* a conjunction that connects ideas about space, if you are talking about time.

Not: New Year's Eve, 1986, was the time <u>where</u> I resolved to quit smoking.
But: New Year's Eve, 1986, was the time <u>when</u> I resolved to quit smoking.

TABLE 10–1 Subordinating Conjunctions

Space: where, wherever
 Time: after, before, once, since, until, when, whenever, while, as soon as
Ideas: although, as, as if, because, even though, if, in order that, no matter how, since, so that, than, though, unless, while

EXERCISE 18:   Combine the following sentences using subordinating conjunctions to make a single complex sentence. You may compound parts of any sentence, but do not write a compound sentence.

1. The blue whales sing. They swim in the Antarctic Ocean. They play in the Antarctic Ocean.
2. Aladdin rubbed the lamp. The lamp was ancient. A genie sprang from the spout.
3. Humans could not live on Jupiter. The atmosphere is made of gases. The gases are poisonous.
4. The blue of a blue topaz is created by exposing smoky topaz to radiation. The stone is still considered a natural gem.
5. The hang gliders leaped from the cliff top. An updraft caught them. They soared over the treetops.

Complex sentences are also formed using words like *that, what, which, who, whom,* and *whose* as connectors. These words are called *relative pronouns,* and they may replace the subject or a predicate word so that one sentence idea may be embedded in another.

> The recording won the contest. The recording had the loudest beat.
>
> *Combined:* The recording <u>that</u> had the loudest beat won the contest.

That replaces the subject, *recording,* in the second sentence, allowing us to combine the sentences smoothly and avoiding repetition.

> The composition won the contest. He wrote the composition.
>
> *Combined:* The composition <u>that</u> he wrote won the contest.

That replaces the predicate word, *composition,* in the second sentence. When the relative pronoun replaces a predicate word, the order of the embedded sentence is changed, and the pronoun precedes the subject.

EXERCISE 19:   Combine the following sentences using relative pronouns to make a single complex sentence.

1. The mail order firm sent me a credit slip instead of a refund. The firm sold me mismatched seat covers.
2. Boll weevils eat the buds and bolls of young cotton plants. The weevils migrated from Mexico around 1880.
3. Sourdough bread is made with a starter. The starter is kept in a crockpot. It is kept warm. It is fed.

4. The mail carrier refused to come near our house. The mail carrier was bitten by our dog, Peaches.
5. Hans Selye spoke to the TOPS (Taking Off Pound Sensibly) Club. His book on stress is a national best-seller.

Clauses

The basic structural building blocks of the simple, compound, and complex sentences you have been studying are called *clauses*. A clause is a group of words that has either a subject and a verb or a subject, a verb, and a predicate word. An *independent clause* is a complete sentence. It is independent because it can stand alone and make sense. A simple sentence is an independent clause, and a compound sentence is made up of two or more independent clauses.

A *dependent clause*, on the other hand, has a subject and a verb but cannot stand alone. When you embed one sentence in another by adding a subordinating conjunction or a relative pronoun, you have made the embedded sentence a dependent clause. A complex sentence, therefore, is made up of an independent and a dependent clause.

Because dependent clauses do not stand alone, they must serve some function in the sentence they are part of. Dependent clauses that begin with subordinating conjunctions are usually adverbs, telling how, when, where, or under what condition.

After they sank the *Rainbow Warrior*, the terrorists escaped. (adverb clause telling when the terrorists escaped)

I will review your portfolio if you will review mine. (adverb clause indicating a condition for reviewing the portfolio)

Dependent clauses that begin with relative pronouns may function in a sentence either as nouns or as adjectives.

The terrorists who sank the *Rainbow Warrior* were French agents. (adjective clause describing which terrorists)

Who ordered the attack will probably remain a mystery. (noun clause serving as subject of verb, *will remain*)

EXERCISE 20: Combine the following sets of sentences to make a single complex sentence using the subordinating conjunction or the relative pronoun in parentheses.

1. The whooping crane is making a comeback. It was once thought to be extinct. (which)
2. In 1985 more than a hundred whooping cranes flew south from Canada. The birds have their nesting grounds in Canada. (where)

3. Conservationists are responsible for much of the comeback. They followed the cranes to thcir nesting grounds. (who)
4. They learned an important fact about whoopers. Whoopers will only raise one of their eggs. They lay two eggs. (that)
5. The eggs are laid. A watchful scientist steals one. (after)
6. The egg is then placed in the nest of a sandhill crane. The sandhill crane makes an excellent foster parent. (which)
7. The adopted whoopers winter in New Mexico with the sandhill cranes. The original whooping crane flock winters in Texas. (while)
8. The whooping cranes are being saved. People love their majestic beauty. (because)
9. The grizzly bear is also facing extinction. Few people are very concerned about its fate. (although)
10. The pioneers named the grizzly *ursus horribilus*. People have considered the animal a threat to life. (since)

Compound/Complex

A sentence may be both compound and complex if it includes at least two independent clauses and one dependent clause.

> If the grizzly is to be saved, hunting the shaggy creatures must be banned, and steps must be taken to preserve the animal's natural habitat.

The first clause in this long sentence is easily identified as dependent by the subordinating conjunction *if*. The two clauses joined by the coordinating conjunction *and* are independent. Each has a subject and a verb *hunting/must be banned* and *steps/must be taken*) and can stand alone as a complete statement of thought.

EXERCISE 21: Combine the following sets of sentences to make a single compound-complex sentence.

1. Zoo keepers have rescued the few remaining California Condors from the wilds. The outlook for their future is not good. So far none have bred in captivity.
2. It takes years to become a master potter. Even the most talented beginner will smash her pots. She will refuse all offers of sales.
3. Totem poles look like garish idols. They are actually a family tree. The carvings contain the records of deeds and births.
4. Vermont folk medicine relies heavily on vinegar. It was

popularized by Dr. D. C. Jarvis in his book *Folk Medicine.* Its claims for cures range from arthritis to ringworm.

5. The Rolex gold watch has become a status symbol. It costs $7,500. The less affluent buy counterfeits for a fraction of the price.

EXERCISE 22:   Identify the sentences in the following paragraph as simple (S), compound (CD), complex (CX), or compound/complex (CCX).

1. ____   [1]Playing Trivial Pursuit may be delightful for some, but for
2. ____   me it offers a lesson in humility. [2]I do not remember who played
                  Dobie Gillis's brother in a long-ago television series whose name
3. ____   I have forgotten. [3]I cannot recall and do not care about the
4. ____   height of Pike's Peak. [4]The words of Teddy Kennedy at his
                  brother's inauguration have long ago slipped my mind—if they
                  were ever there to begin with.
5. ____   [5]My friends and co-workers, unfortunately, do not share my
6. ____   distaste for the game. [6]They play it at lunch in the computer
                  room where they can check their answers with the computer's
7. ____   encyclopedia of little-known facts. [7]They discuss their answers
                  over coffee or over the xerox machine, and I have even noticed
                  supposedly busy executives whose computer terminals are
8. ____   displaying pages of *How to Win at Trivial Pursuit.* [8]The mania
                  is everywhere.
9. ____   [9]The person who invents a fad to replace Trivial Pursuit will
10. ____   have my eternal gratitude. [10]In the meantime I will keep playing
                  Monopoly.

TROUBLESHOOTING: *Compound and Complex Sentences*

Two common errors are closely tied to compound and complex sentences.

   1.   An inadequately punctuated compound sentence may result in a comma splice.

Deep sea fishing in the Pacific Ocean requires a spirit of adventure, it also requires a strong stomach.

The two sentences spliced by the comma are closely related, but they are also complete and independent. Placing a semicolon between them eliminates the comma splice without altering the arrangement of ideas.

Deep sea fishing in the Pacific Ocean requires a spirit of adventure; it also requires a strong stomach.

Another kind of comma splice frequently occurs when a transition word like *moreover* or *however* separates the sentences instead of a co-ordinating conjunction.

> A white-haired grandmother caught a twenty-pound steelhead, however, several sporty-looking fishermen caught nothing.

However makes a transition between the ideas, but it is an adverb rather than a conjunction. We can correct the comma splice by exchanging the adverb for a conjunction or by using stronger punctuation.

> A white-haired grandmother caught a twenty-pound steelhead, but several sporty-looking fishermen caught nothing.
> A white-haired grandmother caught a twenty-pound steelhead; however, several sporty-looking fishermen caught nothing.

2. The dependent part of a complex sentence is sometimes incorrectly punctuated as an independent sentence. The result is a fragment.

> The programmers had nothing to do today. Because the computer was down.

The first group of words is a complete sentence. It has a subject, *programmers*; a verb, *had*; and a predicate word, *nothing*. The second group also has a subject, *computer*; a verb, *was*; and a predicate word, *down*. However, it also has *because,* a subordinating conjunction.

To correct the error, we could join the parts to make a complex sentence, or we could remove the subordinating conjunction.

> The programmers had nothing to do today because the computer was down.
> The programmers had nothing to do today. The computer was down.

EXERCISE 23: Troubleshoot for errors in the following student essay. Pay special attention to spelling, word usage, comma splices, and fragments. Read aloud to find awkwardness caused by lack of variety in sentence types. Look carefully for problems with paragraphing and organization. An outline of the content will help you here.

> I believe that Shakespeare stated the problem the best:

> > O! beware, my lord, of jealousy;
> > It is the green-eyed monster which doth mock.
> > (*Othello* III.iii.165)

Shakespeare is telling us that jealousy is a "monster" and "mocks" ourselves. I, like most people, am competitive and am extremely jealous of anyone that can out-perform me in the simplest tasks. This problem is especially acute when I am matched with my arch-rival, Herman Schmeckal, I have a great dislike for Herman Schmeckal in my Chemistry, Math, and English courses.

With the "monster" of jealousy to gnaw at me, I try to mimic Herman Schmeckal's abilities. This just proves my inadiquecy and increases my ill-feelings toward him. Herman Schmeckal is the type of chemistry student that can work in achemistry lab with great ease, efficiency, and economy, I, on the other hand, am constantly having problems with arranging, using, and processing chemicals. I also take twice the time to complete the same tasks and never accomplish what Herman Schmeckal does. His solutions are always correct and mine are "unusual" as the professor would say. Which leads to the second point, that the professor is not very fond of me. Naturally the professor admires Herman Schmeckal's scholarally aptitude and he compliments Herman Schmeckal for being "sapient." I am reffered to as being "less endowed with brilliance" or more in the order of "egregious." I'm not really sure what they really mean, but I do not believe it is a favorable comment.

I did previously state that Herman Schmeckal is economical with all laboratory equipment and supplies and by this, I mean he does not spill, splatter or other wise waste any chemicals. Naturally I am the one that adds new "decorating touches" (as my proffessor would constantly remind me of) to the tables, floors, doors, seats, stools, walls, ceilings, charts, text books, note books, etc., etc. The laboratory exercises is the part of the course where I exceed my professors and Herman Schmeckals expectations. While Herman Schmeckal is working the problem with his usual efficientcy; I, trying to copy his speed and accuracy, am blowing-out the laboratory's back wall along with three tables, four students, my professor and several hundred dollars worth of equipment and supplies. It can be seen, that with all my great abundance of patience and temperance; I have not tried to wring Herman Schmeckal's neck.

To further aggravate my growing dislike of Herman Schmeckal, I am scheduled in the same math class, which is Math 161. Herman Schmeckal sits in the front of the class where he can ask intelligent and relevant questions pertaining to a caliber of mathmatics far above my comprehension. I ask questions which sound less intelligent, like, "where did the three comes from?" and so on. When homework is to be turned-in, I always wait to see Herman Schmeckal put his paper down on the desk first. This way I can take a quick glance at the "correct" answers while I linger at the desk. His papers are always organized, neat and legable while mine arent. His graphs are always elaborite and drawn on graph paper while mine is'nt. My homework looks like an ancient form of chinese manuscript with half the neatness. My graph lines are always bent or crooked. Especially when they are supposed to be straight!

The final aggravating cause of my hatred for Herman Schmeckal is the attendance of the same english class. Herman Schmeckal writes perfect grammar. He also talks and thinks in perfect grammar. He says "whom." I say "whoz-zits." Every student must write a rough-draft essay. Old Herman Schmeckal writes his paper in old English Script. I "chicken-scratch." The final copies are very different too. Herman Schmeckal types his. I write mine in pen. Herman Schmeckal types double-space. Within the margins. I, on the other hand, run off the margined boundaries. I splatter liquid paper on my inevitable mistakes. Herman Schmeckal's grades on essays are always the highest. He is constantly complimented on his "literary accomplishments." I only get baleful looks from the professor. Herman Schmeckal's air of confidence before a grammar test sets me to an unquenchible desire to tear off his errasers from his pencils and pray he makes what he calls a "silly typographical err." To have Herman Schmeckal score lower than me on any exam would be a dream come true.

In conclusion, with such a supreme, transcendent and unequaled intellectul capabilities, that Herman Schmeckal possesses, would cause a sense of inferority in anyone. As Socrates put it,

> Mankind is tolerant of the praises of others so long as each hearer thinks he can do as well or nearly as well himself, but, when the speaker rises above him, jealousy is aroused and he begins to be incredulous.
>
> (Funeral speech of Pericles)

READING TO WRITE

Throughout this chapter you have been reading examples written by student writers who use various methods to develop and organize their ideas.

Professional writers also use these methods; however, they frequently combine methods rather than using one alone.

The first paragraph of Charles Berlitz's article, "The Triangle of Disappearing Planes," on page 334 of the Readings, provides a good example. Berlitz both defines the Bermuda Triangle and explains why the name is shrouded in mystery. The remainder of the article recounts step by step how Flight 19 disappeared and offers and rejects various explanations of why the planes disappeared.

Berlitz also demonstrates the skillful use of simple, compound, and complex sentence structures to bring together and clarify a complicated sequence of actions. Consider, for example, paragraph 7. It begins with a complex sentence, emphasizing the importance of the action and suggesting the probable surprise of the hearers.

> At 4 P.M. the tower suddenly heard that Lieutenant Taylor had unexpectedly turned over command to a senior Marine pilot, Captain Stiver.

The sentence that follows begins with a subordinate clause that helps us "feel" the pilots' distance from the tower—the stretching of the thin thread that still connected them to the base.

> Although obscured by static and strained by tension, an understandable message was received from him: "We are not sure where we are. . . ."

Then a compound–complex sentence expresses some of the complexity of what happened next.

> The flight leader then apparently decided to turn 180 degrees in the hope of flying back over Florida, but as they made the turn the transmission began to get fainter, indicating that they had made a wrong turn and were flying east, away from the Florida coast over the open sea.

Pay attention to both development and sentence structure as you read Berlitz's article. Could you use any of his methods in your own writing? Which ones? Are there any methods you would hesitate using? Are there any sentences that are too complicated, too packed with information, or simply too long? You might try revising one or more of his longest sentences.

WRITING ACTIVITY

For this assignment you will be working to develop your ideas more fully; therefore, you might plan to spend extra time on exploring your subject. The more information you can find, the more you will have to choose from when it comes time to select support and plan your essay.

ACTIVITY: Write about an event that has special significance either to the world, to the country, to people at large, or to you personally. Choose methods of development that will enable you to discuss what the event was, why it is important, how it came about, or how and why it affected people. Some possible topics follow. You may choose one of these or one of your own.

1. Martin Luther King's March on Washington
2. The Boston Tea Party
3. The Firing on Fort Sumter
4. The First Moonwalk

CHECKLIST: Check each draft of your paper carefully for the following:

1. Is the essay well developed and well organized?
2. Is the purpose clear?
3. Does the essay have an effective introduction with a clear thesis statement?
4. Are simple, compound, and complex sentences used effectively?
5. Are there any errors in capitalization or apostrophe usage?
6. Are there any comma splices, run-ons, or fragments?
7. Are there any misplaced or dangling modifiers or errors in adjective and adverb use?
8. Are there any errors in subject–verb or pronoun agreement?
9. Are there any misspelled words, left-out words, or reversed letters?

CHAPTER ELEVEN
Concluding the Essay

Interpreting Meanings and Making Judgments

Once you have found something to say, explored and focused it, developed it fully, and organized it tightly, there is still another step—discovering meaning and your own reactions to that meaning. To Diane Ackerman in the reading selection for Chapter 7, the Ellis Island experience is meaningful because it is at the roots of American life for millions of us. She compares immigrants' passing through Ellis Island to going through the eye of a needle—an important if unpleasant experience and certainly one that cannot be forgotten. Suzanne Britt Jordan, whose article is discussed on page 120 of Chapter 6, makes judgments, some of them dangerous, about fat and thin people, then hints at the end of the article that she might have been joking. "Fat people," she says, "will take you in," hinting that she might not dislike thin people quite as much as she said and might even not mind being thin herself.

Different people will, of course, find different meanings and make different judgments. You might, for example, see the Ellis Island experience as a warning about inequities in immigration laws or of continuing unfair treatment of some immigrants.

Some questions will help you to find your own meanings and make your own judgments. If you have developed an essay using examples or descriptive details, ask yourself, "How does all of this affect me? How does it make me feel? What does it make me want to do? Why do I care?" If you have written about an event, you can ask, "Did this event change my life or that of someone I know? Why is it important to me or my friends or the world?" If you have developed an essay using types of people or things or an essay comparing two items, you might ask, "Which one or which ones do I prefer? Why?" If you have explained how to do something or how something works, you can ask, "Would I advise the readers to do this my way, or should I issue a warning instead? Does it really matter how they do it?"

Your answers to these questions will help you understand what the evidence and opinions you have marshalled in your essay mean to you. Your answers will also help you understand what the evidence and opinions might mean to your readers. If your judgments, based on that meaning, are harsh or extreme, your readers may find it difficult to take you seriously and may discount everything you have said. If your judgments are bland or wishy-washy, your readers may lose interest and forget about what you have said. Moderate judgments that show respect for your readers are often the most effective. Consider Jean's sentences about her experience with a Siamese cat.

> Because of my experience of being bitten by Prince, I have hated Siamese cats every since.
> Being bitten by Prince was quite an experience!
> Since Prince bit me, I walk warily with Siamese cats and pet their regal heads very, very carefully.

The first judgment is extreme; basing an attitude as intense as hatred upon one experience seems narrow-minded and petty. On the other hand, the second judgment is so bland it is not a judgment at all. The reader is left wondering whether the writer means that the incident added excitement to a dull life and she would like to repeat it or the incident was so traumatic that she feels fortunate to have lived through it. The final sentence is both clear and moderate. The writer is not ignoring the incident: she is somewhat afraid of these rather arrogant animals—a feeling the reader can sympathize with. However, she still has affection for them, even if that affection is expressed more cautiously than it was before she was bitten.

EXERCISE 1:   Read and evaluate statements of judgment for their effect upon readers. Choose the statement in each group that seems most effective to you. Discuss your reasons.

1. a. After comparing my car to a Mercedes, I think I'll run mine over the nearest cliff.
   b. My car cannot be compared to a Mercedes.

      c. In performance and looks, the Mercedes is a better car, but I think I'll stick with my Taurus. At least it's paid for.

2. a. I will never forget stumbling as I walked down the aisle.
    b. The embarrassment of stumbling at the wedding ruined my marriage and my life.
    c. Because I stumbled as I walked down the aisle, the happy memories of my wedding day are mixed with embarrassment.

3. a. My first endeavor at making a pineapple upside down cake was such a disaster that I will never make it that way again.
    b. My first endeavor at making a pineapple upside down cake was such a disaster that I will never make it again.
    c. My first endeavor at making a pineapple upside down cake was such a disaster that I will never eat it again.

4. a. Win a few; lose a few.
    b. Although I cannot help being disappointed not to have won the blue ribbon, I plan to try it again next year.
    c. I now know that competition is wrong, and from now on contests are off limits in my house.

5. a. After carefully weighing the evidence, I feel the defendant should be shot.
    b. Who has a right to judge another person? Given similar circumstances, we might have done the same thing.
    c. After carefully weighing the evidence, I feel the defendant is guilty.

FOCUS ON WRITING: *Concluding the Essay*

Although some essays may end with the last paragraph that develops the main idea, most need a concluding paragraph to sum up, interpret, or give a final judgment or comment about the subject. A concluding paragraph makes an essay feel more complete—like the period at the end of a sentence or the awards ceremony at the end of a track meet.

If the concluding paragraph is not the easiest to write, it is certainly the most fun. After writing several hundred words that support ideas with concrete evidence and restrict opinion to thesis and topic sentences, you may finally "cut loose." The concluding paragraph is the place to solve the world's problems ("If these steps are followed, crime in St. Louis will be cut in half"); to play the authority ("My evidence clearly shows that San Francisco is sinking into the Pacific Ocean"); to boast ("My own life-style enables me to fly to Hawaii every weekend"); or to advise the readers ("Try it; you'll like it"). The conclusion may be humorous or serious; it may clinch an argument or simply relate the topic to the readers. The two major things this paragraph can do most effectively are (1) to remind the readers of what has been said and (2) to leave them with the feeling that the essay is finished and that what it said was significant.

The real work is in writing the first sentence of the concluding paragraph. The last paragraph can be shaped like a megaphone, narrow at the top or mouthpiece and broad at the other end. In terms of the overall essay, the first sentence of the concluding paragraph is the counterpart of the thesis statement—narrow and specific, completing the essay's tell-them, tell-them, tell-them-again pattern. The first sentence may do either of two things: (1) restate the thesis in different words or (2) briefly summarize the paper's major idea in a sentence that introduces a final judgment or comment.

Restating the Thesis

Because most essays are actually quite short, using the same sentence for the conclusion that was used for the thesis would sound awkward and lazy—as though the writer were painting by numbers. If, however, you use different words, a concluding paragraph may begin with a simple restatement of the entire thesis, or at least part of the thesis.

Take, for example, Jeanette's thesis about shopping at the Mall.

> *Thesis:* I decided going to the Mall for jeans would pick me up, but the noise, the crowds, and the outrageous prices only increased my depression.
>
> *Restatement #1:* Instead of being picked up by shopping at the Mall, I was thoroughly depressed with the racket, the people, and the exorbitant prices.
>
> *Restatement #2:* Instead of picking me up, shopping at the Mall plummeted me to a psychotic level of depression.

The major difference between the two restatements is that number one restates all of the thesis, including the major causes of the depression, whereas number two restates only the limited subject, shopping at the Mall, and the focus, the author's depression. Either type of restatement will work fine as long as the reader is reminded clearly of the main idea of the essay.

> *Thesis:* There are many different kinds of crazy drivers, but I'll only mention a few: there are the road-hogs, the curb-huggers, the poke-alongs, and the lane-hoppers.
>
> *Restatement #1:* The road-hogs, the curb-huggers, the poke-alongs, and the lane-hoppers are all crazy drivers.

Restatement #2: All of these drivers are dangerously crazy.

Thesis: As I babysit, I begin to have doubts about myself, marriage, family life, and children.

Restatement #1: Babysitting makes me question my traditional dream of marriage, home, and children.

Restatement #2: When I babysit, I come close to rejecting the traditional family lifestyle.

Thesis: A woman would make a good President because women are strong, decisive, and patient.

Restatement #1: Women's strength, decisiveness, and patience qualify them for the U.S. Presidency.

Restatement #2: Women are well qualified by nature to be President.

Sum-up Sentence

The second method of beginning a concluding paragraph is probably easier to write but harder to conceptualize. You still recall the thesis idea, but you do so in a brief phrase or clause that helps to introduce the final comment or judgment; that is, the sum-up becomes part of a topic sentence for the conclusion. Rizzi's essay in Chapter 10 offers a good example.

Thesis: Airplane passengers, I think, can be divided into three main categories: the "I hate to fly" group, the over-active group, and the cool, expert travelers.

First sentence of conclusion: Whenever I fly, I usually try to find three empty seats so I can go to sleep, but I've been in each of these groups also.

These groups reminds us that the writer has been talking about three different kinds of airplane passengers, but the sentence does more than simply restate Rizzi's observation that the passengers may be classified in this way. It actually injects the writer himself into each of the three categories, and personalizes the essay. We may have suspected all along that he was speaking both from experience and observation, but we did not actually know that Rizzi had been an I-hate-to-fly traveler, an over-active traveler, and a cool-expert traveler until the concluding paragraph.

Other examples of thesis statements and sum-up sentences follow:

Thesis: The kinds of students I noticed at Sam Houston High School were the over-achiever, the mediocre, the timid, and the reluctant.

First sentence of conclusion: I noticed one major thing as I observed these different students: there were very few that I would call well rounded.

Thesis: My favorite place at City College is the Reading Lab because the director is friendly and understanding, the exercises help me develop my reading and English skills, I have met many friends there, and I can go there just to relax.

First sentence of conclusion: Because the Reading Lab is my favorite place, I spend at least five hours there every week.

Thesis: As a roller-skater I have been able to study several types of skaters—the coward, the moderate, and the daredevil.

First sentence of conclusion: Of the three different types, I find it best to be a moderate.

EXERCISE 2: Write ten sentences that either restate in different words or sum up the ideas of the following thesis statements.

1. Exercise is very important to our bodies because it burns up calories, firms the muscles, relieves tension, and helps us to relax.
2. On I-5 I saw three different kinds of hitchhikers: the bold adventurers, the scared commuters, and the dangerous opportunists.
3. The problems of living in a tourist-oriented community are some of the worst I have encountered. Housing is poor, jobs are hard to get, work is seasonal, and the cost of living is outlandish.
4. I will always remember the Talk of the Town, a restaurant in Ladonia, Texas, because of the atmosphere, the people, and the good food.
5. I become very depressed when I remember deaths of loved ones.

6. The worst time of my life was on a hunting trip I took last spring. I got trapped in the mountains by a snowstorm, I almost froze to death, and I did not get a bird.

7. Life as a work-study secretary is sometimes fun, sometimes hard, sometimes frustrating, and all the time challenging.

8. If I could live in another time, I would choose the nineteenth century because of the open land and six-gun law.

9. If I could live in another time, I would choose the twenty-fifth century because of the new frontier in the stars, the medical advances enabling people to live to be two hundred years old, the chance to live on the moon, and many living conveniences like housework robots.

10. Dr. Fu Manchu VIII, a Pekinese dog, is my best friend because he is always there when I need him.

Final Comment or Judgment

Writing the first sentence is the hard part; the rest is fun. Be creative; use your imagination; enjoy. This is the writer's soapbox.

One effective way to develop this final paragraph is to relate the subject to your own actions or feelings. Rizzi uses this method in "On an Airplane" (page 210, Chapter 10).

> Whenever I fly, I usually try to find three empty seats so I can go to sleep, but I've been in each of these groups also. The first time I flew I could have certainly been placed among the "I hate to fly" group. My second flight I was the cool, expert traveler. I have been the over-active passenger also; I remember once using up an entire roll of film on clouds, which certainly looked good from the airplane, but once developed, the pictures looked like dirty pieces of paper. Another time when I didn't have a camera, I had a couple of drinks too many, which resulted in my getting completely airsick for the rest of the flight. For me flying is now interesting and, if I could take a parachute with me, it would be almost a pleasure.

Rizzi's personal comment borders on a humorous confession. This works especially well since he is in effect atoning for the fun he has poked at other people by poking fun at himself. Moreover, the tongue-in-cheek confession reinforces the sympathies which the writer engaged in the introduction by admitting to some air fright. Instead of being left with a final picture of Rizzi as a cynical, superior critic of human nature, the reader sees him as human, amused by and involved in human weakness.

A more serious approach is taken by Yvonne in the conclusion to her essay, "Rape in Houston." After explaining the problem clearly in her essay, Yvonne uses the conclusion to offer a solution.

> I believe that the rape level in Houston can be lowered. I think this can be done in several ways. A woman can develop her physical ability. A woman may not be able to fight off a potential attacker, especially if he's armed, but someone who projects physical self-confidence is far less likely to be a victim. Women can also lobby to revise criminal codes that encourage rape: laws that make the prior sexual history of the victim admissible courtroom evidence, laws that require witnesses for this rarely witnessed crime, and laws that make sentences so unrealistically high that prosecution of rapists is difficult. Also a twenty-four hour rape crisis center should be organized, and a female rape squad should be on duty at all times. If these things were done, I for one would feel safer in Houston.

Kenneth concludes his essay "Living in a Tourist Community" with some advice for the readers.

> The tourist community is fun if you don't live there. All the conveniences and many luxuries are available, but you must pay dearly for them. If you don't mind poor housing, no jobs, and high prices, you'll enjoy living in a town like Telluride, Colorado. But if you have to make a living and want to raise a family, try Denver or Salt Lake City. In a tourist community it's too hard to make ends meet.

The conclusion of Donna's essay "My Appetite" simply reasserts the primary idea of her essay: Donna enjoys food.

> Now even at an older age, I still have a large appetite. I worry about it for a day or two at most, but I always return to my regular eating style. Until it becomes hazardous to my health, I shall continue to eat peach cobbler with thick, homemade crust; smothered potatoes baked in milk and butter and topped with cheese; hot-water cornbread; and crusty fried chicken. I don't eat excessively because of personal problems. It's simply because food is good to me and I love to eat.

Other ways that students have developed concluding paragraphs are illustrated in the exercise that follows. Some methods work better than others, but we can learn from all of the attempts.

EXERCISE 3:   Discuss the effectiveness of the following conclusions.

1.   These reasons for my love for my Karmann Ghia all add up to my vision of a dream car. Just imagine; it is economical, aero-dynamically designed, and adored by women. What will your next car purchase be?

2.   I cherish the moments I've spent working in the Reading Lab. The opportunity is there to learn the material I didn't in the past. I still have problems in most of my schoolwork, but as long as I "keep truckin'" on my English, reading, and writing, I will surely celebrate when I graduate. And the Reading Lab director will be one of the first guests for this celebration.

3.   Childhood shall never be forgotten. I felt secure, loved, and happy—especially whenever I stepped into my grandmother's kitchen.

4.   To be a work-study in a job you like can give you exciting and happy times. You can get to know the people you work with real well. It can be a hard job at times, but the good friend you will find in that job is worth it.

5.   As I watch the people at the laundromat, I wonder which group I would fit into—the socializing, the picky, or the impatient washers. If I am in a good mood, I will take my time and wash my laundry like the picky person. If I'm not feeling well or am tired, I will just throw the laundry in and come back later.

6.   Selfishness is at its peak during rush hour. With all of this going on, I avoid 7:30 a.m. and 5:00 p.m. anyway that I can. I might work a little late or just simply relax for a half hour before leaving my building. In the morning I will have my second cup of coffee at the office instead of at home.

7.   Women are half of the population and can contribute much to our country—including leadership in the White House. Women possess strength, courage, and intellect. These qualities are what make a good President and women have proven they are capable of being President. A scientific finding has shown that there is little difference between men and women in the size of their brains or ability to think. It has been found that both sexes are equal, but more interesting was the fact that women are also slightly superior. I believe there is more than enough proof that a woman can and probably someday will make a great President.

FOCUS ON THE SENTENCE: *Predicate Words*

Just as some essays need a concluding paragraph, some sentences need a concluding word or group of words. You have learned to recognize complete sentences by their sound and feeling of completeness, by their expression of complete ideas, and by the basic sentence elements of subjects and verbs. In this section you will study some additional sentence elements, called *predicate words*, which are needed to complete certain sentences.

Sentences Without Predicate Words

Some sentences are complete with just a subject and a verb.

<blockquote>

subj.   verb
<u>Mt. St. Helens</u> <u>erupted</u>.

subj. verb
<u>Lions</u> <u>roar</u>.

subj. verb
<u>Geese</u> <u>fly</u>.

subj.   verb
<u>Thunder</u> <u>rolls</u>.

</blockquote>

We may add modifiers to describe the subject, the verb, or both, but they are not actually needed to complete the sentences.

<blockquote>

subj.   verb
Beautiful <u>Mt. St. Helens</u> <u>erupted</u> violently in May of 1980.

subj. verb
African <u>lions</u> <u>roar</u> in rage, in triumph, and in challenge.

subj. verb
Graceful Canadian <u>geese</u> <u>fly</u> in formation across the river.

subj.   verb
<u>Thunder</u> like the deep bass drums of a symphony orchestra <u>rolls</u> menacingly in the background.

</blockquote>

Sentences that give commands or make polite requests may even be complete with just a verb. The subject is understood to be *you*.

<blockquote>

subj. verb   subj. verb
(you)<u>Help</u>!   (you) <u>Eat</u>.

</blockquote>

EXERCISE 4: Build more interesting sentences by adding adjectives and adverbs, both single words and prepositional phrases, to the following basic sentences.

1. Run!
2. The microcomputers are coming.
3. Dogs bark.
4. The Madisons will wait.
5. Superman can fly.
6. Cows moo.
7. Hurry!
8. The alarm tripped.
9. Millions are starving.
10. Sing.

Sentences That Need Predicate Words

Sometimes we need something more than just a subject and a verb to make a complete sentence.

> Hussein is _____.
> Debbie gave _____.
> Rocky kayoed _____.
> Margaret grows _____.

Most of the completing elements, called *predicate words*, follow the verb. Even if we add modifiers to the sentence, unless we fill in the blanks left by the missing predicate words, the sentences will be incomplete.

Incomplete	*Complete*
Unhappy Hussein is certainly _____ today.	Unhappy Hussein is certainly <u>homesick</u> today.
Debbie, always generous, eagerly gave _____.	Debbie, always generous, eagerly gave <u>us a clock</u>.
With a sharp right Rocky kayoed _____ in the twelfth round.	With a sharp right Rocky kayoed <u>the champion</u> in the twelfth round.
Because of her green thumb Margaret grows enormous _____ in her garden.	Because of her green thumb Margaret grows enormous <u>sunflowers</u> in her garden.

What you can use as a predicate word depends upon the sense of the sentence and upon the verb you are using. In the first sentence an adjective, *homesick*, is used as a predicate word. We might also have used an adverb, such as *here: Hussein is here.* In the second sentence two words, the pronoun *us* and the noun *clock*, complete the idea. And in both the third and fourth sentences, nouns, *sunflowers* and *champion*, are predicate words.

Nouns and Pronouns as Predicate Words

One or more nouns or pronouns may be needed to complete some sentences.

1. When the verb shows an action, a noun or a pronoun will show who or what is affected.

> subj.   verb   noun
> The twister uprooted <u>trees</u>. (uprooted *what?*)

> subj.   verb   pronoun
> The twister uprooted <u>them</u>. (uprooted *what?*)

> subj.   verb   **noun**
> Gina surprised the <u>saboteur</u>. (surprised *whom?*)

> subj.   verb   pronoun
> Gina surprised <u>her</u>. (surprised *whom?*)

When the action continues, another noun or pronoun may be needed to show other people or things that are affected.

> subj.   verb   pronoun noun
> For Christmas Glenda will send <u>him</u> <u>orchids</u>.
> (will send *what?* will send it *to whom?*)

> subj.   verb   noun   noun
> The expedition radioed <u>headquarters</u> the <u>location</u>.
> (will send *what?* will send it *to what?*)

> subj. verb   noun   **noun**
> Pat has done <u>Glenda</u> many <u>favors</u>.
> (has done *what?* has done it *for whom?*)

2. When the verb shows a state of being, a noun or a pronoun after the verb reidentifies—or shows another state, condition, or role—of the subject.

> subj.   verb   noun
> Ms. Jaramillo is the <u>principal</u>.

> subj. verb pronoun
> The principal is <u>she</u>.

> subj. verb noun
> Our sun's name is <u>Sol</u>.

> subj.   verb   noun
> A used car dealer will become our <u>mayor</u> today.

Verbs that show state of being include all the forms of *be* (*am, is, are, was, were, being, been*) and *become* (*became, becoming*).

EXERCISE 5: Underline subjects once and verbs twice. Circle all nouns and pronouns used as predicate words.

If I could be empress for a day, I would accomplish miracles in twenty-four hours. For myself, I would buy a new home. It would be a solar house with a windmill-driven, electrical back-up system. And I would give each member of my family one wish. They could have anything or be anyone for the day of my reign. For nature, I would free all of the animals kept in zoos and laboratories; I would sink every whaling ship; and I would protect the baby seals. For the world, I would become Mother Bountiful. I would send Africa more food and every country more Peace Corps volunteers. And for my country, I would ban the use of private automobiles and close polluting factories. All public employees would truly serve the public for a day. City crews would build shelters for homeless people and animals, and government workers would cook and serve food. To finance the shelters, the military would mine gold and silver, and I would establish a trust fund so that the work could continue after my reign.

Adjectives and Adverbs as Predicate Words

Verbs that show state of being or condition, like *be* or *become,* may be followed by adjectives as well as nouns to complete the sentences.

> subj.   verb   adj.
> The Sandia Mountains become red at sunset.

> subj.   verb   adj.
> Sioux Falls is growing large.

> subj.   verb adj.
> The tiger in *Masters of the Universe* is green.

Adjectives that complete sentences describe the subject. They show what color, what size, what shape the subject is or how the subject looks or feels. Other verbs which may be followed by adjective predicate words include *look, feel, appear, taste, smell, remain, sound,* and *seem.*

> subj.   verb   adj.
> Amin is feeling homesick.

        subj.   verb   adj.   subj.   verb   adj.
The guacamole tastes bitter; the avocados must not have been ripe.

Occasionally an adverb, either a word or a phrase, may complete a sentence in which the verb shows a state of being.

         subj. verb adv.
Humphrey is here.

       subj.   verb   adv. prep. phrase
Humphrey is in the game room.

Adverbs may also be used to complete a sentence idea when the verb shows an action but the action does not affect anyone or anything except the subject.

                     adv.
      subj.   verb   prep. phrase   adv.
Michelle goes to the mall often.

         subj.   verb   adv. prep. phrase
The company will spring into action.

Note: Adjectives and nouns and pronouns acting as predicate words have technical names which your instructor may or may not ask you to learn. When an adjective or noun follows a verb like *be* or *feels* and describes or renames the subject, it is called a *subjective complement* because it adds to or complements the subject. When a noun or pronoun follows an action verb and shows who or what receives the action, it is called a *direct object*. When a noun or pronoun comes between an action verb and a direct object, it is called an *indirect object*. It can be identified easily after you find the direct object. Find the subject, the verb, and the direct object; then ask the questions: to or for whom? to or for what? The indirect object is the answer to those questions.

        subj.   verb   ind. obj.   dir. obj.
The florist brought me a dozen roses.
(The florist brought what? The florist brought *roses; roses* is the direct object. The florist brought roses to whom? The florist brought roses to *me; me* is the indirect object.

EXERCISE 6: Underline subjects once and verbs twice. Circle each adverb or adjective (word or phrase) used to complete the sentence.

1. All of life grows at our doorstep.
2. The rings of Saturn look solid from a distance.

3. The baby harp seal's coat is dazzlingly white.
4. The exploits of the *Rainbow Warrior* and its crew are legendary.
5. The flood waters of the Columbia rose above the bridge.
6. Our guests became ill after a dinner of hobo stew.
7. Mocha mint coffee tastes rich and zesty.
8. Oz is over the rainbow.
9. The burglar crept cautiously into the room.
10. The flight of cranes rode gracefully on a stream of moving air.

EXERCISE 7: Add nouns, pronouns, adjectives, or adverbs as necessary to complete the following sentences.

1. A sharp wind whipped _____.

2. To a chocoholic a hot fudge sundae is _____.

3. Soft, fluffy, and white—the storm clouds appeared _____.

4. The versatile Transformers defeated _____.

5. A generous billionaire gave _____.

6. After last night's defeat, Rocky will be _____.

7. An autumn moon rose _____.

8. Shimmering curtains of aurora borealis lighted _____.

9. The odds–on favorite in the third race is _____.

10. The dutiful host passed _____.

EXERCISE 8: Write two sentences to fit each of the basic sentence patterns described below. Your sentences should match the examples.

1. Subject + verb/The sky is falling.
2. Subject + verb + adjective/The new neighbors seem pleasant.
3. Subject + verb + adverb/The explosion ripped through the building.
4. Subject + verb + noun or pronoun that renames subject/ Francine is a spy.
5. Subject + verb + noun or pronoun that receives the action of the verb/The machine ate my report.
6. Subject + verb + noun or pronoun + noun or pronoun/The company mailed us the contracts.

TROUBLESHOOTING: *Listening for Completeness and Correctness*

Reading aloud is an important troubleshooting technique. It gives you two ways to find problems—with your ears and with your eyes.

Read the following paragraphs first silently and then aloud.

> [1]Our marauding cat Mitzy first discovered the menace of a mouse invasion in our house. [2]She caught a mouse in the kitchen and ate it. [3]She caught a mouse in the bathroom and drowned it in the toilet. [4]She caught a mouse in the greenhouse and killed it and buried it in a pot of geraniums. [5]But there were too many of them. [6]Finally we called the Happy Hunters Roach, Mouse, and Pest Exterminators company for help.

> [1]Dinning out elegantly is an art. [2]Not unlike that of drinking tea without spilling it on your shirt or watching ballet without falling asleep. [3]To become a master, you must work hard. [4]While avoiding the appearance of working.

The eye alone might notice the fragments and misspelled word in the second paragraph. However, the ear would help you find the extra *n* in *dining* since two *n*'s change the pronunciation of the *i* to a short "ih" sound. And your ear would also help you find the unnatural stops after *art* and *hard* that create the fragments, "not unlike that of drinking tea without spilling it on your shirt or watching ballet without falling asleep" and "while avoiding the appearance of working."

But it will take your eyes and your ears working together to find the problems in the first paragraph. The repetition of sounds in sentence 1 is awkward: *marauding, Mitzy, menace, mouse invasion in . . . house.* The repetition of *she caught a mouse* in sentences 2, 3, and 4 is monotonous. And the modifying phrase, *Happy Hunters Roach, Mouse, and Pest Exterminators* in sentence 6 is unpronounceable.

As you read aloud, follow these guidelines:

1. Read slowly.
    If you read quickly, you will tend to skip over problem spots, to concentrate on what you said rather than how you said it.
2. Read words letter by letter and syllable by syllable, being careful to pronounce what is actually on the page.
    Once you have recognized the word, avoid the temptation to get ahead of yourself and say the word without reading it. Reading letter by letter and

syllable by syllable will help you find errors such as *atmoshpere* for *atmosphere* and *studing* for *studying.*

3. Give full sound value to punctuation.

Coming to a full stop for periods and letting your voice fall, as though there were no following sentence, will help you find fragments. Pausing only briefly for commas and not at all when there is no punctuation will help you find run-ons and comma splices.

EXERCISE 9: Troubleshoot for errors by reading the following paragraph and sentences aloud. Mark the errors in the originals, then revise and make corrections.

1. The freeway during the morning rushed hour. Concrete overpasses, underpasses, thoroughways and expressways. Gray river flowing with green, red, white, black, brown, blue, and yellow metal. I join the flow. Darting between a gray semi and an orange Toyota. Wedged there, I am carried along, I cannot change lanes, I cannot move faster or slower than the stream of traffic. I escape with relief at the Irving exit.

2. Watching television is the great American pasttime, many of us watch at least two hours a day, some watch as many as six hours, some never turn the television of.

3. Everyone in town believes there is treasure buried on Thieves' Mountain. For years they have searched for it. Alone, in groups, with mapps, with only a hunch.

READING TO WRITE

Rereading some of the student writing in previous chapters will give you additional examples of effective conclusions. Bernardo's final paragraph about left-handedness (Chapter 7, page 129) makes both a judgment and a final comment. He calls discrimination against left-handed people cruel and unjust and adds information about left-brain/right-brain research to clinch his arguments. Sabrina concludes her essay "Cooking Now and Then" (Chapter 10, page 212) with a humorous comment that sums up her reaction to the recipes in her grandmother's cookbook. The student essay in Chapter 10, Exercise 22, uses a quotation that comments on the writer's envy.

Notice that a conclusion need not be long or complicated to be effective. The conclusion to Laurence Morehouse's "Fitness Is a Piece of Cake" (pages 338–44, Part II) is short and direct. He simply repeats twice the opinion he gives in the first sentence of the article: "I hate exercise."

> I repeat: I hate formalized, rigid, punitive exercise. I hate
> it all the more now that I have the science to support my
> instinctive knowledge that it simply isn't necessary.

Morehouse also gives us examples of effective sentences. His writing is strong and active, using a variety of sentence types and structures.

EXERCISE 10: Use the structures of Morehouse's sentences as models for your own sentences. Use nouns where Morehouse has used nouns, prepositional phrases where he uses prepositional phrases, clauses where he uses clauses, and so forth. You may need to analyze the structure of each sentence before you begin.

1. When the rest of the class did calisthenics with their arms, I mimicked them with my fingers.
2. I repeat: I hate formalized, rigid, punitive exercise.
3. Fitness is determined by what you do twenty-four hours a day, how you live, work, sit, walk, think, eat, and sleep.
4. We esteem those who can ride rather than walk and who can sit rather than stand.
5. The mystique fostered by the fitness cult encourages the belief that good physical condition comes slowly, that work to exhaustion is necessary, that the process requires pain.

EXERCISE 11: Use sentence combining to rewrite the following paragraph in a variety of sentence types and structures. Compare your revision with the original on page 341.

> The pulse rate is important. We all know that. You go to a
> doctor's office. You go for a checkup. There are three things. His
> nurse does these three things. She does them almost invariably.
> She takes your temperature. She weighs you. She takes your
> pulse. Have you ever spent time in a hospital? If so, you become
> aware of something. You become aware of it almost the first
> thing. People are taking your pulse. They do it all day long.
> They awaken you in the morning. They awaken you during your
> afternoon nap. They come in at night. You are just falling asleep.

It's imperative. They compare your pulse rates. They compare them during the course of your treatment.

WRITING ACTIVITY

Make planning an effective conclusion part of your prewriting. Consider how you will sum up or restate your main idea and whether you will make a final judgment, as Morehouse does, or add a final word to strengthen your position, as Bernardo does in his paper about left-handedness. Whether you outline before writing or simply write an idea "map," be sure to think through and include the major points of your conclusion in your writing plan.

ACTIVITY: Write a paper about some aspect of the physical fitness craze. You might write about some technical facet of conditioning (in which case you may need to do some more reading on the subject). You might discuss the experiences of friends who are aerobic dancers or runners or weight lifters. Or you might write about your own experiences in a physical fitness program. Whatever aspect of physical fitness you choose to write about, be careful to support your ideas with facts, examples, and details—that is, with substance rather than opinions (review pages 55–65, Chapter 4).

CHECKLIST: Check each draft of your paper carefully for the following.

1. Is the essay well developed and well organized?
2. Is the purpose clear?
3. Does the essay have an effective introduction and a clear thesis statement?
4. Does the essay have an effective conclusion?
5. Are there a variety of sentence types and structures?
6. Are there any errors in subject-verb or pronoun agreement?

7. Are there any misplaced or dangling modifiers or errors in adjective and adverb use?
8. Are there any comma splices, run-ons, or fragments?
9. Are there any errors in capitalization or apostrophe use?
10. Are there any misspelled words, left-out words, or reversed letters?

CHAPTER TWELVE
Building Bridges

Bridges for Ideas

Remember London Bridge? In childhood games it is always falling down. In history it gave monarchs and common folk alike dry passage across the Thames River. A number of years ago an enterprising American purchased the bridge and had it taken apart stone by stone and reassembled in the Mojave Desert near the Arizona-California border. Why did he do it? Perhaps he was trying to preserve a piece of history, or then again maybe he hoped it would become a tourist attraction, drawing travelers off the Interstate: "200 miles to the Grand Canyon! 100 miles to the world's largest meteor crater! 10 miles to London Bridge!" Whatever the buyer's reasons, London Bridge now sits in a tiny desert community as far in spirit as in miles from the river and city that give it meaning. It has in fact ceased to be London Bridge.

Bridges take their meaning and identity from what they connect. They may be plain or fancy. They may be covered bridges, drawbridges, suspension bridges, or stone bridges. Their importance lies primarily in what two places they connect and what or who passes over them.

In this chapter we will look at building bridges for ideas. You have already studied building bridges between sentences in a paragraph (Chapter 6: Coherence). Now you will look at building bridges between paragraphs in an essay. These bridges, called transitions, do not add to the content of your essay as an example or fact would do; instead transitions help clarify the pattern of your thoughts—the lines of the idea structure you are building—and then help hold those thoughts together. Consider the following pairs of paragraphs.

> The plateau in the San Juan Mountains was a sanctuary. Coyotes hunted desert quail in the arroyos, and pumas watched from the canyon rims for wild burros or antelope. The wildlife's peace was disturbed only by Indians searching the ruins of cliff dwellings for reminders of their ancestors or by boys from a small boarding school exploring on horseback.
> The blue mountains tower over Los Alamos, nicknamed Atomic City. Broad roads marked "Evacuation Route" cut straight across the mesa. There are gray laboratories and low buildings with "Fallout Shelter" signs prominently displayed. The canyons are fenced and posted with warnings: Danger! Radioactive!

> Once the plateau in the San Juan Mountains was a sanctuary. Coyotes hunted desert quail in the arroyos, and pumas watched from the canyon rims for wild burros or antelope. The wildlife's peace was disturbed only by Indians searching the ruins of cliff dwellings for reminders of their ancestors or by boys from a small boarding school exploring on horseback.
> Today the same blue mountains tower over Los Alamos, nicknamed Atomic City. Instead of antelope and burro trails wandering through the pinons, broad roads marked "Evacuation Route" cut straight across the mesa. Instead of cliff dwellings, silent reminders of the Anasazi, there are gray laboratories and low buildings with "Fallout Shelter" signs prominently displayed. And where the wildlife once lived in peace, the canyons are fenced and posted with warnings: Danger! Radioactive!

The descriptions in the first two paragraphs seem unrelated. Unless the readers know that Los Alamos is located in the San Juan Mountains and that it was once the site of a boys' school, they would probably think the writer is describing two different places. However, once the transitions are added, the relationship is clear. The underlined words or phrases draw the paragraphs together by establishing connections in time and in space. They change two independent statements into one statement of contrast.

FOCUS ON WRITING: *Transitions*

Transitions are not only like bridges; they are also like glue. You may build a structure of blocks, but if you do not glue it together, it will topple. The same holds true for essay writing. You build an essay of paragraphs, and if you do not glue those paragraphs together with transitions, the overall effect of the essay will be fragmented and uncertain.

> *Definition:* A transition is a verbal connection or bridge. It is a word or phrase that helps the reader see a relationship between ideas.

In an essay overall the key sentences involved in making the structure hold together as one idea are (1) the thesis statement, (2) the topic sentences of the middle or developmental paragraphs, and (3) the first sentence of the concluding paragraph. These sentences, then, are the best places to make transitions. The simplest ways to do this are by repeating words and phrases or by using transitional words and expressions.

Repetition of Words and Phrases

Drawing an important word or phrase from one sentence and repeating it in a second sentence is an effective way of "gluing" the two sentences together or bridging the gap between them.

> Human <u>selfishness</u> is seen at its worst during rush hour.
>
> The most appalling examples of <u>selfishness</u> are pedestrians.
>
> or: Human <u>selfishness</u> is seen at its worst during rush hour.
>
> The most <u>selfish</u> are the pedestrians.
>
> or: Human <u>selfishness</u> is seen at its worst during <u>rush hour</u>.
>
> One <u>rush-hour</u> menace is <u>selfish</u> pedestrians.

Often, using a pronoun to refer to a noun in the preceding sentence is just as effective as repeating the noun and much less awkward.

> Human <u>selfishness</u> is seen at <u>its</u> worst during rush hour.
>
> <u>It</u> is especially apparent among pedestrians.

In this case, we have actually two connections—one primary and one secondary. The most important is the reference of the pronoun *it* to the noun *selfishness*. But we also have a literal repetition since *its* had already been used in the first sentence to refer to *selfishness*.

EXERCISE 1:   Use repetition to write sentences that follow and make a transition from those listed. Draw lines between the connecting words as in the examples above.

1. Flying is fast, inexpensive, and relatively safe.

2. Status symbols are high on many people's wish lists.

3. Some geologists believe that Mt. Hood near Portland, Oregon, will erupt before the end of the century.

4. The Alaskan Kodiak Bear deserves its reputation for ferocity and size.

5. To commute in the Big Apple requires the strength of an elephant, the courage of a lion, and the tenacity of a bulldog.

Transitional Words and Expressions

Some words and phrases function solely as connectors or ways of making transitions between ideas. These transitional expressions have a distinct advantage over repetition since they not only connect ideas but also show the nature of the connection. For example, *and, also, in addition,* and *moreover* all add one idea to another.

The state government in California has launched an Earthquake Survival Campaign.

Moreover, Californians are now more willing to learn how to survive.

The second sentence in this pair actually uses two methods of transition. *Moreover* tells us that the people of California are adding to the efforts of their government. We also have repetitions of two key words. *California* and *survival,* two important ideas in the first sentence, are emphasized by the words *Californians* and *survive* in the second sentence.

Other transitional expressions such as *but, however,* and *on the other hand* signal contrasting ideas.

The state government in California has launched an Earthquake Survival Campaign.

However, so far Californians are refusing to learn how to survive.

The repetition in this case is the same, but the negative transitional expression and the negative verb *refuse* reverse the meaning.

Therefore, consequently, and *as a result* indicate a cause-effect relationship.

TABLE 11-1 **Transitional Words and Phrases**

Time	*Space*	*Ideas*	
after	above	*Addition:*	and; moreover; also; not only/but also;
afterward	along side		both/and; in addition; too; first, second,
at the same time	around		third, and so forth
before	behind	*Comparison:*	similarly, likewise
earlier	below	*Contrast:*	but, yet, however, on the other hand, on
first	beside		the contrary, nonetheless, in contrast,
in the meantime	between		not withstanding, although,
last	bottom		nevertheless
later	in back of	*Result:*	therefore, consequently, as a result, as
meanwhile	in front of		a consequence, thus then
next	near	*Example:*	for example, for instance, such as
now	nearby	*Conclusion*	
once	next to	*or summary*:	in short, on the whole, in brief, to sum
second	opposite to		up, in other words, as I have said,
soon	over		finally
then	top		
third and so forth	to the left		
today	to the right		
tomorrow	under		
yesterday			

I neglected to submit my income tax returns on time.
<u>Consequently</u>, I was fined by the IRS.

The second statement is a result of the first, as the transitional expression clearly points out.

Words like *then, next, first, second, third* show a sequential or time relationship.

Making a banana nut cake is easy.
<u>First</u>, collect the ingredients.

Whether you make a transition by repeating words or by using a transitional expression, the important thing to remember is to make the relationship clear and true. Nothing confuses the reader more than a false transitional clue. For example, using *however* when you mean *moreover* or using *therefore* or *and* when you mean *but* may send the reader's thoughts in the opposite direction of that intended.

I neglected to submit my income tax returns on time.
Poor: However, I was fined by the IRS.
Better: <u>Therefore</u>, I was fined by the IRS.

The use of *however* in the second sentence implies that the writer had some inside information to the effect that the returns should not be submitted on time. Now he is confused because even though he was late, he still was fined. This, of course, is absurd. Obviously the effect, being fined, was caused by the taxpayer's neglecting the deadline.

EXERCISE 2:   Use transitional words and phrases to write sentences that follow and make a transition from those listed. Underline the transitional expressions.

1. Solar panels provide an inexpensive source of energy.
2. A crystal chandelier hung from a twenty-foot ceiling.
3. The watch is on sale for $39.95.
4. An angry driver shook his fist at the jaywalker.
5. The newspaper headlined the benefit concert.

EXERCISE 3:   Find and correct errors in the choice of transitions in the following sentences.

1. Margo is a blond; on the other hand, Suzanne is a blond.

2. First, peel the apple so that the peeling makes a single corkscrew; meanwhile, slice the apple into bite-sized pieces.

3. Avocados will not be in season until January; consequently, we will buy some now.

4. Rain fell in the Rocky Mountain region today; for instance, the Great Lakes experienced blizzards and sixty-mile-per-hour winds.

5. The Abeytas are dining with us this evening; later the Nguyens had lunch with us; and earlier our other neighbors, the Jorgensons, will join us for coffee and crullers.

6. The designer jeans have a famous label on the hip pocket; similarly, the bargain brand has only wide stitches in orange thread.

7. The price, the location, and the possibilities for expansion match our company's needs; however, our consultant recommends we go ahead with the purchase.

8. The bookcase is filled with first-edition treasures. Nevertheless, I keep it locked at all times.

9. The radio contest host called to ask me the jackpot question; in addition, I was not at home.

10. Open some of Grandmother's wild plum butter; however, make sourdough biscuits to go with it.

Transitions Between First and Second Paragraphs

The first major transition in an essay will be between the first and second paragraphs. Since the thesis statement is already overloaded, the connection will have to be made by the topic sentence of the developmental paragraph. Fortunately, in this case the job is an easy one. Since a topic sentence tells the reader which aspect of the thesis will be covered in the paragraph, repetition of some words is almost automatic.

> *Thesis:* I decided going to the Mall for jeans would pick me up, but the noise, the crowds, and the outrageous prices only increased my depression.

> *Topic sentence:* As I walked through the Mall, I encountered depressing noises.

Mall is repeated literally while *noise* becomes *noises* and *depression* becomes *depressing.* In this case simply naming the topic includes transitions. Richard's essay "Crazed Drivers" gives us another good example.

> *Thesis:* There are many different kinds of crazy drivers, but I will only mention a few; there are the road-hogs, the curb-huggers, the poke-alongs, and the lane-hoppers.
>
> *Topic sentence:* Of the four kinds of drivers I've mentioned, the road-hog is second to the worst.

In this case the transition is made clearly by repetition.

EXERCISE 4: Identify and discuss the transitions between the thesis statements and topic sentences below. If the transition is inadequate, try to improve it.

1. *Thesis:* As I babysit, I begin to have doubts about myself, marriage, family life, and children.

   Topic sentence: As I look around the room, the surroundings appear warm and cozy.

2. *Thesis:* A woman would make a good President because women are strong, decisive, and patient.

   Topic sentence: A good example is ERA.

3. *Thesis:* The hair-dos I noticed at the Foxy Lady Beauty Salon were either glamorous or wash-and-wear.

   Topic Sentence: I have two friends who wear the wash-and-wear style.

4. *Thesis:* I will always remember the Talk of the Town, a restaurant in Ladonia, Texas, because of the atmosphere and the good food.

   Topic Sentence: The interior and exterior of the cafe are very old.

5.   *Thesis:* I become very depressed when I remember the
                          deaths of loved ones.
        Topic Sentence: I remember the day it happened.

Transitions Between Middle Paragraphs

Although the task of the topic sentence in the second paragraph is fairly simple, the topic sentences of the other middle paragraphs of your essay must do double duty. They must name which aspect of the thesis will be dealt with in each paragraph, and they must also make the transition from the preceding paragraph. Going again to Jeanette's essay about shopping at the Mall, we can see how one writer solves the problem.

Thesis:	I decided going to the Mall for jeans would pick me up, but the noise, the crowds, and the outrageous prices only increased my depression.
Topic Sentence Paragraph #2:	As I walked around the Mall, I encountered depressing noises.
Topic Sentence Paragraph #3:	In addition to the noises, the expressions on people's faces were unbearable.
Topis Sentence Paragraph #4:	The people were bad, but the prices were worse.

In each case Jeanette simply repeats a key word from the preceding paragraph, like *noise* and *people,* and then adds the subject for the new paragraph.

EXERCISE 5: Discuss the transitions in the essays "Against Left-handers," on pages 128–29; "Surrogate Parents," pages 132–33; and "Cooking Now and Then," pages 211–12.

EXERCISE 6: Write topic sentences that show transitions for each of the thesis statements. Follow the example on this page of the topic sentences for Jeanette's essay about shopping at the Mall.

1. Money means two things to George—freedom and status.
2. Salespeople at Mann's Department Store fall into three distinct categories—high pressure, low pressure, and no pressure.
3. You can fool some of the people all of the time, and all of the people some of the time, but you can't fool all of the people all of the time.
4. Overcoming my fear of flying has not been easy.
5. My ambition is to be a television news anchor because of the glamor of being famous, the high salaries, and my interest in journalism.

Transitions and the Conclusion

Like the topic sentence of the first developmental paragraph, the first sentence of the concluding paragraph by its very nature is transitional. If you restate the thesis totally (although in different words), you must draw ideas from every paragraph to tie them together again in this sentence. For example, Richard begins the conclusion of his essay about crazy drivers by renaming each of the types he observed.

> The road-hogs, the curb-huggers, the poke-alongs, and the lane-hoppers are all crazy drivers.

Restating only part of the thesis or simply summing up will have the same effect if done skillfully. Rizzi uses the phrase *these groups* to sum up and recall the different groups of airplane passengers he has discussed.

> Whenever I fly, I usually try to find three empty seats so I can go to sleep, but I've been in each of these groups also.

EXERCISE 7:   Write concluding sentences for each set of thesis and topic sentences in Exercise 6.

The way all of these transitions bridge the gaps between paragraphs and glue the essays can be represented by a diagram, with the addition of new paragraphs for each additional aspect of the thesis to be covered (see Figure 12–1). When the areas to be covered are named in the thesis, repetition of the areas strengthens transitions.

Transitions contribute to the sense of unity and oneness in an essay. They not only hold the essay together by clarifying or emphasizing relationships but also keep the reader on track. If your reader is constantly and persistently pointed and repointed in the direction you are going, the reader is less likely to mistake your purpose, thereby getting lost in the communication process.

EXERCISE 8:   Rewrite the following sets of paragraphs to make them fit and hold together.

> 1. The mall is empty. The shops are closed, their open fronts covered with barred gates. The sound of falling water, cascading in the fountain on the quadrangle, echoes down the deserted walkways.
>   The mall overflows with shoppers. The open fronts of the Hallmark store, the candy shop, and the jewelers merge together in the flood of moving people. On the quadrangle the fountain

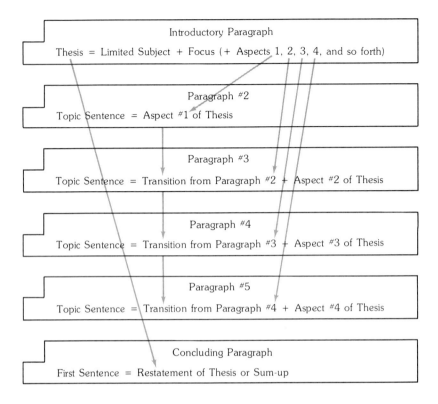

FIGURE 12-1.   Transitions in essays.

cascades and sparkles silently, its soft voice lost in the tramp of feet and the din of humanity.

2. Each December the end-of-the-year car sales pose a temptation and a dilemma. Should I keep my old car, or should I buy a new one?

My old car still runs well. Its engine purrs on the road, skimming over the miles in July heat and January cold without a complaint. It is paid for.

The new cars look better. They have no scratches or tiny dents. There are no stains on the seat covers, and the clocks still work. If I buy now, I do not have to make any payments until February.

What should I do?

FOCUS ON THE SENTENCE: *Meaningful Mechanics II*

Transitions are needed to hold essays together and to show relationships among ideas. Punctuation serves the same functions within a sentence, showing the direction of your thoughts and focusing the readers' attention on key elements.

Punctuating a Series, List, or Compound

You discovered on page 220 that a series is three or more words, phrases, or clauses that serve the same function in a sentence—subjects, verbs, modifiers, and so forth. Putting commas between the parts of a series shows that each part is equal but separate.

Pine needles, mint leaves, and birch bark make nourishing teas. (subjects)
The arrow shot through the knothole, through the curtain, and into his shoulder. (prepositional phrases)
If we cut down on expenses, if we hold back on buying a new car, and if we both take extra jobs, we can afford a Hawaiian vacation this summer. (dependent clauses)

Occasionally, you might write a series in which one or more of the parts is already punctuated with commas.

For our picnic Jeanette brought a chocolate cake, which had fallen in the middle, barbecued chicken, which had been burned and then soaked in sauce to disguise the taste, and a lettuce salad, in which the lettuce was brown and wilted.

The parts of the series are *chocolate cake, barbecued chicken,* and *lettuce salad.* However, each part is followed by a modifier that is set off by commas. Using additional commas to separate the parts of the series would be confusing, making it appear that there are six rather than three parts. We need a stronger punctuation mark to separate the parts and their interrupting modifiers from each other. Semicolons eliminate the confusion and mark the divisions clearly.

For our picnic Jeanette brought a chocolate cake, which had fallen in the middle; barbecued chicken, which had been burned and then soaked in sauce to disguise the taste; and lettuce salad, in which the lettuce was brown and wilted.

EXERCISE 9: Combine the following sets of sentences to make one, correctly punctuated sentence that includes a series.

1. Samson broke his eyeglasses on the trampoline. Laurie broke her eyeglasses on the trampoline. Gil broke his eyeglasses on the trampoline. Hannah broke her eyeglasses on the trampoline.

2. The guest list includes Robert. I do not like him. The guest list includes Phyllis. I do like her. The guest list includes the Rupperts. I do not know them.
3. On Sunday I like to relax. First, I must attend church. Then I always eat a huge meal. Then I work off the calories with a run around the park.
4. My golf game is off. I may take up needlepoint. I may become a gourmet cook. I may stay home. I may play solitaire.
5. The bells rang. The people shouted. The revolution had begun.

When a long list or series comes after or before a sentence, you will need two types of punctuation—one to separate the items in the series and one to set the list off from the rest of the sentence.

> For the real estate seminar, please bring the following materials: two pens, a note pad, a clipboard, and the classified section of a daily newspaper.

> To make a devil's food cake, you will need these ingredients: 1¼ cups of flour, sifted twice; 1 cup of sour milk, curdled and thick; 1 teaspoon of soda, dissolved in the milk; a pinch of salt; 1 cup of white sugar; ½ cup of shortening (not the butter-flavored variety); 4 tablespoons of nonsweetened cocoa; and 1 egg, to be beaten in last.

In both examples the colon points toward the list, setting it off and preparing the reader for what follows. The first list is a simple series of items, so commas are all we need to divide the parts. But the second list is much more complicated with several of the items followed by interrupting modifiers; the stronger semicolons are needed to separate the items.

When a list comes before a subject, we also must set it off.

> Circle K, Safeway, the Motor Vehicle Department, the City Parks and Recreation Center—all have allowed us to put up posters and leave brochures.

In this case a dash (—) sets off the list and draws attention to the subject, *all.*

EXERCISE 10: Write sentences modelled on the examples above.

1. A sentence in which you use a colon to set off a list and commas to separate the items

2. A sentence in which you use a colon to set off a list and semicolons to separate the items
3. A sentence in which you use a dash to set off an introductory list and commas to separate the items

Most compounds with only two parts do not require any punctuation.

<u>Waltzing and tap dancing</u> are becoming lost arts. (compound subjects)
The chairperson <u>hammered on the table and broke his gavel.</u> (compound verbs and predicate words)
<u>Into the kitchen and around the table</u> scrambled the puppy. (compound prepositional phrases)

However, there are two exceptions.

1. A comma is used before the conjunction in a compound sentence.
   The sun is shining downtown, yet it is snowing in the Northeast Heights.
   I must finish planting my herb garden, or there will be no mint for our iced tea this summer.
2. When there is no conjunction, a comma separates two adjectives that describe or modify the same word.
   The antique, mahogany table sold for $650. (adjectives modifying *table*)
   The captain ordered the angry, embarrassed steward from the cabin. (adjectives modifying *steward*)

Be careful, though, to use the comma only when the adjectives could be joined by *and* or could be reversed. If they cannot, they probably do not modify the same word in the same way.

The mahogany coffee table sold for $650.
The old merry-go-round horses have become antiques.

You cannot insert *and* between *mahogany* and *coffee* or between *old* and *merry-go-round*. Nor can the order of the adjectives be reversed. Therefore, no commas are needed.

EXERCISE 11: Insert commas, dashes, colons, and semicolons as needed in the following sentences.

1. Lizanne Carlos and Massi all three will be jumping during the big Fourth of July skydiving exhibition.

2. Kate and Lee crept cautiously through the old battered door.

3. You have a choice of four costumes for Friday's masquerade the goblin outfit which has horns and a pointed tail the exotic skimpy harem girl costume the Supergirl suit or a fake leopard skin and tights which are supposed to make you look like a female Tarzan.

4. The mail carrier climbed into his boat and tied down the mailbags for the trip upstream.

5. The telephone rang and I nearly forgot my grocery list.

6. I plan to make several substitutions in the devil's food cake recipe brown sugar for white carob for cocoa and whole wheat for white flour.

7. Skiing snowshoeing backpacking playing tennis horseback riding these are all winter sports in high desert country.

Punctuating Interruptions

Earlier in this chapter you practiced writing sentences that are interrupted by transitional words or expressions or by groups of words that describe or modify. Interruptions may be set off within a sentence with commas, parentheses, or dashes.

Setting off a word or word group with commas means it interrupts the sentence and is not essential to the meaning. Transitions, verbal phrases, some noun phrases, and dependent clauses are often set off with commas.

This hair dryer cost $21.95. (no interruptions)
This hair dryer moreover cost $21.95. (interrupted by transition word)
This hair dryer on the other hand cost $21.95. (interrupted by transitional phrase)
This hair dryer blistering my head cost $21.95. (interrupted by verbal phrase)
This hair dryer the top of the line model cost $21.95. (interrupted by noun phrase)
This hair dryer which is blistering my head cost $21.95. (interrupted by dependent clause)

Sometimes modifiers are essential to meaning. When a word or a group of words is needed to identify a noun or pronoun—when it tells specifically which one we are talking about—no commas are needed.

The book *Crime and Punishment* is too long to be read in one
night. (tells which book specifically)
The car crashing into your fence is mine. (tells which car
specifically)
The doctor that you recommended is a quack. (tells which doctor
specifically)

Using parentheses is like whispering. Parentheses de-emphasize an
interruption. Minor notes, lists, statements, or questions that interrupt a
sentence may be set off with parentheses.

Cornflowers (called bachelor buttons in the Northwest) are
growing wild in the field beside my house.
I brought my tools (hammer, level, saw, and so forth) to work on
your cabinet.
Fourth of July Canyon in October (did you see it?) rivals
fireworks for color.

On the other hand, using dashes is like shouting. Setting off an interruption with dashes emphasizes it.

My winnings—a Hawaiian cruise, a television, and a Transam—
total $41,000.
I won—can you believe it?—$41,000 on *The Wheel of Fortune.*

EXERCISE 12: Add commas to show interrupters or delete them for essential modifiers in the following sentences.

1. The one, who finishes first, will receive a bonus.

2. Angela who wrote from Los Angeles says she has received a
    promotion.

3. *The Journal* a paper that emphasizes investigative reporting has
    been sued by a politician who was featured in an exposé article.

4. The author, Tony Hillerman, created my favorite mystery-novel
    cops.

5. Sergeant Jim Chee and Lieutenant Joe Leaphorn officers with
    the Navajo Tribal Police patrol a district that extends for
    hundreds of miles.

EXERCISE 13: Add commas, parentheses, or dashes to set off interruptions in the following paragraphs.

1. My three-speed bicycle which I have had for fifteen years cost me $95 in 1977. Newer models the ten-speed bikes with hand brakes and plenty of chrome look better and promise more, but can they really I mean *really* do more for me personally? My bike still takes me where I want to go up the street, down the street, to the market, and to the park without the brakes' locking or the wheels' falling off. If a new bike moreover could serve me better and I have my doubts what would it cost me? Will I be paying an arm and a leg $200, $300, $500 and still have a vehicle that does essentially the same things as my old bike?

2. Cynthia Adopolis our next door neighbor is having a garage sale. The oak end tables that I have been coveting for years will go for $20 each, and she is getting rid of her son Phillip's comic book collection. Some old favorites I had a sneak preview will go for no more than a dollar each. We could fill in the gaps in our collection the *Superman* anniversary issue, *Jungle Girl and the City of Gold,* and *Huey, Dewey, and Louie find Atlantis,* and in addition we will be helping out a friend.

Punctuating Introductions

A comma or a dash after an introductory word or group of words tells the reader two things: (1) the introduction is over and (2) get ready for the main idea of the sentence. A comma is used after introductory conversational words, transitions, verbal phrases, long prepositional phrases, and dependent clauses.

Yes, I am travelling by Amtrak. (conversation word)
Consequently, it will take me two days to arrive. (transition)
Traveling by train, I have time to prepare my speech. (verbal phrase)
On a narrow trestle high over a canyon, the train stopped. (long prepositional phrase)

If I had known about the danger of train robbers, I would not
have worn my gold Rolex watch. (dependent clause)

As you saw earlier, on page 268, a dash is used when a list of items,
summed up in the subject, introduces a sentence.

Rings, wallets, watches, briefcases—all were dumped in a sack
by the bandits.
Minette, Tinker Toy, Allegretto—these are the names of three
beautiful, arrogant cats.

EXERCISE 14: Add punctuation as appropriate after introductory words
phrases, or clauses in the following paragraphs.

1. If I send in the coupon that came in today's mail I will get a
free ten-day trial of an automatic juicer. However do I need an
automatic juicer? True I drink juice. Orange juice, carrot juice,
tomato juice these are some of my favorite drinks. But I usually
buy my juice in a can. Considering the cost of the juicer and the
high prices of vegetables and fruits I wonder whether I would be
saving money if I made my own juice.

2. As I see it our company has several options. First we can try to
compete with the giant toy companies like Mattel and Hasbros.
Second we can appeal to a specialty toy market like children who
play educational games. Or third we can get out of the toy
business altogether. If we decide to compete we will need to
come up with a dynamite idea. Gobots, Transformers, Cabbage
Patch Dolls, Trivial Pursuit all are making millions for their
companies. Unfortunately someone else thought of them first.

The Meaning of Quotation Marks

The most important meaning of quotation marks is explained by their
name: quotation marks punctuate quotations. They show where someone's words begin and where they end.

The superintendent said, "Your bonus checks will be at the pay
window by quitting time."
Martin Luther King said: "I have a dream."

Often you will introduce a quotation with a tag phrase that identifies the speaker. When the quotation is informal (the words of a friend or acquaintance), the tag will be set off with a comma. When the quotation is formal (famous words, for example), the tag will be set off with a colon.

A second meaning of quotation marks is unrelated to their name. Quotation marks are used to indicate the titles of short written works: poems, songs, magazine articles, short stories, chapters of books.

> Please explain to me Lewis Carroll's poem "Jabberwocky."
>
> Songs popular in the fifties, like "Catch a Falling Star," are becoming popular again.
>
> Terry has written a magazine article entitled "How to Lose Weight Without Losing Your Mind."
>
> Mark Twain's short story "The Corruption of Hadleyburg" has been filmed.
>
> The Andromeda Nebula are discussed in Chapter 6, "Other Galaxies," of Asimov's book.

The Meaning of Italics or Underlining

Underlining in handwritten or typewritten papers indicates italic type in print. Underlining or italics are used to indicate the titles of longer published works: books, magazines, newspapers, plays.

> <u>Profiles in Courage</u> is a Pulitzer-Prize-winning book by John F. Kennedy.

> The story, with a full spread of photographs, was featured in <u>Newsweek.</u>

Profiles in Courage is a Pulitzer-Prize-winning book by John F. Kennedy.

The story, with a full spread of photographs, was featured in *Newsweek*.

> Most libraries subscribe to the <u>Wall Street Journal</u>.

> According to legend, the cast of any performance of Shakespeare's <u>Macbeth</u> will be plagued by mysterious accidents.

Most libraries subscribe to the *Wall Street Journal.*
According to legend, the cast of any performance of
Shakespeare's *Macbeth* will be plagued by mysterious accidents.

Underlining or italics also help set off a word or a phrase for discussion of its spelling, meaning, or use in a sentence.

I may have used *eminent* when I meant *imminent.*
There are too many *and*'s in this sentence.

EXERCISE 15: Add quotation marks and underlining (to indicate italics) as needed in the paragraphs below.

1. As part of Reading Week, the public library will be having an after-school story hour. We will read to the children as a way to motivate them to read on their own, says Librarian Gini Tafoya. Ms. Tafoya will be reading Through the Looking Glass, the favorite children's book by Lewis Carroll, and folk-tales, such as Davy Crockett Meets Mike Fink and Paul Bunyan Finds Babe.

2. The proofreader on The Daily Lobo needs to read more carefully and to use a dictionary. In just one story, Students Speak Out on Star Wars, I found five typographical errors. Separate was printed separaet; economy, ecoonemy; and, nd; and believable, believible. President Kennedy's famous statement about service to one's country was misquoted: Ask what your country can do for you, not what you can do for your country.

The Meaning of Hyphens

Hyphens show connections. When hyphens connect words or parts of words, they show that one idea is meant. Hyphens are used with numbers from twenty-one to ninety-nine.

Next week our classic Chevrolet convertible will be thirty-one years old, twenty-two years older than our son.

Hyphens also join words that come before a noun and serve as a single adjective.

I am having a birthday party for my thirty-one-year-old car.
The sun-loving Californians had reddish-brown tans and surf-
and-ski wardrobes.

Your dictionary will show you when a hyphen should be used to connect various prefixes and suffixes to a word.

Around mid-June the scent of orange blossoms fills the air.
The treasurer-elect of the Racket Club has resigned before
officially taking office.

And hyphens are used to divide words at the end of a written or
printed line to show that the word is not complete and there is more to
come. Follow these guidelines when you must divide words.

1. Do not divide unless you must.
2. Divide only between syllables as marked in your dictionary:
    pop-u-lar, min-i-ster
3. Do not leave two letters on the first line or carry over one letter
    to the second line.
4. Divide at the hyphen for words that already contain hyphens,
    and divide between most double consonants: self-help, wrap-ping.

EXERCISE 16: Add hyphens as needed in the following sentences.

1. The red faced defendant became confused in the court room and
    pleaded the twenty fifth amendment instead of the fifth.
2. First, the diners ordered a steak and lobster entrée with side
    orders of hush puppies and smoked salmon. Then they called
    for a round of Hawaiian fruit cocktails and not too sweet pine
    apple drinks for dessert.
3. The accident occurred at First and Forty Second. The vehicle at
    fault—a blue and brown, four door coup—attempted to leave the
    scene but was stopped by a blast from the second driver's two
    barrel shotgun.
4. My super expensive, unlisted phone number was discovered
    today by a matter of fact computer with a voice like my ex
    wife's.
5. Our Weight Watchers group fell off the chuck wagon at
    Christmas. Our calorie counting graphs went off the charts, and
    our tapes are measuring at least an inch more than they were
    before our hardtack and cottage cheese diets gave way to tur
    key and dressing feasts.

Other Uses of the Colon

In addition to setting off long lists and formal quotations, the colon is used in a number of conventional ways:

1. To divide minutes from hours:
   8:15 A.M., 9:00 P.M.
2. To divide chapter and verse in Bible quotations:
   Romans 8:28, John 3:16
3. To divide titles and subtitles:
   The Whitmans: Missionaries and Pioneers, New York: The Big Apple

Other Uses of the Comma

Like the colon, the comma has several conventional uses:

1. To divide items in a date or address book from each other and to set off the final item from the rest of the sentence:
   The party left on Monday, May 2, 1988, to climb Mt. Everest.
   The space explorer gave his address as 11615 Asteroid Belt, Solar System, Milky Way, but he gets his mail at 1516 Avenida Del Sol, Albuquerque, New Mexico 87108.
2. To divide large numbers into groups of three digits:
   1,016,933   42,111   1,969   5,000,165,933
3. To show that a word has been left out:
   I ordered a guacamole salad; he, a sirloin steak.

EXERCISE 17: Add colons and commas as needed in the following sentences.

1. The first speaker quoted Psalm 231-2; the second Shakespeare's sonnets.

2. The terrorist mailed the package bomb set to go off at 1215 A.M. to 916 St. Joseph's Place NW De Paul Wisconsin.

3. Sandra's new thriller *The Case of the Lost Diamonds A Sherlock Jones Mystery* has already sold 1342914 copies.

4. The time was 436 A.M.; the date Friday April 13 1986; the place a mountaintop overlooking Los Alamos New Mexico site of a top-secret laser experiment.

5. I read in *Bird Digest A Guide to North-American Birds* that 15623 geese were banded in 1985 compared to 3114 in 1984.

TROUBLESHOOTING: *Asking "Why?"*

Looking for punctuation errors requires a practiced eye and continually repeating the question: Why? Why do I need punctuation here? Why did I use this punctuation mark? Why did I use it in this way? To help you focus on one sentence at a time, remember the technique of reading your essay backward, starting with the last sentence. When you read this way, you are less likely to get involved in content and forget about punctuation.
Consider the sentence:

Every Tomasina, Denise, and Harriet, everyone in town knows the importance of today's special election.

To correct punctuation in the sentence, you must first ask yourself about the nature and the purpose of *every Tomasina, Denise, and Harriet*. Is it the subject of the sentence or is it an introductory list? What is the subject? How can the list be set off from the subject? How should the items in the list be set off from the subject? Are the commas used sufficient, or do we need semicolons?

Every Tomasina, Denise, and Harriet—everyone in town knows the importance of today's special election.

Changing the comma before *everyone* to a dash shows that the list precedes the subject *everyone*. The commas in the list need no changes because the items are simple and can be clearly understood without stronger punctuation.
Deciding whether a word or a group of words is essential to meaning or interrupts a sentence and should be set off with commas creates problems for many writers. Again, asking questions will help you understand the function of the words.

The magazine *Parade* comes with the Sunday paper.

Is the word *Parade* essential or is it not essential to the meaning of the sentence? To find out, try reading the sentence with the word left out.

The magazine comes with the Sunday paper.

We are left with the question, "Which magazine?" Therefore, the word *Parade* is essential and does not interrupt the sentence. No commas are needed to set it off.

Georgina Arms, who has written ten novels, will speak at the seminar.

Georgina Arms will speak at the seminar.

Is the "who" clause essential or nonessential to the meaning of the sentence? In the second example we have left it out without obscuring the identity of the subject; therefore, the clause is an interrupter and should be set off with commas.

EXERCISE 18: Be a peer critic for the following student essay. Evaluate the essay for structure, support, transitions between paragraphs, and coherence within paragraphs. Then troubleshoot for errors in spelling, punctuation, capitalization, sentence structure, and grammar.

I nominate superman for president. Im sure that Clark Kent wouldnt mind giving up his job at the daily planet, for some real action. I doubt if Perry White his boss would object either especially because Clark is never around when he is needed. Im sure Lois Lane would miss him, because I think she has an inkling to who he is. As for Jimmy Olson I don't think he would care who was leaving the office, just so he could be the hero. All in all I think that they would agree with my choice. Everyone knows superman for his honesty, his fight for justice; and his living the american way.

Honesty is a good quality for the president of the United States, he would keep the government which is known for corruption free of disloyalty. Otherwise he'd have someone hanging on a hook. We could even have a new emblem for the United States the S that stands for honesty. The only thing wrong is, I dont know how people would deal with too much honesty. I think it would be hard at first but I think they would get used to it. I dont think superman would let too much get by, because he can use his xray vision and his extra-sensitive ears to detect dishonesty. We would save alot of fuel. Instead of hiring the presidential plane. He could just fly from once city to another.

The criminals would know that his fight for justice is neverending, and that sooner or later they would be caught. The russians would be afraid to attack us, for fear that superman would intecept their missles; He would throw them out into the universe, or would melt them into flowing ore, with the x ray molecules streaming from his eyes. Crime would cease to be. As for the middle eastern crisis he owuld fly over there pick up each one of the hostages, and move them to a safe place, before the terrorists ever knew what hit them.

Im convinced that, jsut because Clark Kent Superman became president, that he would not change his way of being kind to old ladies and animals. I doubt that he would get a <u>big head</u>. There wouldnt be any conflict of a first lady telling the president what to do, unless he decided to make Lois Lane who is his sweetheart his bride. He would also be a good representative to other planets such as Krypton the planet he came from.

These are my reasons for nominating my hero, superman, for the president of the United States of America.

READING TO WRITE

The development of Francine Patterson's "Conversations with a Gorilla" on page 344 differs from that of many of the selections in the Readings section. Dr. Patterson uses narrative or story-like description and dialogue. As you read, consider how this narrative development increases or decreases the chances of our accepting the article's main idea: that Koko the gorilla "talks." Consider also how the narratives reinforce Dr. Patterson's statement that Koko "has become a dear friend."

Indented dialogue, you will notice, is particularly effective for connecting ideas. The order and the punctuation organize what was said, and each item is connected clearly as a response to the preceding comment or question.

EXERCISE 19:   Use these sentences from Dr. Patterson's article as models for your own sentences. Follow the model of both the sentence structure and the punctuation.

1. I've come to cherish her lies, relish her arguments, and look forward to her insults.
2. Quickly sizing me up, the tiny 20-pound gorilla bit me on the leg.
3. Finally, I would estimate that Koko's current working vocabulary—signs she uses regularly and appropriately—stands at about 375.
4. Now the godmother of two gorillas, I weigh my responsibilities to this threatened species.
5. Manipulating hands and fingers, Cathy had asked Koko, "What's this?"

WRITING ACTIVITY

As you write, you will use many transitions naturally and automatically. However, once you have completed a draft, look at each paragraph and sentence to see how you can improve the transitions you have made or add transitions where there is a gap. To test the transitions between paragraphs, you may find it helpful to make a diagram of key sentences like the one on page 266.

ACTIVITY: Write an essay about an abstract concept. You may use personal as well as objective examples and observations to support your ideas. Pay special attention to transitions, both within and between paragraphs. Choose one of the topics below or a topic of your own.

1. Friendship
2. Animal intelligence
3. Honesty
4. Human (or animal) rights
5. Happiness

CHECKLIST: Check each draft of your paper carefully for the following:

1. Is the essay well developed and well organized?
2. Are transitions clear and effective?
3. Does the essay have a clear purpose and an effective introduction and thesis?
4. Does the essay have an effective conclusion?
5. Are there a variety of sentence types and structures?
6. Are there any errors in subject-verb or pronoun agreement?
7. Are there any misplaced or dangling modifiers or errors in adjective and adverb use?
8. Are there any errors in capitalization or punctuation—including comma splices, run-ons, or fragments?
9. Are there any misspelled words, left-out words, or reversed letters?

SKILLS IN ACTION TEST #1

Sentence Completeness: Fragments, Run-ons, Comma Splices

A. Identify fragments (F), run-ons (RO), and comma splices (CS) in the spaces at the left. Label correct sentences *C.*

_____ 1. In the box office overflowing with hysterical fans, eager to see the Rockets in their final performance.

_____ 2. Down the mountain pass, skimming the treetops, came the missing Cessna.

_____ 3. It's broken.

_____ 4. The pilot saw the missing the hiker, the girl waved happily up at him.

_____ 5. Robbery because of the price of modern living.

_____ 6. When Robert found the pre-Columbian artifact, the expedition knew that the lost city was nearby.

_____ 7. Romance novels provide quick escape they often feature exotic remote places with heroines who live glamorous lives.

_____ 8. Running through the fields, scrambling over fences to catch the escaping mare.

_____ 9. *Crazy Like a Fox* will be on cable soon, then we can eat our TV-dinners.

_____ 10. If the producers would only show more shots of beautiful Golden Gate Bridge.

B. Circle the number of any fragments, run-ons, or comma splices in the following paragraph. Add or change punctuation or words, as necessary, to correct the errors.

[1]Before the game had even begun. [2]The home team was at a disadvantage. [3]Bookies all over town were refusing bets. [4]Knowing that the odds were a hundred to one against the unranked Lobos' beating the number three team in the nation. [5]The players were tense as they put the ball into play, they knew the defeatist attitude of the crowd and shared it. [6]Jones passed to Brown, and the basketball seemed to spin away on its own. [7]A turn-over in the first minute of play. [8]The opponents' fans

cheered. [9]And booed at the embarrassed Lobos. [10]"Get a football," they cried derisively, "Wipe the butter off your fingers." [11]The Coach growled at the crowd then he growled at his players. [12]The embarrassing moment stretching to an eternity as the visitors pounded down the court and dunked an easy basket. [13]Making the score two to none, visitors. [14]Then the Lobos woke up. [15]Willis put the ball back in play, Rhodes danced down the court with it. [16]Next a lay-up, executed so quickly that the visitors could only stare. [17]And the score was even. [18]Back and forth the game went in the first half. [19]The Lobos pressing every minute and the visitors becoming rattled. [20]Finally, with thirty seconds left to play, the score was still even, however, the two teams were exhausted. [21]Both coaches had played their top players relentlessly, both coaches had three players in danger of fouling out. [22]Desperate, the visitors tried a long shot. [23]The ball arched gracefully over the court, it hit the rim of the basket, rolled around the edge, and bounced out again. [24]The game went into overtime.

Scoring: Deduct 4 points for errors in Part A and 2 points for each error in correcting or identifying in Part B.

SKILLS IN ACTION TEST #2

Verbs/Subjects

A. Identify subjects and verbs in the following sentences by circling the subjects and underlining the verbs.

1. An angry tiger bounded over the fence and into my neighbor's backyard.
2. The smells of perfume, hairspray, and shampoo assaulted our noses as we walked into the beauty parlor.
3. The calendar has been turned to October for three months now.
4. Are you ever going to change it?
5. The month of October features a black cat in a witch's hat and a dog with a sheet over its head.
6. Both the black cat and the ghostly dog have been staring at me day after day when I visit you in your office.
7. A helicopter with the number XJ-41000 on its side buzzed my house and landed on top of my garage.
8. We could have experienced a disaster if someone with a match had been close to the leaky gas pipe and ignited the gas.

B. Identify subjects and verbs in the following paragraph by circling the subjects and underlining the verbs. (The sentences are numbered for easy reference.)

[1]I was shopping at the Coronado Mall when the twister struck. [2]It bounced across San Pedro and ripped up trees and tore off the roof of an apartment building as it came. [3]The funnel was long and dark. [4]It writhed like an ugly, gray snake. [5]At the large plate windows of the Broadway, I watched in awe. [6]I did not realize that I should move away from the window, and, therefore, when the glass was shattered, I was taken completely by surprise and received several cuts.

Scoring: Deduct 2 points for each error in identifying subjects and verbs.

SKILLS IN ACTION TEST #3

Subject/Verb Agreement

A. Find and correct any errors in agreement of subjects and verbs in the following sentences. Mark any sentence that is correct *C.*

1. A flock of crows have landed in my backyard and are scaring away the birds from my feeders.

2. Everyone of us who came today wish that Omero had stayed home.

3. *The Dawn and the Deer,* one of Yazz's latest paintings, are done in pastel tones on a gray background.

4. There is undoubtedly several ways to set up your letter.

5. Neither the roses nor the spring bouquet were fresh.

6. Neither the spring bouquet nor the roses were fresh.

7. A tuba player as well as sixteen majorettes and ten trombone players is marching in the parade.

8. The problems of financing the new credit union building is the first item on tonight's agenda.

9. Rodriguez in addition to Nguyen, Johnson, and Mohdavi are competing in the billiards tournament.

10. Playing Trivial Pursuit and listening to Mozart on the stereo is my favorite way to spend a quiet evening at home.

B. Circle the number of any sentence in which there is a problem with subject-verb agreement; then correct the error.

[1]Reading romance novels are epidemic in the United States and Canada. [2]Housewives, career women, schoolgirls, grandmothers—each have added to the increasing sales across the counter and through the mail. [3]"Social problems is my daily diet," said one research sociologist; "when I want to relax, I

prefer fantasy to socially significant themes." [4]There has, of course, been romantic novels as long as there has been novels. [5]In the early part of the last century, *romance* and *novel* was nearly synonymous. [6]"A novel by a lady, for the discriminating feminine reader" were often written on the title page—a guarantee that there was a hero and a heroine and ample romantic scenes inside the covers. [7]The Regency romance—still popular today in the works of Georgette Heyer, Joan Smith, Clare Darcy, and others—probably owe much of its substance and some of its style to one of those ladies who wrote anonymously. [8]Jane Austen's witty tales of grand country houses, great fortunes, and Cinderella-style marriages set the pattern for books still being written in the 1980's. [9]Her intelligent heroine and arrogant hero—like Elizabeth and Darcy in *Pride and Prejudice*—is echoed in the characters of literally hundreds of books. [10]Neither the romance writers nor the romance reader seem to mind that the story has been told before. [11]In fact, assuring the reader that a tale is like *Pride and Prejudice* and promising that the writing is in the manner of Georgette Heyer is a sure way to increase sales. [12]There are no other area of publishing, including science fiction, that have such a loyal following of readers. [13]A true romance fan—the buyer of Harlequins and Silhouettes as well as Regencies—read two or three novels in a sitting and buy ten to twelve novels at a time. [14]A few are closet readers, keeping a copy of *Moby Dick* close by to pick up in case someone should catch them reading, but everyone of them are dedicated readers—"romance novel junkies," as one female critic put it. [15]Her favorite novels, by the way, are the Regencies.

Scoring: Deduct 4 points for each error in Part A and 2 points for each error in identifying or correcting problems in Part B.

SKILLS IN ACTION TEST #4

Pronoun Agreement

A. Find and correct any errors in agreement of pronouns and the words they refer to. Mark any sentence that is correct *C*.

1. None of the players has broken their training by partying before the game.

2. When the Public Service Company announced the increase, they neglected to say that it had not been approved by the Commission.

3. Either the senator or one of her aides is bringing their briefcase-sized PC to the meeting.

4. There is a large Canadian gander making her nest in my chicken coop.

5. I began my presentation by explaining how you analyze the audiences of business communications.

6. The television broadcaster was only one of those donating his time to the Special Olympics.

7. One's first formal charity ball is not the time to wear your new shoes with the squeaky soles.

8. Tweedle-dee along with Tweedle-dum and the Chesire Cat made their big film debut in Disney's *Alice in Wonderland*.

9. Bread-and-butter flies and dog-and-caterpillars lived their lives in a garden of talking flowers in the same film.

10. Roberto and Monica of Chez Roma will be hosting the *Good Eating* show on PBS this afternoon to share their insights about healthy eating habits.

B. Circle the number of any sentence in which there is a problem with agreement; then correct the error.

[1]The pilot of a two-seat aircraft radioed her position at one o'clock. [2]They were over the Malpais and experiencing some turbulence. [3]At 1:05 his voice was picked up again, faint and distant. [4]"My passenger has bailed out," air traffic controllers picked up the transmission. "We'll try to land her alone." [5]Then the blip left the screen. [6]Finding a small plane in the Malpais, an area of lava beds mixed with canyons, is something like finding your grain of white sand in a salt shaker. [7]But minutes after the plane was reported down, our Civil Air Patrol was in the air. [8]They spotted a parachute in a canyon, but there was no sign of the passenger. [9]Oddly a final radio transmission was picked up from the pilot. [10]She gave their coordinates, but the signal was too faint. [11]The searchers continued to fly in grid patterns until darkness halted your search. [12]Each of the Patrol pilots was haunted by the knowledge that they could be the ones in distress. [13]But in spite of days of diligent searching, neither the pilot nor his passenger was found.

Scoring: Deduct 4 points for each error in Part A and 3 points for each error in identifying and correcting agreement problems in Part B.

SKILLS IN ACTION TEST #5

Verbs

A. Find and correct errors in verb form or tense in the following sentences.

1. The runner has broke the track record for the mile.

2. Tomorrow the workmen had wallpapered the kitchen and tiled the bathroom.

3. After Rupert broke the mirror, his luck will be bad for seven years.

4. Unfortunately, Rupert breaks two mirrors, which has been resulting in fourteen years of bad luck.

5. The balloon bursted, spraying red paint over the singer's white ball gown.

6. The singer sung two medleys in spite of the booing audience and then rung a bell to announce the next act.

7. The roads had been slick as we are driving through the Siskiyou Mountain pass.

B. Circle the number before sentences in which there is an error in verb form or tense. Then correct the errors.

¹The hikers sat out at dawn to follow the La Luz Trail to the summit. ²There will be four in the party. ³The leader is a veteran hiker and bird watcher who is making the trip to look for raptors. ⁴The other three hikers were students in a wilderness survival class. ⁵At the start the leader lay down the rules: no smoking, no loitering, and no detours. ⁶He don't say whether he will allow brief rests.

⁷They are half way up the mountain, and the sun was half

way to its zenith when one of the hikers notices that he had forgot his canteen. [8]He seed what he thought was a shortcut and starts back to get the canteen. [9]That shortcut begun two days of wandering, lost on the mountainside.

Scoring: Deduct 4 points for each error in Part A and 3 points for each error in identifying sentences with problems or in correcting those problems.

SKILLS IN ACTION TEST #6

Dangling and Misplaced Modifiers

A. Identify sentences with dangling or misplaced modifiers and rewrite to correct the errors. Mark correct sentences *C.*

1. While brushing his teeth, George's house was robbed.

2. The Senator postponed the speech which he was to have given tonight for a week.

3. I saw a beautiful red-leafed maple walking down Rio Communities Boulevard.

4. Watching the peaceful scene from outside the bowl, the goldfish seemed perfectly happy in its water world.

5. To buy the new car, I sold my coin collection and mortgaged my house.

6. Between the covers of *Moby Dick,* I began to understand the sea-goer's fascination with whales.

7. With my golf club in hand, the day looked and felt like singing.

8. The dog was chased up the tree with the black and white spotted coat by a mean-looking cat.

9. Besides the problem of producing a show, finding a sponsor can be a problem for a production company.

10. The next morning, dizzy from lack of sleep, the computer would not do anything right.

B. Circle the number before any sentence with a dangling or a misplaced modifier; then correct the error.

[1]Stammering excuses, the dawn-to-dusk radio station came on the air an hour after sunrise. [2]"This is Randall in the Round, bidding a late but hearty good morning to you in the studios of KARS," the disc jockey rattled into the microphone trying at the same time to select records and rewind tapes. [3]Driving in to work on the freeway, his car had been stopped at a highway patrol roadblock. [4]The officers were checking on motorists' compliance with the new buckle-up seat belt law with every intention of giving out tickets. [5]Randall, who had been caught trying to pull the belt quickly around himself, had tried to protest. [6]"Knowing the law has only been in effect since midnight, shouldn't this time be just a warning?" [7]But the officers had refused to listen, anxious to fill up their ticket

Name _____

books. [8]"That will be fifty dollars by the driver for violation of the seat-belt law and fifty dollars by the passenger," the officer had said. [9]Angry at the officer and at himself, the speed limit had then been exceeded by Randall. [10]Another ticket—this time for speeding—came next without protesting. [11]"After two tickets in one hour, a lesson is learned. Buckle up, and drive the speed limit," Randall told his audience.

Scoring: Deduct 4 points for errors in Part A and 3 points for errors in identifying or in correcting problems in Part B.

SKILLS IN ACTION TEST #7

Apostrophes

A. Find and correct errors in apostrophe usage in the sentences. Mark any sentence without errors *C*.

1. The womens softball team beat the mens during an after-work match.

2. There are three Robert's and two Marian's in this office.

3. It's canvas filled with a Pacific breeze, the clipper ship sailed through San Franciscos Golden Gates.

4. Although the players behind, shes still in the running for the grand prize.

5. They're defiance of the law will cease when they're arraigned by the judge.

6. The poet used &s instead of *and*s, which was a daring thing to do in the 20s.

7. Rupert and Greg's office's are at opposite ends' of the building.

8. Isnt the sunset a vivid blaze of color through you're window?

9. It's been a long day of answering your phones, typing your letters, and trying to finish making entries in your books.

10. The editor-in-chiefs' comments' were bluepenciled all over the reporters story.

B. Circle the number before any sentence in which you find one or more errors; then correct the errors.

¹If your the kind of person who enjoys an adventure, make your reservations on the Cumbres-Toltec Railroad. ²The ride begin's in Chama, New Mexico, just south of the Colorado line and wind's it's way through the twisting, plunging Rio Grande Gorge. ³The

track is narrow gauge, and the engine is powered by steam. [4]An intriguing assortment of antique cars', many bearing the names' of long-forgotten railways', carries' the passengers' on a ride that rivals' the thrills of many roller coasters'. [5]Theirs a wooden trestle so high and so rickety that one of the engine's must be uncoupled to make the crossing and the train its'self must creep carefully over. [6]There are hairpin turns and steep grades, and at one point the track clings like a snake to the side of a thousand-foot cliff. [7]If its adventure you're looking for, you'll find it on the Cumbres-Toltec Railroad.

Scoring: Deduct 2 points for each error in Part A and 3 points for each error in identifying or correcting errors in Part B.

SKILLS IN ACTION TEST #8

End Punctuation / Capitals

A. Add end punctuation and capitals as appropriate.

1. the book *mission mia* begins in a cambodian prison camp

2. will dr simpson be in mitchell hall for the reading of her poem, "who am i"

3. the note in the bottle that washed up on brookings beach said, "help i'm being held in the bermuda triangle by descendents of the inhabitants of the lost continent, atlantis"

4. at 8:00 a m, m s t, sergeant jim chee of the navajo tribal police found the victim in a battered 1972 ford pick-up

5. in january the roberts family spent its last winter in snowy michigan in june they will move to the southwest

6. mr jones, chairman of the board of trustees, called a tuesday meeting at the hollywood hilton

B. Identify sentences with errors in end punctuation or capitalization by circling the number of the sentence; then correct the errors.

[1]It was mid-July of a hot, muggy Summer. [2]At the edge of the bosque, beside the Rio Grande river, a single fisherman sat motionless, his fishing line trailing in the muddy water, his nose in Terry Brooks's fantasy novel, *The Elfstones of Shannara*, his name was Greg Candela, Ph D, and he was an instructor of english.

[3]Beside Dr. candela sat a large but short Hound named Sebastian. [4]Sebastian shuffled his stubby legs and flicked his long ears as a squadron of mosquitoes dove and circled about his head. [5]"I wish we could go home," Sebastian thought, glancing

plaintively at his Master, "the fish aren't biting, but the mosquitoes are."

⁶Suddenly there was a tug on the fishing line, and a ten-pound golden carp pushed its head above the water. ⁷My name is Waldo, o mighty captor," the carp told Sebastian. ⁸"If you will release me. I will grant you one wish."

⁹"Woof!!!" replied the Hound, and he clawed at his Master's leg. ¹⁰But Dr Candela was deep in the adventures of the half-elf hero of his Random House Novel and did not hear.

¹¹Left to his own devices, Sebastian, who was clever with his paws, released the golden carp from the hook and lure—a deadly model called the fish magnet. ¹²The grateful Carp immediately granted Sebastian's wish to go home, and in the time it takes a Frog to swallow a Fly, he and his master were back in their air-conditioned living room.

¹³Dr Candela never figured out how he had gotten home that day. ¹⁴Leaving his Ford Truck on the riverbank and losing his fishing pole in the quicksand at the bottom of the River.

Scoring: Deduct 1 point for each error in Part A and 1 point for each error in identifying or correcting problems in Part B.

SKILLS IN ACTION TEST #9

Sentence Structures

A. Circle subjects; underline verbs once and predicate words twice.

1. The potter with infinite care and the skill of a lifetime molded the red, slippery clay.

2. It was the best of times; it was the worst of times. (Dickens)

3. Over the river and through the woods, to Grandmother's house we go.

4. For her birthday Augustine gave Jenny a dozen American beauty roses in an elegant silver vase.

5. The odds-on favorite in the sixth race was looking sleepy and bored.

6. Errol Flynn played romantic, swashbuckling heroes in films like *Captain Blood* and *Robin Hood.*

7. But the best swashbucklers were Kirk Douglas in *The Crimson Pirate* and Gene Kelly in *The Three Musketeers.*

8. Kelly horrified his producers by doing his own stunts.

B. In the space provided at the left, identify the sentences in the following paragraph as simple (S), compound (CPD), complex (CX), or compound/complex (CPD/CX).

1. _____   [1]One of the mightiest of all the volcanoes in the
2. _____   Cascade Range of the Pacific Northwest has nearly
            been forgotten. [2]While Mt. Shasta, Mt. Hood, and
            Mt. Rainier are household words, few people have
3. _____   even heard of Mt. Mazama. [3]Coming between Shasta
            and the Three Sisters, Mazama was one of the tallest
            volcanoes in the chain as well as one of the most
4. _____   violent. [4]Scientists estimate a period of continuous
            eruptions twenty thousand years ago, but Native
            American folklore recalls more recent periods of

5. ____   intense activity. [5]In Klamath Indian legends a spirit
that was embodied in Mt. Mazama warred with a
6. ____   similar, but milder spirit at Mt. Shasta. [6]In both
legend and geological history, the violence escalated
7. ____   until it reached catastrophic proportions. [7]Mt.
8. ____   Mazama literally blew its stack. [8]In a massive series
of eruptions, the mountain threw ash over most of
North America, spewed molten lava that scoured the
country for hundreds of square miles, and set forest
fires that must have devastated a large part of what
9. ____   is now Oregon. [9]When the eruptions were over, only a
shell of the mountain remained—a *caldera*, or heart,
that eventually was filled to a depth of nearly four
10. ____   thousand feet with water. [10]Mt. Mazama had become
Crater Lake.

Scoring: Deduct 2 points for each error in Part A and 4 points for each error in Part B.

SKILLS IN ACTION TEST #10

Series, Compound, and List Punctuation

A. Add series, compound, and list punctuation as appropriate.

1. For the potluck please bring the following a smoked turkey, smothered in dressing a pumpkin pie two quarts of your famous delicious cranberry sauce and stuffed mushrooms.

2. Be sure to peel the potatoes carefully for some of us are allergic to the skins.

3. If we can collect the money in time, the society will build a chain of comfortable rustic bird hotels put bird feeders in every public park and also, if the right person can be found, hire a full-time energetic bird warden to ensure the safety comfort and health of the city's bird population.

4. The concert series began with a Beethoven sonata and ended with a Stravinsky symphony.

5. Ford or Chevrolet Mercury or Pontiac Toyota or Honda these are the options within my price range.

6. Handcrafting moccasins weaving rugs making pottery and carving fetishes are crafts to be featured at the state fair.

7. A precious antique clock will be placed on the block at the auction and I plan to bid vigorously and wrecklessly on it.

8. You will find the cookie jar in the top right-hand corner of the cupboard.

B. Circle the number of any sentence that contains a punctuation error, and correct the error.

[1]The invitation list for the banquet was impressive, a prince, two sheiks, an ambassador, six senators, and a prime minister.

303

²Protocol was a nightmare for each dignitary was very conscious of his or her status, and also that of their colleagues. ³To avoid the worst problems of the seating arrangement, the banquet officials opted for a gigantic, round table. ⁴With no head of the table, there should have been no difficulty with ranking the guests, yet a few squabbles arose inevitably. ⁵The prime minister, whose country was 100,000 square miles in size, felt she should outrank a sheik whose country was a mere 10,000 square miles, the prince was annoyed to find himself seated next to the ambassador, and the six senators, accustomed to seeing each other every day, were bored with one another's company. ⁶For weeks after the banquet, the young twenty-five-year-old organizer insisted that her black hair had turned white with the strain, and wore a white wig to prove the point.

Scoring: Deduct 2 points for each error in Part A and 3 points for each error in identifying or in correcting errors in Part B.

SKILLS IN ACTION TEST #11

Interrupting and Introductory Punctuation

A. Add interrupting and introductory punctuation as appropriate.

1. Walking along the river bank I encountered one of the nearly extinct whooping cranes.

2. The crane which ignored my presence was in the middle of a flock of sandhill cranes.

3. The whooper however did not blend into the crowd; its white feathers and elegant stature both distinctive features identified it immediately as something special.

4. If you are ever traveling through the bosque along the Rio Grande River keep an eye open for whooping cranes.

5. On the other hand formations of the geese that fly each year from Canada to their winter home in the Bosque del Apache attract little attention.

6. All of the birdwatchers who are surveying for the Audubon Society should meet for a training session also an enjoyable social function at the Holiday Inn.

7. Georgina, Samantha, Lupe, and Carmen all will participate in the fundraiser.

8. The $6,000,000 ? collected by the foundation should be earmarked for public service projects.

9. The committee Rolf, Sandy, Homer, Curt, and Jo Ann adjourned the meeting immediately following the food fight.

10. Moreover the major troublemaker you know whom I mean is running for reelection next year.

B. Circle the number of any sentence that contains a punctuation error and correct the error.

¹Painting which used to be Jenny's hobby has now become her profession. ²Speaking on a local talk show the artist described her early years as an artist. ³"In 1981, I sold my first painting," Jenny told the interviewer. ⁴"Until that happened I had practically paid people to accept my work. ⁵Then (all of a sudden) things had changed. ⁶I was no longer just a dabbler; I had become the real (!) thing. ⁷*River Peace, Sky City, Old Town, Good Friends,* I can still remember the names of those first paintings I sold and even the prices I got for them, $10, $12.50, $25.00, $15.00 and the people who bought them." ⁸When asked whether her love for painting had decreased as her income increased Jenny replied, "No I enjoy painting now more than ever. ⁹However now I do get burdened down sometimes with all of the work." ¹⁰The artist whose latest show opens Wednesday at the Brandywine Galleries will be on hand to talk with art collectors, a group Jenny says she still views with awe.

Scoring: Deduct 2 points for each error in Part A, 3 points for each error in identifying a problem in Part B, and 3 points for any sentence in which an error remains in Part B.

SKILLS IN ACTION TEST #12

Quotation Marks/Italics/Hyphens

A. Add quotation marks, italics, and hyphens as appropriate.

1. The song On the Street Where You Live is from the musical My Fair Lady.

2. The ex Canadian told us, the British burning of Washington in the second American British war was in retaliation for the American burning of Toronto.

3. The famous Mona Lisa painting inspired the song Mona Lisa, which is best remembered in the Nat King Cole recording.

4. We will be leaving for our tour of the pineapple factory at 9:45 a.m., the guide told us. Please do not say, That's too early. We have to go when the factory manager tells us.

5. The soon to be completed freeway will within a week connect Los Angeles with San Clemente.

6. The writer of the journal wrote & instead of and and left out the e's in the ed's of his verbs—for example, jumpd.

7. The Spirit of St. Louis carried Lindbergh over the Atlantic.

B. Circle the number of any sentence that contains a punctuation error, and correct the error.

[1]Being posted at a weather station on the far, northern coast of Alaska requires a better than average dose of individualism. [2]When I first accepted the post, I was skeptical. [3]Ever the party person, I was not in the least bit sure I could exist without people. [4]But the only company I had during the long, Arctic night was myself and two other members of the weather team—Arthur Rudolf Kreisman and Bruce Miner. [5]Art was a college student, and he spent his time reading War and Peace and The Rise and Fall of the Roman

Empire. ⁶Bruce's adjustment was more questionable. ⁷From dawn-to-dusk he sang the same song, Raindrops Keep Falling on My Head. ⁸Surprisingly, I dis covered a deep affection for the Arctic nights with their vividly-flashing auror- a borealis. ⁹And I even did the all American thing by signing up for a second tour of duty.

> *Scoring:* Deduct 2 points for each error in Part A and 3 points for each error in identifying or in correcting errors in Part B.

Readings

Reading like writing is a process. It involves more than beginning at the beginning and reading one word at a time until you reach the end. Good reading like good writing requires preparation and planning, identifying purpose and main ideas, even reviewing and revising as you search for over-looked information and adjust ideas.

SQ3R

One reading method that helps involve you in the reading process is called SQ3R: Survey, Question, Read, Rehearse, Review. You begin by *surveying* what you will read, finding out what the article or chapter is about. Then you look for or think of *questions* that your reading should help you answer. Then *read* actively; jot down answers to the questions as you find them and comments as you think of them. In this text, questions are placed at the side of the article, instead of at the end, to help you interact with the material as you read. Once you have finished reading, *rehearse* what you have learned—the main ideas, key supporting points, answers to the questions you or the author posed. Finally, *review* the article for information you overlooked or do not remember.

Follow the SQ3R method as you read each of the articles in this section. Reading the articles in the order printed will give you a short reading-improvement course. Most of the articles also will be read as part of your preparation for the writing activities at the end of each chapter.

BAT HABITAT

by Irene Brady

What is a
colony?

From the ceiling of a cave in the canyon rim, a colony of big-eared bats hung by their toes. Where they were clustered, the cave was only a narrow slit. But it widened out below to make a dark den for the old mother bobcat and her young. It was mid-June when the female bats gathered in the slit to have their babies. They swung their ears backward and forward nervously as the six-week-old bobcat kittens wrestled and growled and chased feathers far below. For one of the bat mothers, it was almost time.

Why doesn't the bat
have her baby on
the cave floor?

Reaching up with the thumbs on the front edges of her wings, she hooked them into the rough stone ceiling. Now her body was in the shape of a cup, with all ten toes and both thumbs holding tight. The tiny, hairless batling was born into the cup, and she leaned forward and licked him dry.

Where are the bats'
heads?

Then the batling found a nipple and clung to it with his mouth. His thumbs dug deeply into her fur. The mother bat slowly swung back down to hang by just her hind feet. The batling's hind feet crept upward until he could hook his sharp toenails into a crack in the ceiling close beside her.

What do the bats
eat?

He was several hours old when she left him to fly out into the dusk to catch insects. He tried to reach out for her and one foot slipped from the stone ceiling. For a few seconds he hung by five toes, squeaking with fright as he twisted and turned. But he found the crack again and hung on. If he had fallen, the bobcat kittens would have eaten him.

Why must the bat
mother squeak to
find her baby?

His mother returned to the cave and squeaked loudly for her baby. When he answered, she lit beside him and wrapped a wing around him to warm him. A cave is a cold home for a hairless batling and he was very small—only two inches from the end of his nose to the tip of his tail. The skin that stretched between his fingers to make wings and between his legs to connect them with his tail was velvety, thin, and wrinkled. His ears were soft and floppy, not firm and alert like his mother's. When he hung beside her, her nipple was in just the right place for him to reach out and nurse. As she cuddled and licked him, he drank the warm, sweet milk and then went to sleep.

Why do you
suppose there is a
difference in the
mother's and the
baby's ears? Why is
this important?

When the batling was eight days old he fell, fluttering and squeaking, to the floor of the bobcat den. The kittens were asleep and their mother was out hunting when it happened.

Why didn't the baby
fly back on his own?

The mother bat swiftly zig-zagged down to rescue her squeaking baby. As the kittens crept closer, the mother bat spread her wings like an umbrella over her baby. The batling grabbed her nipple in his mouth and clutched her fur with his thumbs and toes. Then she flapped to the top of the cave with her heavy baby. The kittens meowed loudly, but the bats would not come back to be eaten.

A big-eared batling grows very fast. It must be able to fly before it is a month old so that it can practice in the cave before going out in the summer nights to catch its own food. When it is seven weeks old it is chasing moths through the sky, and when it is two months old, its mother will no longer let it nurse.

How are bats useful animals to have living nearby?

When they were about eighteen days old, the young batlings began to try their wings. They spent long minutes opening and closing them in the dim cave. Then one would flutter down a few feet, catch itself in midair and flap its way back up to the cluster of bats. When the baby bats flew for the first time, they had to learn all at once how to use their wings and also how to listen for things that they might bump into. If they had landed on the ground, they might have been eaten by other animals or unable to get back up into the air.

Why must the bats "listen" to keep from bumping into things?

As August with its hot days and short nights passed, the young big-eared bat began to learn the lessons he must know. He couldn't land on the bank of a pond to drink. A weasel or raccoon could catch him easily on the ground. He learned instead to fly low over a smooth stretch of water, open his mouth, and scoop up a drink. Once he dipped too low and flipped into the water. But a bat's wings make good paddles and he beat his way to shore quickly and climbed up a tree to dry in safety before flying again.

Why is the bat so easy to catch?

Why must he dry before flying?

Autumn was coming. All of the bats must be fat enough to get through the winter. Some bats go south when cold weather comes. Big-eared bats hibernate, coming out on warm winter nights for a snack. The little big-eared bat was very good by now at catching insects. Squeaking, he would follow the echoes to his prey. Scooping it into the pocket of skin between his legs, he would reach down while flying and eat it. The soft moth wings drifted down like petals in the evening air. Let winter come. The big-eared batling was ready.

Why must the bat be fat before winter comes?

Questions for discussion:

1. If the bobcats might eat the batlings, why do the bats make their home in the bobcats' den?
2. A feeling of mystery and even terror surrounds the bat. Why are people afraid of bats?
3. How do you feel about bats? Has reading this article made any difference in your feelings?

LITTLE RED RIDING HOOD

by Charles Perrault

Why does Perrault tell us she is from the country?

Once upon a time in a small village there lived a little country girl, the prettiest you've ever seen. Her mother adored her, and her grandmother doted on her even more. This good woman had made for her granddaughter a little red riding hood, which became her so well that everyone called her Little Red Riding Hood.

One day her mother, having baked some cakes, said to her, "I hear that your grandmamma has been ill. Take her a cake and this little pot of butter and see how she is doing." Little Red Riding Hood set out immediately for her grandmother's house, which was in another village.

Why is she a "poor" child?

As she was going through the forest, she met a sly old wolf, who longed to eat her but dared not because of some woodcutters who were close by in the forest. He asked her where she was going. The poor child, who did not know that it was dangerous to stop and pay attention to a wolf, told him, "I am going to see my grandmamma and take her a cake and a little pot of butter, which my mamma sends her."

"Does she live far away?" asked the wolf.

Why does she tell the wolf where her grandmother lives?

"Oh, yes," said Little Red Riding Hood, "It is beyond the mill that you see yonder, the first house in the village."

"Well!" said the wolf, "I shall go to see her also. I shall go by this path, and you, my dear, go by that path, and we shall see who will be there more quickly."

What do these activities tell you about the girl?

The wolf raced at top speed by the shorter path, and the little girl disappeared along the longer path, amusing herself by gathering hazelnuts, chasing butterflies, and making bouquets of the little flowers she found.

The wolf did not take very long to arrive at the grandmother's house. He knocked: tap, tap.

"Who is there?"

Is this wolf a master of disguises?

"It is your granddaughter, Little Red Riding Hood," said the wolf, mimicking the girl's voice, "who brings you a cake and a little pot of butter, which my mamma sends you."

What does the unlocked door tell you about Grandmother?

The good grandmother, who was in bed because she felt a bit ill, cried, "Pull the latch; the bobbin will fall." The wolf pulled the latch and the door opened. He threw himself on the good woman and devoured her in a second, for it had been more than three days since he had eaten. Then he closed the door and got into Grandmother's bed, expecting Little Red Riding Hood, who some time later came to knock on the door: tap, tap.

Does he don a disguise?

"Who is there?"

Little Red Riding Hood, who heard the wolf's gruff voice, was at first afraid but, thinking that her grandmother had a cold, responded,

Why does the girl decide it is her grandmother? Is this a reasonable decision?

Why does he ask her to come into bed?

Why does she get undressed?

Why would the wolf hug her?

Why does she still address the wolf as "Grandmamma"?

"It is your granddaughter, Little Red Riding Hood, who brings you a cake and a little pot of butter, which my mamma sends you."

The wolf cried, softening his voice a little, "Pull the latch; the bobbin will fall."

Little Red Riding Hood pulled the latch, and the door opened. The wolf, seeing her enter and hiding himself in the bed under the covers, said, "Put the cake and the little pot of butter on the hutch, my dear, and come to bed with me."

Little Red Riding Hood undressed and lay down in the bed, where she was astonished to see how her grandmother looked in her nightgown. She said, "Grandmamma, what big arms you have!"

"That is to hug you better, my dear girl."

"Grandmamma, what big legs you have!"

"That is to run better, my child."

"Grandmamma, what big ears you have!"

"That is to hear better, my child."

"Grandmamma, what big eyes you have!"

"That is to see better, my child."

"Grandmamma, what big teeth you have!"

"That is to eat you, my dear."

And saying these words, the evil wolf pounced on Little Red Riding Hood and gobbled her up.

Questions for discussion

1. Is this story believable? If not, why does it continue to be popular?
2. Although "Little Red Riding Hood" is an ancient fairy tale, Perrault wrote his version for the court of Louis XIV. Do you find any indications there might be a double meaning in the tale—one appropriate for a sophisticated group of aristocrats?

THE LITTLE GIRL AND THE WOLF

by James Thurber

How does this beginning differ from Perrault's?

Why did this little girl tell the wolf where her grandmother lived?

One afternoon a big wolf waited in a dark forest for a little girl to come along carrying a basket of food to her grandmother. Finally a little girl did come along and she was carrying a basket of food. "Are you carrying that basket to your grandmother?" asked the wolf. The little girl said yes, she was. So the wolf asked her where her grandmother lived and the little girl told him and he disappeared into the wood.

When the little girl opened the door of her grandmother's house she saw that there was somebody in bed with a nightcap and nightgown on. She had approached no nearer than twenty-five feet from the bed when she saw that it was not her grandmother but the wolf, for even in a nightcap a wolf does not look any more like your grandmother than the Metro-Goldwyn lion looks like Calvin Coolidge. So the little girl took an automatic out of her basket and shot the wolf dead.

Moral: It is not so easy to fool little girls nowadays as it used to be.

> How does her recognizing the wolf change the story?
>
> What is the Metro-Goldwyn lion? Who is Calvin Coolidge?

Questions for discussion

1. Which is the more violent version of "Little Red Riding Hood"— Perrault's or Thurber's? Why?
2. Thurber's tale is shorter than Perrault's. Would "The Little Girl and the Wolf" have been more effective if Thurber had retold more of the original story? Why or why not?
3. What does the moral of Thurber's tale have to tell us about both stories?

THE WORLD'S DUMBEST PRODUCT IS A ROLEX WATCH

by Mike Royko

If poverty, an unhappy childhood or being dropped on my head as an infant had forced me into a life of crime, I know what my racket would be.

> Is he serious?

I would have specialized in stealing Rolex watches from the wrists of those who flaunt them.

> Why is he offended?

Why the Rolex watch? Because of all the ostentatious products that are available in our materialistic society, the Rolex watch is the most offensive to me. By stealing them, I would be able to engage in a life of crime while still having no pangs of conscience.

> Why shouldn't it take 24 months to pay for a watch? Is a watch less important than a stove? What is his point?

The full silliness of owning a Rolex watch struck me a few days ago when I saw an ad for them in my newspaper.

The ad said that if you bought a Rolex now, you could take up to 24 months to pay. Why should it take 24 months to pay off a wristwatch? A car maybe. Or a stove, refrigerator and bedroom set. But a watch?

That's because the cheapest Rolex costs $550, and the top model costs $7,100. And for that, what do you get? You get a device that you wear on your wrist and it tells you the time of day.

> Is a Rolex just a device that tells time?

I used to work with an executive who had a Rolex—the top of the line, gold, $7,000-plus model.

We used to have lunch in the same corporate lunchroom. And whenever we sat near each other, I'd say, "Got the correct time?" He'd look at his $7,000-plus watch and give me the time. I'd look at my $32 Japanese-made, battery operated watch, nod, and say, "Yep, that's what my $32 watch says, too." Then I'd say something like, "Do you happen to know what 95.2 multiplied by 33.8 is?"

He'd look exasperated because he knew what I was up to. "No, I don't" he'd say. I'd jab at my watch, which had a mini-calculator on it, and in a few seconds I'd triumphantly say, "The answer is 3,217.76."

Then I'd hit another button, and my watch would play a song. I concede that it didn't sound like the Chicago Symphony, but tinny as it sounded, it was a song.

"Does your watch play a song?" I'd ask.

He'd sigh and say, "You know it doesn't."

"A Rolex," he would say haughtily, "doesn't do tricks. It tells the time."

No, it does far more than that. It permits the wearer to make a social statement. It says, "Admire me. Envy me."

How crass. And how obscene, considering the terrible social deprivation that exists in our society. Why, for the cost of that one watch, some poor wino could stay looped for 10 years.

One day, my Rolex-wearing friend came to the lunchroom without his watch.

"Were you mugged?" I asked in a voice filled with hope.

"I'm having it cleaned," he said.

I took my watch off and slammed it against the table. It shattered.

"Why did you do that?" he asked.

"I've had it two years and the battery was running down."

"Couldn't you replace the battery?"

"Why bother?" I said, reaching into my pocket and withdrawing another watch. "I already bought the latest model. Four alarm clock modes. Four different songs. An improved calculator. Plus all the other features. $32.50."

I also pointed out that if I replaced it every two years, at the end of 20 years I would be $6,600 ahead of him and his Rolex. And by then, the improved model would probably include a TV screen and a laser death beam to ward off hostile street urchins.

We worked in the same place for several more years. Then he moved to a city on the West Coast. When he left, he still had his fancy Rolex.

And that's one of the things that bugs me about Chicago: When you really need a mugger, there's never one around.

Questions for discussion

1. What is the major point of Royko's article? Do you agree with him? Why or why not?

Why does his friend's watch annoy the writer? Can his $32 watch do everything the Rolex can?

Which would you rather have—the Rolex or the watch that can play songs? Why?

Do you agree that owning a Rolex is crass?

Does Royko's argument make giving up a Rolex seem noble? Why did he mention the wino instead of hungry people?

What was the purpose of destroying his watch?

Would you find all of these features useful?

Would the writer be ahead after 20 years?

Is it the Rolex the writer is objecting to or something else?

2. Does Royko see himself as totally right and Rolex wearers as totally wrong? Can you find any clues in the article that suggest he may be questioning his own motives?

A KIOWA GRANDMOTHER

from The Way to Rainy Mountain *by N. Scott Momaday*

What is an anvil? How could a prairie be like an "anvil's edge"?

Why does Momaday use the word *isolate* instead of *desolate*?

What does *proportion* mean?

A single knoll rises out of the plain in Oklahoma, north and west of the Wichita Range. For my people, the Kiowas, it is an old landmark, and they gave it the name Rainy Mountain. The hardest weather in the world is there. Winter brings blizzards, hot tornadic winds arise in the spring, and in summer the prairie is an anvil's edge. The grass turns brittle and brown, and it cracks beneath your feet. There are green belts along the rivers and creeks, linear groves of hickory and pecan, willow and witch hazel. At a distance in July or August the steaming foliage seems almost to writhe in fire. Great green and yellow grasshoppers are everywhere in the tall grass, popping up like corn to sting the flesh, and tortoises crawl about on the red earth, going nowhere in the plenty of time. Loneliness is an aspect of the land. All things in the plain are isolate; there is no confusion of objects in the eye, but *one* hill or *one* tree or *one* man. To look upon that landscape in the early morning, with the sun at your back, is to lose the sense of proportion. Your imagination comes to life, and this, you think, is where Creation was begun.

I returned to Rainy Mountain in July. My grandmother had died in the spring, and I wanted to be at her grave. She had lived to be very old and at last infirm. Her only living daughter was with her when she died, and I was told that in death her face was that of a child.

Why does Momaday want to think of his grandmother as a child?

How can war be "sacred"?

I like to think of her as a child. When she was born, the Kiowas were living the last great moment of their history. For more than a hundred years they had controlled the open range from the Smoky Hill River to the Red, from the headwaters of the Canadian to the fork of the Arkansas and Cimarron. In alliance with the Comanches, they had ruled the whole of the southern Plains. War was their sacred business, and they were among the finest horsemen the world has ever known. But warfare for the Kiowas was preeminently a matter of disposition rather than of survival, and they never understood the grim, unrelenting advance of the U.S. Cavalry. When at last, divided and ill-provisioned, they were driven onto the Staked Plains in the cold rains of autumn, they fell into panic. In Palo Duro Canyon they abandoned their crucial stores to pillage and had nothing then but their lives. In order to save themselves, they surrendered to the soldiers at Fort Sill and were imprisoned in the old stone

How could she know this without experiencing it?

corral that now stands as a military museum. My grandmother was spared the humiliation of those high gray walls by eight or ten years, but she must have known from birth the affliction of defeat, the dark brooding of old warriors.

What makes them mysterious?

Her name was Aho, and she belonged to the last culture to evolve in North America. Her forebears came down from the high country in western Montana nearly three centuries ago. They were a mountain people, a mysterious tribe of hunters whose language has never been positively classified in any major group. In the late seventeenth century they began a long migration to the south and east. It was a journey toward the dawn, and it led to a golden age. Along the way the Kiowas were befriended by the Crows, who gave them the culture and religion of the Plains. They acquired horses, and their ancient nomadic spirit was sud-

Why would the sun be an attractive deity for the Kiowas?

denly free of the ground. They acquired Tai-me, the sacred Sun Dance doll, from that moment the object and symbol of their worship, and so shared in the divinity of the sun. Not least, they acquired the sense of destiny, therefore courage and pride. When they entered upon the southern Plains they had been transformed. No longer were they slaves to the simple necessity of survival; they were a lordly and dangerous society of fighters and thieves, hunters and priests of the sun. According to their origin myth, they entered the world through a hollow log. From one point of view, their migration was the fruit of an old prophecy, for indeed they emerged from a sunless world.

How could such a migration turn hunters into fighters and thieves?

How can a memory be "in her blood"?

Although my grandmother lived out her long life in the shadow of Rainy Mountain, the immense landscape of the continental interior lay like memory in her blood. She could tell of the Crows, whom she had never seen, and of the Black Hills, where she had never been. I wanted to see in reality what she had seen more perfectly in the mind's eye, and traveled fifteen hundred miles to begin my pilgrimage.

Why does Momaday say his grandmother saw the land "more perfectly in the mind's eye"?

Yellowstone, it seemed to me, was the top of the world, a region of deep lakes and dark timber, canyons and waterfalls. But, beautiful as it is, one might have the sense of confinement there. The skyline in all directions is close at hand, the high wall of the woods and deep cleavages of shade. There is a perfect freedom in the mountains, but it belongs to the eagle and the elk, the badger and the bear. The Kiowas reckoned their stature by the distance they could see, and they were bent and blind in the wilderness.

How does the change of landscape of Oklahoma probably affect their way of life and their self-perception?

Descending eastward, the highland meadows are a stairway to the plain. In July the inland slope of the Rockies is luxuriant with flax and buckwheat, stonecrop and larkspur. The earth unfolds and the limit of the land recedes. Clusters of trees, and animals grazing far in the distance, cause the vision to reach away and wonder to build upon the mind. The sun follows a longer course in the day, and the sky is immense beyond all comparison. The great billowing clouds that sail upon it are shadows that move upon the grain like water, dividing light. Farther down, in the land of the Crows and Blackfeet, the plain is yellow. Sweet

In what ways would the new land require the Kiowas to change their lives?

What do *lees, caldron,* and *solstice* mean?

How can a land be like "iron"?

Is this true? How do you know?

For the purpose of the legend, why would the boy turn into a bear rather than a bear come around the rock and chase them?

In what ways does this legend mirror the physical reality of the Kiowas' migration?

In what way is the legend comforting to the Kiowas? In what way is it not?

clover takes hold of the hills and bends upon itself to cover and seal the soil. There the Kiowas paused on their way; they had come to the place where they must change their lives. The sun is at home on the plains. Precisely there does it have the certain character of a god. When the Kiowas came to the land of the Crows, they could see the dark lees of the hills at dawn across the Bighorn River, the profusion of light on the grain shelves, the oldest deity ranging after the solstices. Not yet would they veer southward to the caldron of the land that lay below; they must wean their blood from the northern winter and hold the mountains a while longer in their view. They bore Tai-me in procession to the east.

A dark mist lay over the Black Hills, and the land was like iron. At the top of a ridge I caught sight of Devil's Tower upthrust against the gray sky as if in the birth of time the core of the earth had broken through its crust and the motion of the world was begun. There are things in nature that engender an awful quiet in the heart of man; Devil's Tower is one of them. Two centuries ago, because they could not do otherwise, the Kiowas made a legend at the base of the rock. My grandmother said:

Eight children were there at play, seven sisters and their brother. Suddenly the boy was struck dumb; he trembled and began to run upon his hands and feet. His fingers became claws, and his body was covered with fur. Directly there was a bear where the boy had been. The sisters were terrified; they ran, and the bear after them. They came to the stump of a great tree, and the tree spoke to them. It bade them climb upon it, and as they did so it began to rise into the air. The bear came to kill them, but they were just beyond its reach. It reared against the tree and scored the bark all around with its claws. The seven sisters were borne into the sky, and they became the stars of the Big Dipper.

From that moment, and so long as the legend lives, the Kiowas have kinsmen in the night sky. Whatever they were in the mountains, they could be no more. However tenuous their well-being, however much they had suffered and would suffer again, they had found a way out of the wilderness.

Questions for discussion:

1. Momaday uses many descriptive details in his writing. What does this tell you about him and about his subject?

2. Compare the Kiowa legend of the eight children with any legends you might know. How are they alike or different?

3. Do you know any "things in nature that engender an awful quiet in the heart of man"? Explain.

HALO (HIGH ALTITUDE—LOW-OPENING) JUMP

From **Mission MIA** *by J. C. Pollock*

Would you like to do this?

Callahan exited the plane in a graceful swan dive, his back arched and his head high; his arms and legs pulled upward into a spread-stable position. The others followed a split second later.

What does *terminal* mean in this context?

Caught in the slipstream of the aircraft, they were pulled along for three hundred meters before falling free and reaching terminal velocity—120 miles an hour—twelve seconds into the jump.

What senses are appealed to here?

The sound of the aircraft's engines faded in the distance, and the rush of freezing air roared in their ears, tearing at their jump suits and stinging the exposed skin on their necks and foreheads.

Why might it be called a "spider" position?

Jack quickly assumed a "spider" position, reversing the arch in his back while stretching his arms and legs as wide as possible. He positioned himself for a slow turn, bringing his hands back slightly, lowering his left hand and shoulder, and looking into the turn. Once headed toward the drop zone, he stopped the turn and pulled himself into the tracking position.

What does *tracking* mean?

Bending slightly at the waist, he rolled his shoulders forward and placed his arms back along his sides with the contour of his body, and cupped his hands, palms downward, while bringing his head back and stretching his legs out, holding them shoulder-width apart.

What is lifting him?

He felt the lift developing as his speed increased. The airfoil configuration gave forward motion to his fall as he tracked thirty-five degrees horizontal to the ground, the force of the rushing air increasing as he reached 135 miles an hour.

What does *airfoil* mean?

He scanned the ground twenty-five thousand feet below, searching for his visual reference point which would give him his bearing on the drop zone. His eyes moved quickly over the silhouetted mountainous jungle terrain until he spotted the broad, winding river he had seen in the satellite photograph. The murky water, luminous in the bright moonlight, cut a distinct swath through the valley, in clear contrast to the dark, shadowy jungle canopy.

Why does he need a reference point?

His eyes followed the river upstream to a sharp bend he knew lay a few hundred feet directly below the plateau where the drop zone was located.

Looking to his right, he found his predesignated opening point—a horseshoe-shaped ridgeline west of the bend in the river—and tracked steadily toward it. . . .

Why is his altitude so important?

Callahan read his rapidly moving altimeter needle as he came abreast of the horseshoe-shaped ridgeline. He was twenty-five hundred feet from the ground when to the east of the ridgeline he spotted the plateau and the fast-approaching drop zone.

What happened to the sound?

Pulling his arms forward against strong resistance, and arching his

How did his changing position slow his descent?

back, he flared from the track position into a spread-eagle, and effectively stopped his forward motion and slowed his vertical rate of descent.

Within six seconds he dropped twelve hundred feet to the opening point that would put him under canopy at the altitude he wanted. Reaching up with his right hand, he grabbed the D-ring and pulled his rip cord.

What does the term *pilot chute* suggest about its function?

The pilot chute streamed out, followed by the rustle and snap of nylon as it drew the sleeved canopy after it. The suspension lines unraveled and the sleeve slid off. The canopy inflated with a loud *pop!* pulling Callahan upright with a sudden jolt.

The roar of rushing air ceased, and Jack swung gently beneath the risers in the silence of the night sky. He looked up to check his canopy, and then to his right to see the others stacked above him. Removing his oxygen mask and pushing his goggles up onto his helmet, he looked

Do you think the fourth man is directly above Callahan? Why or why not?

again. He couldn't locate the fourth man, and thought one of the team might be out of position directly above him, although he couldn't see him through the cutaway sections of his canopy. He turned his attention to the approach to the drop zone and concentrated on his landing.

Experience told him that on his present course he would overshoot the clearing. Reaching up, he pulled all the way down on the right steer-

How does "spiraling down" correct his position?

ing toggle, taking air out of the canopy. He spiraled down in a small circle, releasing the toggle when the correction had been made.

Halfway across the clearing he turned into the wind and pulled both steering toggles down to a quarter brake, a half, then a three-quarter brake position, and almost to a stall. The canopy buffeted in the wind as he settled to touchdown and released both toggles, then surged, filling with air as he landed firmly on both feet in a standing position.

Why is their dropping-in "silent"?

As he gathered his chute, the other men dropped silently in, landing within a twenty-yard radius of where he stood. A quick glance told him someone was missing. He searched the sky, finding no trace of another canopy.

Questions for discussion:

1. What might be the purpose of a HALO jump, such as the one described here?
2. Pollock writes about the actions of the jump, but he says little about the emotions. What do you think those might be? Do you think Callahan is scared? Why or why not?

THAT LEAN AND HUNGRY LOOK

by Suzanne Britt Jordan

About what was
Caesar right?

Caesar was right. Thin people need watching. I've been watching them for most of my adult life, and I don't like what I see. When these narrow fellows spring at me, I quiver to my toes. Thin people come in all personalities, most of them menacing. You've got your "together" thin person, your mechanical thin person, your condescending thin person, your tsk-tsk thin person, your efficiency-expert thin person. All of them are dangerous.

Do you agree
that fat people
are more fun
than thin people?

In the first place, thin people aren't fun. They don't know how to goof off, at least in the best, fat sense of the word. They've always got to be adoing. Give them a coffee break, and they'll jog around the block. Supply them with a quiet evening at home, and they'll fix the screen door and lick S&H green stamps. They say things like "there aren't enough hours in the day." Fat people never say that. Fat people think the day is too damn long already.

What does *inert*
mean?

Thin people make me tired. They've got speedy little metabolisms that cause them to bustle briskly. They're forever rubbing their bony hands together and eying new problems to "tackle." I like to surround myself with sluggish, inert, easygoing fat people, the kind who believe that if you clean it up today, it'll just get dirty again tomorrow.

Are all fat people
nice?

Some people say the business about the jolly fat person is a myth, that all of us chubbies are neurotic, sick, sad people. I disagree. Fat people may not be chortling all day long, but they're a hell of a lot *nicer* than the wizened and shriveled. Thin people turn surly, mean and hard at a young age because they never learn the value of a hot-fudge sundae for easing tension. Thin people don't like gooey soft things because they

Are all thin
people hard,
mean, and dull?

themselves are neither gooey nor soft. They are crunchy and dull, like carrots. They go straight to the heart of the matter while fat people let things stay all blurry and hazy and vague, the way things actually are. Thin people want to face the truth. Fat people know there is no truth. One of my thin friends is always staring at complex, unsolvable problems and saying, "The key thing is. . ." Fat people never say that. They know there isn't any such thing as the key thing about anything. Thin people

What does
nebulous mean?

Does the writer
intend us to take
this paragraph
literally as a
serious statement
of her beliefs?

believe in logic. Fat people see all sides. The sides fat people see are rounded blobs, usually gray, always nebulous and truly not worth worrying about. But the thin person persists. "If you consume more calories than you burn," says one of my thin friends, "you will gain weight. It's that simple." Fat people always grin when they hear statements like that. They know better.

Fat people realize that life is illogical and unfair. They know very well that God is not in his heaven and all is not right with the world. If

God was up there, fat people could have two doughnuts and a big orange drink anytime they wanted it.

What do *spouting* and *reel* mean? Where do the words come from?

Thin people have a long list of logical things they are always spouting off to me. They hold up one finger at a time as they reel off these things, so I won't lose track. They speak slowly as if to a young child. The list is long and full of holes. It contains tidbits like "get a grip on yourself," "cigarettes kill," "cholesterol clogs," "fit as a fiddle," "ducks in a row," "organize" and "sound fiscal management." Phrases like that.

What kind of happiness do thin people talk about? Why wouldn't fat people want it?

They think these 2,000-point plans lead to happiness. Fat people know happiness is elusive at best and even if they could get the kind thin people talk about, they wouldn't want it. Wisely, fat people see that such programs are too dull, too hard, too off the mark. They are never better than a whole cheesecake.

What is the "mystery of life"?

Fat people know all about the mystery of life. They are the ones acquainted with the night, with luck, with fate, with playing it by ear. One thin person I know once suggested that we arrange all the parts of a jigsaw puzzle into groups according to size, shape and color. He figured this would cut the time needed to complete the puzzle by at least 50 per cent. I said I wouldn't do it. One, I like to muddle through. Two, what good would it do to finish early? Three, the jigsaw puzzle isn't the important thing. The important thing is the fun of four people (one thin person included) sitting around a card table, working a jigsaw puzzle. My thin friend had no use for my list. Instead of joining us, he went outside and mulched the boxwoods. The three remaining fat people finished the puzzle and made chocolate, double-fudged brownies to celebrate.

Who do thin people oppress?

The main problem with thin people is they oppress. Their good intentions, bony torsos, tight ships, neat corners, cerebral machinations and pat solutions loom like dark clouds over the loose, comfortable, spread-out, soft world of the fat. Long after fat people have removed their coats and shoes and put their feet up on the coffee table, thin people are still sitting on the edge of the sofa, looking neat as a pin, discussing rutabagas. Fat people are heavily into fits of laughter, slapping their thighs and whooping it up, while thin people are still politely waiting for the punch line. Thin people are downers. They like math and morality and reasoned evaluation of the limitations of human beings. They have their skinny little acts together. They expound, prognose, probe and prick.

How does liking math and morality make thin people downers?

What does *convivial* mean?

In what way does this list of words that start with *g* emphasize the writer's opinion of fat people?

Fat people are convivial. They will like you even if you're irregular and have acne. They will come up with a good reason why you never wrote the great American novel. They will cry in your beer with you. They will put your name in the pot. They will let you off the hook. Fat people will gab, giggle, guffaw, gallumph, gyrate and gossip. They are generous, giving and gallant. They are gluttonous and goodly and great. What you want when you're down is soft and jiggly, not muscled and stable. Fat people know this. Fat people have plenty of room. Fat people will take you in.

Does the phrase "take you in" have any hidden significance?

Questions for discussion:

1. Is Jordan really writing about size or about personality?
2. Is Jordan creating stereotypes? Are the stereotypes justified in your opinion?
3. Are we supposed to take Jordan's comments seriously? Why or why not?
4. The title and first paragraph refer to Shakespeare's play *Julius Caesar.* Look for the references in the play; then explain what they have to do with Jordan's main ideas.

THE GREATEST TEAM I EVER SAW

by Dick Schaap

Who were "they"? What was "it all"?

They had it all. They had the ultimate bachelor, Paul Hornung—blond-haired, green-eyed and peacock handsome, the all-American Golden Boy from the Golden Dome of Notre Dame, the most explosive scorer in the history of pro football.

Should we take this praise literally? Why or why not?

They had the ultimate family man, Bart Starr, who rose from Alabama, virtue personified, self-effacing and dependable, the most efficient passer in the history of pro football.

They had an offensive tackle (Forrest Gregg), a defensive end (Willie Davis), a linebacker (Ray Nitschke), a fullback (Jimmy Taylor) and a cornerback (Herb Adderley) who, like Starr, wound up in the Pro Football Hall of Fame. And they had a guard (Jerry Kramer), a defensive tackle (Henry Jordan) and a safety (Willie Wood) who, like Hornung, deserve to be in the Hall of Fame.

Is being "feared" positive or negative?

They had Vince Lombardi, the most feared and respected and successful coach in the history of the game.

They were the 1966 Green Bay Packers, and they were, in my opinion, the greatest team that ever lived.

What does this distinction between "greatest football team" and "greatest team" mean?

Not the greatest *football* team. The greatest *team*. In any sport. The almost perfect blend of individual and collective talent, character and personality.

In the last 30 years, as writer and broadcaster, I have observed—on the field and off—the Yankees of Mantle, Ford and Berra, the Canadiens of Richard, Beliveau and Geoffrion, the Celtics of Russell, Cousy and Havlicek, the Steelers of Bradshaw, Harris and Swann. Awesome teams, all of them: athletic dynasties. Certainly, on the basis of championships and glory, I would rate them with the Packers or above.

Do these credentials qualify the writer to make sweeping judgments?

But the 1966 Green Bay Packers transcended championships, tran-

What does
transcend mean?

What does it
mean to be
"greater than the
sum of its parts"?

How is Schaap
using the word
champion here?

What is *infinity*?

What is Schaap
trying to show
with these
comments about
the team today?

How do the 1966
Packers embody
"the American
dream"?

How do these
incidents support
Schaap's
opinion?

scended glory. I have never seen gathered together—in sports or publishing or television or any other business—a group of men or women so unspoiled, so motivated, so unified, so prepared, so eager to learn and to feel and to achieve, a group so much greater than the sum of its parts, 40 distinct and intriguing human beings.

If I had to spend a week or a month or a year with any team, sharing the players' hopes and fears, thoughts and words, social life and professional life, I would pick them, the Packers of 1966, the team that won the first Super Bowl game, the team that won for Green Bay the second of three straight National Football League championship games, a feat performed by no other team.

They were champions then.

They are champions now.

Forrest Gregg, whom Vince Lombardi called the greatest player he ever coached, is the head coach of the 1985 Green Bay Packers and hopes to make Super Bowl XX his fifth Super Bowl, three as a player, two as a coach.

Willie Davis, whose father earned 50 cents a day as a laborer during the Depression, owns five radio stations and a beer distributorship and sits on the board of MGM/United Artists.

Max McGee, who caught two touchdown passes in Super Bowl I, started ChiChi's, a chain of Mexican restaurants, and sold most of his stock for between $10 million and infinity.

Ron Kostelnik, a starting defensive tackle in Super Bowl I, is president of Mainline Industrial Distributors, a company grossing $18 million a year.

Doug Hart, a reserve safety, is president and chief executive officer of Satellite Industries Inc., the world's largest supplier of portable restrooms.

Tommy Joe Crutcher, a linebacker, raises grain sorghum on a Texas farm that is slightly larger than Manhattan.

More members of the 1966 Packers are millionaires than are in the Hall of Fame. They are the embodiment of the American dream, living clichés, tangible proof that if one aims high enough and works hard enough, he is capable of achieving almost anything.

I knew the Packers in 1966. I know them better now. During the last two years, writing a book called *Distant Replay* with Jerry Kramer, the former right guard, I spoke with 38 of the team's 40 players—all except the right side of the starting defensive line: tackle Henry Jordan, who had died, and end Lionel Aldridge, who had vanished. I played golf and poker with the others, ate and drank with them, enjoyed laughs and memories and came away exhilarated, buoyed by their achievements, by their spirit. I came to love them almost as much as they loved each other.

A year ago, in Green Bay, I went to their first full-scale reunion in almost 18 years, and I watched them hug and kiss each other, black and white, trim and stout, bald and bearded, watched them smile and giggle, watched them actually cry, they were so happy to be together again. "This team had more love than any team that ever played the game," said the man who organized the reunion, Fuzzy Thurston, a left guard whose zest for life has overcome bankruptcy and cancer of the larynx.

What does love have to do with a football team?

The reunion was dominated by a man who wasn't there—a man dead for 14 years—Vince Lombardi, their coach, their mentor. "Do you think of him often?" I asked Herb Adderley, and Adderley said, "Every day. And I love my father, who is also deceased, but I don't think about my father every day."

How can a man who is dead dominate a reunion?

"Every time I start a sales meeting," Dave Robinson, a linebacker in 1966, operator of a beer distributorship now, told me, "I find Lombardi conducting it. It's eerie."

If any one man made the 1966 Packers the greatest team, it was Lombardi. Five first-string members of the 1966 team were also members of the 1958 team, which, the year before Lombardi arrived in Green Bay, won one game, tied one and lost 10. They lacked discipline, direction and leadership. Before they met Lombardi, very few of the 1966 Packers had experienced great glory or success, in pro football, in college football, or in life.

Do the Packers still sound like the "American dream" come true? What is the dream?

Ten of the Packers had lost their fathers before they reached their teens, to death or divorce or drunkenness. More than a dozen had fathers who worked in coal mines, steel mills, on tenant farms or assembly lines. Two had fathers who worked as high school coaches. They were the aristocrats of the crowd.

When Schaap calls these players aristocrats, does he mean their fathers were lords?

Not one of the starting players had been on a team that won a national collegiate championship. Only one was a first-string all-American in college. Only three knew the satisfaction of winning a major college bowl game. Most had football credentials that had to be exaggerated to be considered modest. One came from Philander Smith, a college none of his teammates had ever heard of. One was the first pro football player from Valparaiso. Most were barely noticed in college, and many had been discarded by other pro teams.

Why does Schaap go into detail about the players' college accomplishments?

Lombardi took the unsung and the unknown and made them into champions, into heroes. He taught them the beauty of teamwork, drove them to work together, to respect each other, to sacrifice individual goals for the common good. He taught them to persevere, to execute. He taught them to win. They rose from so little to become so much, and that may be the finest measure of their greatness. They didn't know, until they met Lombardi, what special people they were.

How did Lombardi accomplish such a miracle?

Willie Davis may be the most special of all, not only for his credentials, which are dazzling, ranging from an MBA from the University of Chicago to citations from every civic organization known to man, but for his wisdom, his thoughtfulness. "One of my fears," he told me, "is that my kids have it too easy. They don't have to deal with uncertainty. They assume it's gonna be there. And, of course, one of the driving forces in my life is to make sure it is there. I constantly try to bring the possibility

Why is Davis worried about his children's not struggling?

of uncertainty into their lives, but a manufactured fear is never the same as a real fear."

Max McGee is the most fun of the old Packers, the compleat free spirit, a gambler by nature and avocation, incapable of taking himself too seriously. He is a master of understated, self-deprecating wit. How did it feel to be one of the greatest all-around high school athletes in Texas history? "I really wanted to be in the band," Max said. "That's where the girls were." When he became a college star at Tulane, did he dream of playing pro football? "I figured I'd go back to White Oak, Tex.," he said, "and start working in a gas station, like all my idols."

Is Schaap saying we should share Max's idols and dreams so that we will become champions?

Ron Kostelnik is the most sensitive of the group, the most emotional. When he heard that Henry Jordan had died at 42 of a heart attack, he felt, he said, like "a piece of me was chopped out," and he jumped in his car and drove 100 miles to Henry's home. "He wanted to know if we were OK financially," Jordan's widow told me. "Henry had taken good care of everything, but if he hadn't, Ron wouldn't let us go hungry."

What does Kostelnik's sensitivity have to do with the article's main idea?

Later, when Kostelnik learned that Lionel Aldridge had suffered a mental breakdown that cost him his marriage and a promising broadcasting career, Kostelnik agonized. And when he heard a few months ago that Aldridge had returned to Milwaukee and was working for the post office, he again drove 100 miles to see if he could help, to offer encouragement. Kostelnik weighs more than 300 pounds, and every pound cares.

Red Mack is the most moving, a little man with an enormous heart who looks old beyond his years. Mack spent part of his childhood in an orphanage. Knee surgery stopped him from being a star in college or pro football, but nobody could stop him from making two tackles on kickoffs in Super Bowl I. After the game, he cried and told his teammates, "I'm so happy. I've never been part of anything like this before." He never played another football game. He never enjoyed the financial success of so many of his teammates. But he is fiercely proud of his Super Bowl ring. "A guy once offered me a Porsche for it," Red said, "but I wouldn't trade it for all the money in the world."

Why wouldn't Red Mack trade his Super Bowl ring for a Porsche?

Then there is Jerry Kramer, who is a blend of all the other Packers. He has some of Davis' dignity, McGee's wit, Kostelnik's sensitivity and Mack's pride. We first met a quarter of a century ago in Green Bay, and we have played golf and tennis and gin rummy and poker and boasted and caroused and still found time to collaborate on four books. I think we know each other as well as two men can, our strengths and our weaknesses. His strengths, physical and mental, are awesome, but the one that impresses me most is his willingness to search within himself, probing his dreams and his fears, attempting to understand himself. Aside from my wife, Jerry Kramer is my closest friend. I love him like a brother, and not least of all for allowing me, through him, to get to know the men who were his teammates on the 1966 Green Bay Packers. Whenever I'm feeling low, all I have to do is call one of them up, and I feel better. Their spirit is infectious.

Is this paragraph off the subject?

What about their spirit is infectious? Who is infected? What are the effects of this infection?

Questions for discussion:

1. Does Schaap write objectively—that is, focusing on facts without comments about personal feelings or opinion? Why or why not?
2. Schaap emphasizes the concept of a team. What is a team? What does it mean to be a team member? What makes team spirit so important?
3. What made this team so great? Do you agree with Schaap that it was "the greatest"? Why or why not?
4. Why does Schaap use fragments in his writing? How do you think these fragments affect his work? Would it be better without them?

WHERE A NEW WORLD BEGAN

by Diane Ackerman

Is this picture an inviting one? Why or why not?

What does *zigguratlike* mean?

Why would immigrants have expected "a golden turnstile"?

How might the place described here have affected the immigrants?

At first glance, Ellis Island's main building looks like an Oriental mansion, with four domed towers rising like cobras and ornate limestone-and-granite windows set into the brick and ironwork. The roof speaks as many dialects as the immigrants who passed under it—peaks, arches, zigguratlike steps, green sawteeth, parapets—and is so studded with square, porthole and half-moon windows that it's hard to take it all in in one eye-gulp. Surely this is an arcade at a seaside resort fed by gondolas and hovercraft, not a former immigration station in New York Harbor.

But this is what millions of immigrants saw when they first stepped onto American soil, and it must have enthralled them. What greeted them was not a golden turnstile with two gigantic gates spread open in an embrace, as they half-expected, but a mist-hung fortress and 32 outlying buildings, which together served as a self-enclosed world, a city-state for the stateless. There were medical rooms, dining rooms, a baggage room, a power station, a restaurant, dormitories, a bath house, a railroad ticket office, a room for sterilizing linens, even a morgue. There was also a Main Hall, in which three globed chandeliers floated below cathedral windows through which sunlight streamed down to long, parallel rows of wooden benches, a maze designed to keep body and belongings in line.

Inside was bedlam: children crying, megaphones blaring, people searching for family members, interpreters juggling as many as 10 languages, the ambient din of household goods being dragged across cement floors, and perhaps a thousand immigrants from all over Europe, Asia

How does the
contrast of
immigrants to
Americans add
to the picture?

and Africa, many in native costumes speaking languages full of squeaks and pops and guttural scrapes, all noisily chattering and eyeing each other. And there were the Americans: the doctors and nurses, wardens and guards, firemen, immigrant aid society agents, cooks and waiters, and even miscellaneous con men and swindlers luring them toward imaginary paradises on the prairie. There were no porters, so they had to carry all of their hand luggage, as well as their children, with them through the entire immigration process, whose first and most dreaded step was the medical exam.

What kind of
physician is a
"rough-and-ready
diagnostician"?

A doctor wearing a blue uniform and holding a piece of chalk first watched them climb the staircase from the Main Hall in what came to be known as "the six-second physical." A rough-and-ready diagnostician, he pored over hands, feet, eyes, face, scalp, gait, posture and asked questions, to separate the healthy from the suspect. Horrified, they watched him approach with a sterilized buttonhook, then felt him lift up each eyelid to look for trachoma. The chalk was poised in his hand. An "E" chalked on their backs would mean eyes, "S" senility, "H" heart, "L" limp (in a child, perhaps a sign of rickets), "Pg" pregnant, "Sc" scalp. A circle with a cross in it meant feebleminded—and instant deportation. Although they couldn't see or understand the code letters on their backs, they soon wore the ingredients of their fate. Some had complete formulas, a medical history in shorthand.

How accurate do
you suppose
these medical
histories were?

What might
make a case
"suspicious"?

Suspicious cases were detained for further scrutiny, and if they failed to pass, they were denied entry. A golden drawbridge snapped shut with them outside. How could they return to shame, destitution or perhaps even death at the hands of a regime they fled? In despair, some committed suicide by leaping into the harbor.

But millions did go on to Stage 2—the Immigration Inspector, who was more ferocious and whimsical than God himself. Names were checked against the ship's manifest, and it was at this point that so many names changed. Some officers couldn't spell foreign names and suggested American versions. A Turkish "Suleman" became a Jewish "Solomon." A nervously uttered *"Ich vergesse"* (German for "I forget") became "Ferguson." Some names were cropped, others spelled phonetically, and real tongue-twisters were changed to an immigrant's milder-sounding hometown.

How do you
suppose the
immigrants felt
about the name
changes?

How do you
suppose the
lucky ones felt by
this time?

If they could prove they weren't diseased or feebleminded and could support themselves and knew where they were headed (Was "Pringvilliamas" really Springfield, Mass.?), they were free to step through that final, longed-for green door marked PUSH TO NEW YORK. It might have been their slogan.

Why does
Ackerman compare
New York to
Baghdad?

A short ferry ride later, they landed in a Manhattan of fatted zebras and Aladdin's lamps, "Baghdad on the Subway," as O. Henry called it. Most had never seen a two-story building before, let alone some that sprawled straight up to 60. They were fascinated by the dandified look of clean-shaven American men; in Europe, adult men wore beards. Most

saw blacks and Orientals for the first time. On Ellis Island, they wore
tags around their necks and filed through mazes like cattle, sometimes
living only on bread and ladles of prunes. And now suddenly they were
in the cornucopia of their dreams, a futuristic world of cars, towers, uproar and plenty. They had crossed not only an ocean but also an era, and
it would take all the stoic candor they possessed to adjust.

Ellis Island was the eye of a needle, and the miracle is that 17 million passed through it between 1892 and 1954, adding layer by layer to
the ethnic prism of the country. Half the people now alive in the United
States are descended from those immigrants.

What is a cornucopia?

In what ways was Ellis Island like the "eye of a needle"?

What is an ethnic prism?

Questions for discussion:

1. How would you have felt about being an immigrant at Ellis Island?
2. Did any of your ancestors pass through Ellis Island? Do you know how they felt about it?
3. Which immigrants probably received the best treatment? Why?
4. What do you think awaited the immigrants in New York?
5. Do you think that most felt that immigrating was worth the trouble? What about those who were denied entry? What happened to them?

DEVILS IN FUR COATS?

by Erwin A. Bauer

North American history has been vastly affected by certain wild animals.
Much of the continent was first explored by beaver trappers and fur trad-
ers. And everyone knows about the economic importance of the buffalo
to the Indians—and the near elimination of the species. Later, market
hunting for waterfowl and passenger pigeons became a great industry.
But no animal has excited men's fears and imaginations more than the
grizzly bear. No native animal has ever been surrounded by more legend
and colorful lore. And maybe no beast is more misunderstood.

The grizzly, *Ursus horribilis,* or more recently *Ursus arctos* to some
authorities, is one of the largest carnivores on earth. Only the Alaskan
brown bear (if indeed it isn't only a bigger grizzly) and the polar bear are
larger. Potentially, the grizzly is the most dangerous and formidable creature to walk on four feet. It is unpredictable and when full grown is as
magnificent a brute as any outdoorsman will ever encounter. I have met

What happened to the buffalo? The passenger pigeons?

Why are people afraid of grizzlies?

What do these scientific names mean?

Why might a grizzly be more awesome than a lion or a rhinoceros?

Who were Lewis and Clark? What were they doing on the Missouri River in 1805?

What would you have done in this situation?

How is a possum treed?

If you lived through a grizzly attack, how would you feel about grizzlies?

How might *grisly* become *grizzly*?

Have you ever seen a black bear? A grizzly?

lions and rhinos, jaguars and elephants at close range, but a large grizzly always seems more awesome.

The early explorers found it hard not to encounter grizzlies, and there are many quaint and interesting accounts of these meetings. In 1805 Lewis and Clark met this "tremendiously looking anamal," [*sic*] and it wasn't exactly a cordial contact. The bruin chased Lewis back into the Missouri River. Lewis later wrote: "There was no place by means of which I could conceal myself from the monster until I could charge my rifle. In this situation I thought of retreating in a brisk walk until I could reach a tree about 300 yards below me, but I had no sooner terned myself about but he pitched at me, open mouthed and full speed. I ran into the water to such depth that I could stand and he would be obliged to swim, and that I could in that situation defend myself with my espontoon."

Luckily for Captain Lewis, he didn't have to use his espontoon, which is a short pike. But some frontiersmen who followed weren't so fortunate. Kit Carson was treed like a possum a number of times, and old Jim Bridger regarded the bears with great respect. "Grizzlies," he told a friend, "is nothing but devils in fur coats."

Another of the greatest mountain men, Hugh Glass, survived a brush with a grizzly that seems incredible. In 1825 Glass shot a bear but only wounded it, and the bear dragged Glass from a tree into which he tried to escape. The animal proceeded to maul and mutilate Glass beyond recognition, breaking bones and tearing most of his scalp away. His condition appeared so hopeless that his companions (including Jim Bridger) abandoned him for dead.

But somehow, unattended, and after lying in a coma for days, Glass survived and crawled more than one hundred miles on his belly down the Missouri to Fort Pierre, South Dakota. There he continued his recovery, and he later went back to trapping and exploring in the Rockies.

It is hard to say how the grizzly first received its name. Earliest accounts used the terms "gray bear" or "white bear," both of which were probably translations of Indian names for the animal. But more than likely, grizzly is derived from one of two sources: from *grisel*, an old French word meaning "gray"; or from the Old English *grislic*, which meant "horrible" or "demonlike." Some early writers called the brute a "grisly" rather than "grizzly" bear. Later on, during the era of Jim Bridger and the Mountain Men, a grizzly was called Ephraim, or Old Ephraim, or Old Eph. A common term today is "silvertip," a name that describes the animal when the sun backlights the long guard hairs on its back.

Actually, grizzlies come in various colors, from almost black through all shades of brown to almost light blond. Occasionally younger bears are bicolored: dark brown underneath with a blond or near-yellow saddle.

An adult grizzly is truly impressive and remarkable. He can run with startling speed, and an actual charge must be a chilling, fearsome thing. I have watched a female grizzly negotiate a rimrock that appeared difficult even for a bighorn sheep. Still more remarkable, a pair of small cubs followed her.

It isn't easy to confuse grizzlies with the black bears that often share the same range. The wide dished-in face and shoulder hump of the grizzly are highly distinctive. And to me at least, a grizzly has a bolder, more confident and rolling gait. Even the pawprints are distinctive from a black bear's, because the long claws of a grizzly's front feet are etched in soft earth. A black bear's claws do not show unless he is scratching or is injured.

How do you define provocation?

Will a grizzly attack without provocation?

Probably there are more opinions on this than there are grizzly bears, but the wisest answer might be "No—not ordinarily." A lot depends on how you define provocation.

What would you do if you saw a grizzly in the wilderness?

Is it provocation when a cub wanders into your path and cries out in surprise? Next thing you know, Mama may be on your back. Is it provocation if you unknowingly stumble on a bear's meat cache? Or if you meet a grizzly that has just been stung by a whole hive of hornets and is furious with the world? Or how about the big old sow I shot in British Columbia several years ago—the one with abscessed, almost completely hollow teeth? My dentist examined the skull and reported that the bear must have been suffering incredible pain. If that bear had attacked out of pure desperation, would it have been provoked or not?

What does persecuted mean?

Do you feel that grizzlies are persecuted?

Does the grizzly have a place in the civilized world?

Because grizzlies are potentially dangerous to men and even more so to livestock, they have always been relentlessly hunted and persecuted. And probably—tragically—this will continue until all are gone. Everything has been used from helicopters to poison cartridges and electronics. Some people will not mourn the passing, those who shudder every time they hear of a rare grizzly incident and then remark that such a dangerous beast doesn't have a place in the civilized world.

Are the comparisons here appropriate?

Well, airplane and car crashes kill human beings wholesale, and no one suggests that we save the civilized world from flying and driving. In addition, many times more humans are killed or injured every year by domestic cattle—and even by bumblebees—than have been injured by bears in the last half-century. Like plane crashes, bears simply make headlines. They always have.

Questions for discussion:

1. Bauer says the grizzlies are misunderstood. Does the article support this claim? What is the misunderstanding? Are grizzlies not fierce or dangerous, as legend says?
2. Does the writer think the grizzlies are treated fairly, that they get what they deserve? What similarities does he find between the grizzly and the passenger pigeon? How should grizzlies be treated?

CASE HISTORY: THE DONORA SMOG EPISODE

by Amos Turk, Jonathan Turk, Janet T. Wittes, and Robert E. Wittes

How might this location make Donora foggy?

Donora is an industrial town of about 14,000 people, located on the inside of a sharp horseshoe bend of the Monongahela River, about 48 km (30 miles) south of Pittsburgh, Pennsylvania. The area along the river bank . . . is occupied by a steel-and-wire plant and by a zinc-and-sulfuric-acid plant. Taken together, the plants extend for some 5 km (3 miles) along the river bank. Across the river . . . the hills rise sharply to a height of some 105 meters (350 ft) above the river bank; on the Donora side the elevation is a bit higher, though the rise is more gradual. These hills tower

What is an *atmospheric inversion*? What are *pollutants*?

far above the factory chimneys, and as a result, any atmospheric inversion threatens to convert Donora into a basin that collects pollutants from the stacks along the river bank. Anyone familiar with the hill country of Pennsylvania and West Virginia knows that foggy days are common there, especially in the fall. The blackened houses and treeless hills of Donora show vividly that the atmospheric stagnations which shelter these fogs do in fact trap the pollutants that come from the chimneys.

Why might such a fog occur in October?

One such polluted fog settled over the area during the last week of October, 1948. It started Tuesday morning, October 26, and seemed somewhat heavy and motionless, but the townspeople had seen many such fogs before. By the next day, however, there was such a dead calm that it was considered unusual, even for Donora. Streams of sooty gas from locomotives did not even rise, but hung motionless in the air. The visibility was so poor that even natives of the area become lost. Such

What makes dense fog worse than darkness?

dense fog is much worse that mere darkness, which can be pierced by a flashlight beam. During such episodes, a driver cannot see the side of the road, nor even the white line that marks the center. If he leaves his car to explore the immediate area, he may become disoriented and lost

Might he have trouble hearing as well as seeing in the fog? Why or why not?

and be unable to find his way back unless he can hear the sound of the idling engine.

The smog continued through Thursday, when it seemed to become thicker with what may be called chemical "sensations," for such perceptions go beyond the sense of smell: they involve various receptors in the nose and mouth and give rise to sensations of tickling, scratchiness, irritation, and even taste. Sulfur dioxide, particularly, is a gas that imparts

Why is sulfur dioxide mentioned particularly?

a bittersweet taste at the back of the tongue. The fog had piled up in height as well, and the mills, except for the tops of their stacks, had become invisible.

Some illnesses had begun, rather gradually, on Tuesday, and their number had increased on Wednesday and Thursday, but they were yet too scattered to alarm the community. On Friday, however, the rate of illness soared, so that altogether about 40 percent of the exposed population developed some symptoms of illness before the episode was over. The symptoms included smarting of eyes, nasal discharge, constriction in the throat, nausea and vomiting, tightness in the chest, cough, and shortness of breath.

The first death came to a retired steelworker named Ivan Ceh at 1:30 Saturday morning; the second occurred an hour later. By 10 A.M. nine bodies lay at one undertaker's, one at a second undertaker's, and another, the eleventh death so far, at a third. Knowledge of the extent of the disaster gradually spread through the town. It was a long time before the citizens of Donora, accustomed as they were to smog, began to realize that a real calamity was at hand. Help then began to come in from neighboring towns and hospitals (there was none in Donora) and an emergency-aid station was in operation by Saturday night. The death toll that day reached 17. Two more people died on Sunday, and at six o'clock on Sunday morning the factories finally began to shut down. By afternoon it started to drizzle. It really rained Sunday night and Monday, and then it was all over, except for the lingering illnesses and one more death, which occurred a week later.

There are two sequels to the Donora episode. One involved Donora itself and its people. The other involves all of us, everywhere.

To Donora, after the killing smog lifted, came teams of investigators from the U.S. Public Health Service and the Pennsylvania Department of Health. They studied the clinical evidence, the sources of the pollutants, and the local weather patterns. They found that of the nearly 6000 people who became ill during the air pollution episode, most did so because of severe irritation of the respiratory tract; those who became sickest tended to be older than 60 and to have pre-existing disease of the heart and/or lungs which rendered them more sensitive to the irritant effects of the pollutants. The study of pollutant sources identified the emissions from the various manufacturing operations and made specific recommendations for their reduction. The meteorological study confirmed what everyone knew, namely that "a definite relationship . . . existed between the concentration of contaminants and atmospheric stability."

In spite of these studies, however, the *specific* cause of the disaster was not identified. It is important to understand what this statement means and what its implications are. It tells us that the study did not reveal enough for a chemist to be able to duplicate the killer smog in a laboratory flask by mixing together a collection of known ingredients. In kitchen parlance, one may say that the study did not furnish the recipe for the smog. Why would one want to have such a recipe? The answer is: to know what must be *avoided* in the atmosphere.

This brings us to the second, broader sequel to Donora, because it presents a general question. If it is not known exactly what it is in air pollution that harms people, how does one know what standards to set?

Why would this smog cause illness?

Why didn't people become alarmed when the first deaths occurred?

How many days did the crisis last?

What was the total number of deaths?

What are *sequels*?

Why did the investigators visit Donora?

Why did older people become sickest?

What is meant by the *specific* cause?

What does *parlance* mean?

The clinical study of the Donora episode led to the following conclusion, as stated in the government report:

**What does
syndrome mean?**

> It does not appear probable from the evidence obtained in the investigation that any one of these substances (irritant or nonirritant) *by itself* was capable of producing the syndrome observed. However, a combination of two or more of these substances may have contributed to that syndrome.

**In what way was
the Donora
episode a
landmark?**

There have been deaths caused by air pollution before and since, but in the United States, Donora was a landmark in public attitudes toward air pollution. The incident shocked people into the realization that air pollution can be deadly, that simplified experiments with laboratory animals exposed to individual pollutants do not predict how humans will be affected in polluted outdoor atmospheres, that factories should shut down during air pollution episodes before deaths occur, and that the establishment of air quality standards must take into account, to the extent that good judgment can serve as a guide, the possibilities of unknown and subtle effects.

Questions for discussion:

1. Could the disaster in Donora have been avoided? What could have been done on Tuesday to prevent the deaths?
2. What significance does this case history have for you? Have you ever experienced a smog-induced illness? Is your home smoggy?
3. We think of smog as being the special problem of big cities, but Donora was a small town. Has this article changed any of your ideas or attitudes about smog?

THE TRIANGLE OF DISAPPEARING PLANES

by Charles Berlitz

**What is a
triangle? What is
the Bermuda
Triangle?**

The Bermuda Triangle received its name as the result of the disappearance of six Navy planes and their crews on December 5, 1945. The first five planes that disappeared, apparently simultaneously, were on a routine training mission with a flight plan designed to follow a triangular flight pattern starting at the Naval Air Station at Ford Lauderdale, Florida, then 160 miles to the east, 40 miles to the north, and then back to their base, following a southwest course. Bermuda has given its name to what has been variously called "The Devil's Triangle," "The Triangle of Death," "The Hoodoo Sea," "The Graveyard of the Atlantic," and various other appellations, principally because it was noticed at the time

What do
appellations and
apex mean?

What does
inexplicably
mean?

In what way were
the planes
"doomed"?

Why is it
important for us
to know that
conditions were
"ideal flying
weather"?

Why was nothing
of an unusual
nature expected?

What does
vengeance mean?

that the apex of the triangular flight plan from Fort Lauderdale was in a direct line with Bermuda, and partly because Bermuda seems to be the northern boundary of both earlier and later disappearances of ships and planes in very unusual circumstances. But no incident before or since has been more remarkable than this *total* disappearance of an entire training flight, along with the giant rescue plane, a Martin Mariner with a crew of thirteen, which inexplicably vanished during rescue operations.

Flight 19 was the designation of the group of doomed planes which left their base at Fort Lauderdale on the afternoon of December 5, 1945. They were manned by five officer pilots and nine enlisted crew members, the latter detailed two to each plane but on this day short one man, who had requested removal from flying status because of a premonition and who had not been replaced. The planes were Navy Grumman TBM-3 Avenger torpedo bombers, and each carried enough fuel to enable it to cruise over a thousand miles. The temperature was sixty-five degrees, the sun was shining, there were scattered clouds and a moderate northeast wind. Pilots who had flown earlier the same day reported ideal flying weather. Flight time was calculated as two hours for this specific mission. The planes started taking off at 2 P.M. and by 2:10 P.M. they were all airborne. Lieutenant Charles Taylor, with over 2,500 hours flying time, who was in command, led the planes to Chicken Shoals, north of Bimini, where they were first to make practice runs on a target hulk. Both pilots and crews were experienced airmen and there was no reason to expect anything of an unusual nature to happen during the routine mission of Flight 19.

But something did happen, and with a vengeance. At about 3:15 P.M., after the bombing run had been accomplished and the planes had continued east, the radioman at the Fort Lauderdale Naval Air Station Tower, who had been expecting contact from the planes regarding estimated time of arrival and landing instructions, received an unusual message from the flight leader. The record shows the following:

> FLIGHT LEADER (LIEUTENANT CHARLES TAYLOR): Calling Tower. This is an emergency. We seem to be off course. We cannot see land. . . . Repeat . . . We cannot see land.
> TOWER: What is your position?
> FLIGHT LEADER: We are not sure of our position. We cannot be sure just where we are. . . . We seem to be lost. . . .
> TOWER: Assume bearing due west.
> FLIGHT LEADER: We don't know which way is west. Everything is wrong. . . . Strange . . . We can't be sure of any direction—even the ocean doesn't look as it should. . . .

At about 3:30 the senior flight instructor at Fort Lauderdale had picked up on his radio a message from someone calling Powers, one of the student flyers, requesting information about his compass readings and heard Powers say, "I don't know where we are. We must have got lost after that last turn." The senior flight instructor was able to contact the Flight 19 instructor, who told him, "Both my compasses are out. I am trying to find Ford Lauderdale. . . . I am sure I'm in the Keys, but I don't know how far down. . . ." The senior flight instructor thereupon advised him to fly north—with the sun on the portside—until he reached the Fort Lauderdale Naval Air Station. But he subsequently heard: "We have just passed over a small island. . . . No other land in sight . . ."—an indication that the instructor's plane was not over the Keys and that the entire flight, since they were unable to see land, which would normally follow a continuation of the Keys, had lost its direction.

It became increasingly difficult to hear messages from Flight 19 because of static. Apparently Flight 19 could no longer hear messages from the tower, but the tower could hear conversations between the planes. Some of these messages referred to possible fuel shortages—fuel for only seventy-five miles, references to seventy-five-mile-per-hour winds, and the unnerving observation that every gyro and magnetic compass in all the planes were off—"going crazy," as it was reported at the time—each showing a different reading. During all this time the powerful transmitter at Fort Lauderdale was unable to make any contact with the five planes, although the interplane communications were fairly audible.

By this time the personnel of the base were in an understandable uproar as news spread that Flight 19 had encountered an emergency. All kinds of suppositions concerning enemy attack (although World War II had been over for several months), or even attacks by new enemies, suggested themselves, and rescue craft were dispatched, notably a twin-engined Martin Mariner flying boat patrol plane with a crew of thirteen, from the Banana River Naval Air Station.

At 4 P.M. the tower suddenly heard that Lieutenant Taylor had unexpectedly turned over command to a senior Marine pilot, Captain Stiver. Although obscured by static and strained by tension an understandable message was received from him: "We are not sure where we are. . . . We think we must be 225 miles northeast of base. . . . We must have passed over Florida and we must be in the Gulf of Mexico. . . ." The flight leader then apparently decided to turn 180 degrees in the hope of flying back over Florida, but as they made the turn the transmission began to get fainter, indicating that they had made a wrong turn and were flying east, away from the Florida coast over the open sea. Some reports claim that the last words heard from Flight 19 were "It looks like we are . . ." Although other listeners seem to remember more, such as: "Entering white water . . . We are completely lost. . . ."

Meanwhile the tower received a message only minutes after takeoff from Lieutenant Come, one of the officers of the Martin Mariner, dispatched to the general area where the flight was presumed to be, that there were strong winds above 6,000 feet. This, however, was the last message received from the rescue plane. Shortly after this all search units

---

Marginal notes (left column):

How might a compass be "out"?

Why keep the sun on the portside?

Why was this observation "unnerving"?

How might the problems with radio contact have contributed to the sense of unreality that clings to the incident?

Why were they worried about an attack?

Why might Taylor have given up command?

What could account for the differences in these reports?

received an urgent message stating that six planes instead of five were now missing. The rescue plane, with a crew of thirteen, had disappeared as well.

No further message was ever received from the Flight 19 training mission or from the Martin Mariner that was sent to rescue them. Some time after 7 P.M., however, the Opa-Locka Naval Air Station in Miami received a faint message consisting of: "FT . . . FT . . ." which was part of the call letters of the planes of Flight 19, the instructor's plane being FT-28. But if this message was really from the "lost patrol," the time period in which it was received would indicate that the message was sent two hours *after* the planes had presumably run out of fuel.

The original air search, initiated on the day of disappearance, was suspended because of darkness, although Coast Guard vessels continued to look for survivors during the night. The next day, Thursday, an enormous search effort was started at "first light," i.e., daybreak. But in spite of one of history's most intensive searches, involving 240 planes and sixty-seven additional planes from the aircraft carrier *Solomons,* four destroyers, several submarines, eighteen Coast Guard Vessels, search and rescue cutters, hundreds of private planes, yachts, and boats, and additional PBMs from the Banana River Naval Air Station and help by R.A.F. and Royal Navy units in the Bahamas, nothing was found. . . .

A Naval Board of Inquiry, after examining all available evidence and incidentally debating the court-martial of the instrument officer (who was later exonerated when it was established that all his instruments had checked out before takeoff) ended up as much in the dark as ever as to what had really happened. Part of the report states: "A radio message intercepted indicated that the planes were lost and that they were experiencing malfunctioning of their compasses." Captain W. C. Wingard, an information officer, was somewhat more direct in a subsequent press interview: ". . . Members of the Board of Inquiry were not able to make even a good guess as to what happened." Another Board member rather dramatically commented: "They vanished as completely as if they had flown to Mars," thereby introducing the intriguing elements of space travel and possible UFOs which have since become very much a part of the Bermuda Triangle legend. Serious investigators and oceanographers have offered a variety of opinions as to how these and so many other ships and planes could disappear without trace, and how so many pilots and passengers could completely vanish. Lieutenant Commander R. H. Wirsching, a training officer at the Fort Lauderdale Naval Air Base at the time of the incident, who has considered the case for many years, thinks that the word "disappear" is an important factor concerning the fate of the crew of Flight 19 as no proof has ever been adduced that they effectively perished. (A mother of one of the lost pilots who attended the naval hearing stated at the time that she had received the impression that her son "was still alive somewhere in space.") And Dr. Manson Valentine, a scientist who has watched the area for many years from Miami, was quoted in the Miami *News* as saying: "They are still here, but in a different dimension of a magnetic phenomenon that could have been set up by a UFO." A Coast Guard officer, a member of the Board of Inquiry, expressed himself with rather refreshing frankness as he observed simply, "We don't know what the hell is going on out there." And a final, more formal statement from another officer of the Board expressed the consensus of the investigating officers: ". . . This unprecedented peacetime loss seems to be a total mystery, the strangest ever investigated in the annals of naval aviation."

What does
phenomenon mean?

Why is strangest
an appropriate
description for
the incident?

Questions for discussion:

1. Which of the statements from Naval Board of Inquiry members seem most pertinent to you? Why? Which seem least helpful? Why?
2. How does the way in which Berlitz writes add to the drama and the mystery of the incident?

FITNESS IS A PIECE OF CAKE

by Laurence E. Morehouse and Leonard Gross

I hate to exercise. I always have. In high school, I was the gym-class rebel. When the rest of the class did calisthenics with their arms, I mimicked them with my fingers. My friends thought I was hilarious. My gym teacher didn't think so. One day he called me into his office and said, "I notice that you like to lead your little group. I'm going to give you the opportunity to lead the entire class."

How would he
mimic
calisthenics with
his fingers?

It was one thing to be a cut-up. It was another to be a fool. I spent the weekend reading books on physical conditioning. When the teacher called on me the following Monday, I was ready. From then on, I led the class in calisthenics, and he sat in his office and read the newspaper.

Why did the
author study
books about
physical
conditioning all
weekend?

I didn't know it at the time, but that assignment shaped my life. For the last forty-three years, I have studied human performance and how it can be enhanced. I've worked with world-class champions to improve their speed or power or skills. I've helped corporate executives develop their energy and concentration. I've designed a program to maintain the fitness of America's astronauts in space, on the moon and during their eventual trip to Mars. But nothing I have done in this interval has in any way changed my bias against structured exercise; to the contrary, what I've learned has only deepened it.

How did this
assignment
shape his life?

Do you share
this bias?

Most Americans share my bias—women in particular. Newspapers and magazines make much of statistics indicating that millions of Americans are on a fitness kick. That isn't really true. The figures, from a survey made for the President's Council on Physical Fitness and Sport, show that fifty-five percent of the nation's adults engage in some form of exercise. But when the activities themselves are analyzed, it's apparent that at least eighty percent of the adult population isn't exercising sufficiently or properly to arrest physiological decay.

What does physiological mean?

In their resistance to exercise, Americans show a certain amount of commendable intuitive sense. Exercise, as it is generally taught and practiced, is not simply boring; it is punitive, dangerous and ineffective.

What do intuitive and punitive mean?

How Exercise Became Such a Bore

Calisthenics originated in Sweden during the nineteenth century. Swedish landowners found the sight of their stooped and sagging peasants offensive; they investigated physical drills to improve the peasants' posture and counteract the effects of work. They wanted the peasants to bear themselves like soldiers. As a consequence, calisthenic drills and movements became militaristic: by the numbers, shoulders back. That's not just philosophically offensive, it's physiologically harmful. Precise, geometric movements are unnatural and inefficient; movement should be accomplished in a flowing manner and in a circular plane. As to posture, holding the chest up, shoulders back and head erect puts an extra burden on the muscles. The straight, flat back esteemed by the military is a painful back. The best position for the shoulders is hanging loose to the sides, not braced to a point that puts a harmful weight on the spine. The vertical posture is not meant to be exaggerated; man was constructed to be only somewhat upright.

Why did it matter what the landowners thought? Why would the peasants do calisthenics if they did not enjoy them?

What posture does the writer advocate?

Exercise programs are often so rigorous that those who attempt them are injured. The goals of fitness are placed beyond the average person's reach. The mystique fostered by the fitness cult encourages the belief that good physical condition comes slowly, that work to exhaustion is necessary, that the process requires special equipment, space, supervision and an abundance of time. Men should look like Tarzan. Women should resemble his Jane. It's all nonsense.

What does mystique mean? What mystique does the fitness cult foster?

The science of physical fitness concerns itself primarily with athletes. Physical-fitness "experts" are usually athletic coaches. Books on jogging are written by track coaches. The training they impose on the public reflects their orientation. But an athlete is a different person, psychologically and physiologically, from the nonathlete. Athletes will take the time to train. They will sacrifice social pleasures, endure discomfort, even punish themselves in order to create the tolerances required for record-breaking performances. These attributes do not characterize the majority of people.

How is the science of physical fitness biased?

Should we all be like athletes?

A secondary emphasis of the science of fitness is in therapy for persons recuperating from illness. In therapy, you concentrate on the injured or diseased part, rather than on the body as a whole. Those fitness programs that focus on isolated body parts stem from a therapeutic orientation. Once again, the objectives and techniques of exercise have almost no bearing on the needs of normal people.

So we find exercise concentrated at two extremes of the human condition—superbly fit athletes at one end, and hospital patients on the mend at the other. In the center of the spectrum are the overwhelming majority of nonathletic Americans who are healthy and capable of exertion and yet do almost no exercise at all.

Our cultural values reinforce their lassitude. We esteem those who can ride rather than walk and who can sit rather than stand. The higher one rises in the hierarchy, the greater one's comfort and ease. Wealthy golfers drive golf carts. We hire athletes to perform for us so that we can enjoy sports vicariously. We buy expensive, fuel-costly devices promoted as energy "savers." They're not saving us a thing; they're depriving us of the movement and exertion we need to live an energetic life.

What does therapeutic mean?

What does lassitude mean? What cultural values reinforce it?

What do hierarchy and vicariously mean?

What energy savers do we buy?

Heart Rate: A Loud and Clear Signal of Effort

When a man works on the surface of the moon, three signals indicate the extent of his effort: his consumption of oxygen, his body heat and his heart rate. The measurement of oxygen consumption is about as revealing as watching the fuel gauge on your automobile. The gauge tells you how much gas you have left, but it doesn't say anything about the efficiency or condition of the engine. The temperature of the fluids in your system that cools the astronaut inside his space suit tells you how much heat he's giving off, which gives you an idea of the amount of energy he's using. But it takes ten to fifteen minutes to obtain these figures and decide what has happened ten or fifteen minutes earlier. By then it may be too late to make an adjustment. The same problem exists in measuring oxygen consumption.

What does consumption mean?

The third signal is heart rate. It's loud and clear.

It takes a while for the body to heat up. Oxygen usage occurs over a prolonged period. But heart rate is an immediately available indicator of the level of physical effort as of that very moment.

What are the signals of effort?

If an astronaut is working too fast, a doctor in Houston monitoring the mission can tell him to slow down. If the astronaut's heart rate is below what has been gauged acceptable for that task and that astronaut, the doctor can advise the astronaut that he could work a little harder without impairing his condition.

It was the problem of maintaining the fitness of astronauts during prolonged space flights that turned my thinking around. We know that a man who does nothing for a month will lose eighty percent of his physical condition. An astronaut who did little or nothing active in Skylab or on trips to distant planets would quickly become too weak to perform

How did this problem turn the author's thinking around?

his mission. How to keep him fit? It occurred to me that traditional fitness programs wouldn't work. Each time he did an exercise, the astronaut would do it more easily. His body wouldn't be exercised sufficiently. Making the exercise progressively more arduous was helpful, but it still wouldn't tell us whether the workout was sufficient—or too strenuous. It became evident to me that exercise should not be controlled on the basis of time, distance, physical load or other external scales, but on the degree of physiological effort as indicated by physiological signals.

What do arduous *and* strenuous *mean?*

NASA adopted a program based on these principles in 1965. Its efficacy was confirmed eight years later, when three U.S. astronauts returned from a twenty-eight-day mission in Skylab. It was thought that they might have to be carried from their capsule in stretchers. But they had maintained an activity schedule I helped develop for them, based on physiological effort. They walked away from the capsule, a little wobbly, but under their own power.

What does efficacy *mean?*

How did heart rate affect the astronauts' exercise?

The physiological signal used by the astronauts to monitor their maintenance programs was their heart rate. Using heart rate to monitor exercise in ordinary people is a research bonus of the space program.

What Your Pulse Signals

Heart rate and pulse rate, technically, are separate phenomena. But the difference, for our purpose, is not significant. Your pulse tells you how fast your heart is beating.

What is the pulse?

We all know that pulse rate is important. When you go to a doctor's office for a checkup, there are three things his nurse almost invariably does: she takes your temperature, weighs you and takes your pulse. If you've ever spent any time in a hospital, one of the first things you become aware of is that people are taking your pulse all day long. They awaken you in the morning, or during your afternoon nap, and they come in at night just as you're falling asleep. It's imperative that they compare your pulse rates during your course of treatment.

Why do they want to compare your pulse rates?

We know now that pulse rate is not related merely to illness, but also to health. Sickness is indicated by a too rapid pulse, or one that's not beating rhythmically. Health is indicated by one's pulse-rate response to stress.

Should everyone's pulse rate be the same?

Your pulse is as singular as your signature or your fingerprint. It has a characteristic wave form. The wave may have a sharp peak, or be relatively flat. It might have subpeaks. It beats with a certain rhythmicity peculiar to your system. So distinctive is each pulse that a nurse in a ward filled with patients she had attended for some time could be blindfolded, led through shuffled beds and not only identify each patient from his pulse, but tell whether the patient was doing well or poorly that day.

With five minutes' training, you can learn to interpret your own well-being by taking your pulse. You can also note the difference in your

How are
excitement and
calmness
reflected by pulse
rate?

emotional state from day to day. If you're excited, your pulse races. When you're calm and tranquil, your pulse reflects that rhythm. In a sense, the pulse is an aspect of your countenance.

Your normal pulse rate may be extremely fast or extremely slow compared to the norms—and yet be normal for you. You could have a pulse rate of ninety beats a minute while seated and yet be in better condition than someone with a normal rate of forty-five beats a minute.

Your Pulse Rate Guides Your Program

However it beats at rest, it's your pulse rate during exercise that enables you to structure your fitness program exactly to your requirements. Your pulse rate is your individualized guide to fitness.

What does he
mean by being in
good condition
"relative to" your
condition at the
beginning of the
program?

This program applies equally to men and women. The only persons who shouldn't attempt it are those whose doctors have forbidden exertion, or who fail the pulse test you'll be taking later on. Beyond that, the program is open regardless of age or physical condition. Those who are in the worst shape, in fact, will show the most dramatic and rapid improvement. If you haven't exercised once in the last twenty years, you are nonetheless just two hours away from good physical condition, relative to the condition you were in when you began. At the end of twelve hours, you'll be in excellent shape by any standards. You'll look and feel younger. Your waist will be thinner, your hips and thighs firmer. And you'll be permanently rid of many pounds of fat.

What does
cumulative mean?

Is it better to
exercise every day?

Those hours represent the cumulative time of three bouts of exercise a week of ten minutes each, during three courses of eight weeks each. You can do more if you wish. But the data say that you don't get much more good out of exercising every day than you do from exercising every other day. This is one program that discourages overzealousness.

What is the price
of neglect?

The only price you pay for years of neglect is that it takes you a little longer to come back and you have a little further to go. You've already paid the price of low performance and a poor state of health for all the time you were out of shape. There are no further penalties, such as hard exercise.

Why would an
accountant spend
April at his or
her desk?

The least little thing you do will measurably improve you. Consider the accountant who spends a solid month at his desk prior to the April 15th deadline for filing personal income tax. If he's been totally without exercise, his condition will be only twenty percent of what it was when the month began. But half an hour of activity that wouldn't normally be considered exercise—running errands or shopping—would restore twenty percent of the fitness he's lost. The first thirty feet of walking by a man who's recovering from surgery or been bedridden for several weeks will have a marked effect on his system. When your fitness is low, the least bit more of activity of any kind will change your strength, your muscular and cardio-respiratory endurance, help solidify your bones and resurrect your circulatory vessels.

What is cardio-
respiratory
endurance?

The Joys of Pulse-Rated Exercise

What is pulse-rated exercise?

The maximum level of trainability for any man or woman is when he or she starts training at the age of ten and trains ever thereafter without getting sick. No one ever does that. All of us can only approach our potential. None of us ever reaches it. If you are fifty and you haven't worked out for twenty years, you can never get to the level of condition you would have achieved had you continued to play the tennis you played in college. If you had wanted to be the best possible sixty-year-old, the time to start was when you were ten. But you can start at fifty, having **What does** *slough off* **mean?** sloughed off since you were twenty, and be an astonishingly splendid sixty. You'll be in better shape than you were at fifty—even forty.

Actually, you may not be in such bad shape as you thought you were. If you've been climbing stairs or hauling heavy bags of groceries or polishing your car or even swinging a baby, you probably don't have far to go to be in decent shape.

There's no reason not to be in shape. It's so easy. It takes so little time. The response you get from the slightest amount of exercise is so great. You're immediately rewarded with a feeling of increased well-being. With exercise, you're livelier longer. The period during which you're half dead is reduced. And you reduce the prospects of premature death.

What is an *infinitesimal* **increase?**

We'll start you with what you can do, no matter how little that is. Each day, you'll do just a little more, but so little that you'll scarcely notice. This all but infinitesimal increase is known as "overload." It's the foundation of pulse-rated exercise, and the key to its success.

Fitness is determined by what you do twenty-four hours a day, how you live, work, sit, walk, think, eat and sleep. Its purpose is to help you enjoy life, not to punish you or make you feel guilty. Life has enough burdens and prohibitions without adding to them. Just as you can become temporarily ill when you stop smoking, you can add to your deteriorative state by feeling anxious and guilty about skipping an exercise session, or by forcing yourself to do something you don't really enjoy doing.

Is "grin and bear it" a good motto for exercisers?

Why become fit?

This is not a young athlete's program. It's for the individual—man or woman—who wants a substantial reserve of fitness. It dispels late-day drag, makes physical recreation more enjoyable, gives you a sense of muscle tone, self-awareness and readiness, makes you more comfortable and secure because you know that if there's an emergency, you're better able to handle it. If you have to change a tire in the rain, you can do it without exhausting yourself. You can play an extra few sets of tennis with ease. You can stay up late when you have to. You can work an occasional eighteen-hour day and not need a week to recover. One not unimportant dividend is that you'll be a better lover.

I repeat: I hate formalized, rigid, punitive exercise. I hate it all the more now that I have the science to support my instinctive knowledge that it simply isn't necessary.

Questions for discussion:

1. Does the authors' approach to physical fitness appeal to you? Why or why not?
2. How is fitness "a piece of cake"? How is it not?
3. What do the examples about fitness in space and exertion on the moon tell you about at least one of the author's (Morehouse's) qualifications?
4. How does science support the "instinctive knowledge" that formalized exercise "simply isn't necessary"?

CONVERSATIONS WITH A GORILLA

by Francine Patterson

What makes Koko special?

Koko is a 7-year-old "talking" gorilla. She is the focus of my career as a developmental psychologist, and also has become a dear friend.

How does Koko talk?

Through mastery of sign language—the familiar hand speech of the deaf—Koko has made us, her human companions, aware not only that her breed is bright, but also that it shares sensitivities commonly held to be the prerogative of people.

What does *empathy* mean?

Take Koko's touching empathy toward fellow animals. Seeing a horse with a bit in its mouth, she signed, "Horse sad." When asked why the horse was sad, she signed, "Teeth." Shown a photo of the famous albino gorilla Snowflake struggling against having a bath, Koko, who also hates baths, signed, "Me cry there," while pointing at the picture.

What are *motivations*?

But Koko responds to more complicated motivations too. She loves an argument—and is not averse to trading insults.

At six o'clock on a spring evening last year, I went to the trailer where Koko lives to put her to bed. I was greeted by Cathy Ransom, one of my assistants, who told me that she and Koko had been arguing.

What is an *altercation*?

Lest I be alarmed at the thought of an altercation between this slight young woman, who is deaf, and a robust 6-year-old female gorilla, Cathy laughingly pointed to the notebook in which Koko's utterances in sign language are logged. The dispute began when Koko was shown a poster of herself that had been used during a fund-raising benefit. Manipulating hands and fingers, Cathy had asked Koko, "What's this?"

"Gorilla," signed Koko.

"Who gorilla?" asked Cathy.

Why might Koko reply *bird* when asked to identify a picture of herself?

"Bird," responded a bratty Koko, and things went downhill from there.

"You bird?" asked Cathy.

"You," countered Koko.

"Not me, you are bird," rejoined Cathy, mindful that "bird" can be an insult in Koko's lexicon.

"Me gorilla," asserted Koko.

"Who bird?" asked Cathy.

"You nut," replied Koko, resorting to another of her insults. (For Koko, "bird" and "nut" switch from descriptive to pejorative terms by changing the position in which the sign is made.)

"Why me nut?" asked Cathy.

"Nut, nut," signed Koko.

"You nut, not me," Cathy replied.

Finally Koko gave up. Plaintively she signed, "Damn me good," and walked away signing, "Bad."

What does lexicon mean?

What does pejorative mean?

"When She Is Good. . . ."

Why does the writer agree with Koko?

I fully agree with Koko, if she meant that she is good even in a bad situation. I've come to cherish her lies, relish her arguments, and look forward to her insults. While these behaviors demonstrate occasional lapses from sweetness, they also provide reassuring benchmarks in the formal and controlled scientific testing that has monitored Koko's progress since I began to teach her American Sign Language in July 1972.

. . .

Why was the author "undeterred" after being bitten?

On our first meeting, Koko did nothing to advance the cause of gorilla public relations. Quickly sizing me up, the tiny 20-pound gorilla bit me on the leg. But I was undeterred. People often ask if I am worried about dealing with Koko when she reaches full growth, perhaps 250 pounds. The answer is no, though at 130 pounds she already outweighs me and is astonishingly strong. While many captive chimpanzees become difficult to work with as they mature, gorillas seem to be of quite a different temperament.

What does quelled mean?

Soon after starting work with Koko, I met Carroll Soo-Hoo, the man who had donated Koko's mother to the San Francisco Zoo. Mr. Soo-Hoo brought out photos of himself, a slight man, romping with three 200-pound gorillas. That quelled whatever doubts I may have had about the danger of working with these immensely strong animals.

Pupil Begins to Learn — Reluctantly

What does contentious mean?

Koko at first seemed to prefer men to women. While often contentious with me, she was beautifully behaved with Ron Cohn, my close friend and the photographer who has documented Koko's history.

Most bite attempts resulted from the method I used to get Koko to make signs — the "molding" technique the Gardners used with Washoe. The experimenter takes the hands of the subject and shapes them into the proper configuration for the sign representing an activity or an object while in its presence. As the animal comes to associate the hand

How is an animal taught to use sign language?

movement and its meaning, the teacher gradually loosens his or her hold on the ape's hands until the animal is making the sign by itself. At first, every time I would take Koko's hands to mold a sign, she would try to bite me.

Another early problem—before we left the zoo for more satisfactory quarters—was distraction. I found it hard to keep Koko's attention while visitors to the glass-enclosed nursery stared, knocked, and commented on the curious tableau we presented. I grew weary of smirking people (who thought we could not hear them) saying, "Which one is the gorilla?" So it was with great relief that I moved Koko into her own trailer.

Why might it be difficult to train an animal in a zoo?

Are Apes Capable of Language?

What do *sanguine* and *dexterity* mean?

My colleagues were not very sanguine about teaching Koko sign language. Some questioned the gorilla's dexterity as compared with the chimpanzee's. Others were skeptical about the animal's intellect.

In 1959 Hilda Knobloch and Benjamin Pasamanick had reported: "There is little question that the chimpanzee is capable of conceptualization and abstraction that is beyond the abilities of the gorilla."

My experience has been totally at odds with this assumption. While Koko certainly has been contrary at times, I believe that such brattiness may indicate intelligence rather than its absence.

How might "brattiness" indicate intelligence?

In 1929 the great primatologists Robert and Ada Yerkes wrote: "It is entirely possible that the gorilla, while being distinctly inferior to the chimpanzee in ability to use and fashion implements and to operate mechanisms, is superior to it in certain other modes of behavioral adaptation and may indeed possess a higher order of intelligence than any other existing anthropoid ape." Now, fifty years later, Koko is bolstering evidence of the gorilla's intellectual primacy.

What is a primatologist?

Koko Becomes a Star

From the start I have daily recorded Koko's casual signing, conversations, and self-directed utterances. I have also recorded her signing on videotape and film. Grants from the National Geographic Society and other private foundations have enabled me to meet the heavy costs—especially for equipment—to keep Project Koko going.

Vocabulary development is one of the best indexes of human intelligence. Koko's vocabulary grew at a remarkable pace. Over the first year and a half, she acquired about one new sign every month. After 36 months of training, Koko was reliably using 184 signs—that is, she used each spontaneously at least once a day, 15 days out of a month. By age 4½, she had 222 signs by the same criterion. By 6½, she had used 645 different signs. This figure refers simply to the total number of signs she had ever emitted correctly, in my judgment, not signs qualified by frequency of use. Finally, I would estimate that Koko's current working

What does the author mean by *reliably use?*

Why does Patterson estimate Koko's working vocabulary rather than state it exactly?

Why measure Koko's intelligence using a human intelligence test?

What does *fluctuation* mean?

How might a human IQ test be culturally biased against gorillas?

Why does the writer consider some of Koko's incorrect responses jokes?

What does it mean to "program her actions"?

What can the scientists learn from Koko?

vocabulary—signs she uses regularly and appropriately—stands at about 375. . . .

From the start I monitored Koko's performance on human intelligence tests. In February 1975 Koko's intelligence quotient was 84 on the Stanford-Binet Intelligence Scale. Five months later, at the age of 4, her IQ rose to 95, only slightly below the average for a human child. By January 1976 the IQ was back to 85, which is not an uncommon fluctuation. Her scores on other tests confirmed the general range established by the Stanford-Binet scale.

Testing Koko's IQ has not been easy. There is, for instance, a cultural bias toward humans that shows up when tests are administered to a gorilla. One quiz asked the child, "Point to the two things that are good to eat." The depicted objects were a block, an apple, a shoe, a flower, and an ice-cream sundae. Koko, reflecting her gorilla tastes, picked the apple and the flower. Another asked the child to pick where he would run to shelter from the rain. The choices were a hat, a spoon, a tree, and a house. Koko naturally chose the tree. Rules for the scoring required that I record these responses as errors.

Koko has made numerous other "errors" that offer insight into the personality of an adolescent gorilla. One day my associate Barbara Hiller saw Koko signing, "That red," as she built a nest out of a white towel. Barbara said, "You know better, Koko. What color is it?" Koko insisted that it was red—"red, Red, RED"—and finally held up a minute speck of red lint that had been clinging to the towel. Koko was grinning.

Another time, after persistent efforts on Barbara's part to get Koko to sign, "Drink," our mischievous charge finally leaned back on the counter and executed a perfect drink sign—in her ear. Again she was grinning. Sometimes Koko will respond negatively, but without a grin—leading me to believe her intent is not to joke but to be disobedient.

She seems to relish the effects of her practical jokes, often responding exactly opposite to what I ask her to do. One day, during a videotaping session, I asked Koko to place a toy animal under a bag, and she responded by taking the toy and stretching to hold it up to the ceiling.

With Koko in a contrary mood I can almost program her actions. For example, Ron Cohn got her to stop breaking plastic spoons by signing, "Good break them," whereupon Koko stopped bending them and started kissing them. On such occasions Koko knows that she is misbehaving, and once when I became irritated with her negativity, she quite accurately described herself as a "stubborn devil."

Even had I not come to know and love Koko as a witty, sweet, and trusting personality, I cannot foresee terminating Project Koko. Nothing indicates that Koko has reached the limit of her learning capacities. We have a great deal yet to learn from *her.*

Now there is the challenge of new areas of language use. Professor Patrick Suppes and his colleagues at Stanford's Institute for Mathematical Studies in the Social Sciences have designed a keyboard-computer linkup that permits Koko to talk through a speech synthesizer by pressing buttons. Simultaneously, all her utterances are transferred to a computer data file.

What is a speech synthesizer?

I noticed early that Koko responded appropriately to things I said in English, and often spontaneously translated spoken phrases into sign. For example, when asked in English, "Do you want a taste of butter?" Koko responded, "Taste butter."

Can Koko understand spoken English?

Now with the auditory keyboard, which produces spoken words when she presses keys, Koko can talk back as well as listen. The 46 active keys bear the usual letters of the alphabet and numbers. But in addition, each key is painted with a simple, arbitrary geometric pattern in one of ten different colors representing words for objects, feelings, and actions, as well as pronouns, prepositions, and modifiers. . . .

Can Koko read?

If I place, say, an apple before her, she may push the keys representing "want," "apple," "eat," and the computer-generated female voice speaks these words. Thus Koko can produce the spoken English for objects, ideas, and actions already banked in her sign vocabulary.

Typing usually with the index finger of her right hand, but always reserving one hand for signing, Koko can sign and speak simultaneously. As she signs, she can type out an identical or complementary phrase, and the synthesizer will vocalize her message. An ambidextrous and bilingual gorilla!

What does *complementary* mean?

Koko responds to hundreds of spoken words independent of the auditory keyboard, but her vocabulary of spoken English that she can generate (it will surely expand) is now restricted to 46 words. A major objective is to evaluate the gorilla's sense of spoken word order.

Then there is Michael, the 5½-year-old male gorilla we acquired in September 1976 as a companion for Koko. Michael has been receiving sign-language instruction from Ann Southcombe—and from Koko, who has taken it upon herself to coach Michael's execution of the signs for "Koko" and "tickle," So far, Mike's vocabulary is only about 35 signs, and he doesn't always sign fast enough for Koko.

How does Michael's progress compare to Koko's?

Early this year Mike was fumbling for the right sign to convince Ann to let him in to play with Koko. After Mike signed, "Out," Koko, waiting in her own room, began to get impatient. She signed to Mike through the wire mesh, "Do visit Mike hurry, Mike think hurry," imploring him to come up with the right sign. Then she said, "Koko good hug," and it finally dawned on Mike to say, "Koko." A relieved Koko signed, "Good know Mike," and then, "In Mike."

Why would Koko sign to Mike?

Now the godmother of two gorillas, I weigh my responsibilities to this threatened species. I have set up the Gorilla Foundation to protect the future of Koko and Michael. My fondest hope is to establish Koko and Michael, myself, and my associates in a place set aside for the study of gorillas and for their preservation in circumstances of relative freedom. It is sad that the gorilla's best present prospect for survival is un-

Why does the writer call herself the gorillas' godmother?

der the active protection of man. Yet it would be tragic should these animals disappear before we fully understand them.

"Fine Animal Gorilla"

That understanding enlarges as Koko grows ever more flexible and sophisticated in communication. Her recent progress is nothing short of astonishing.

Koko is defining objects. "What is a stove?" I ask her. She points to the stove. "What do you do with it?" "Cook with."

"What is an orange?" "Food, drink."

I ask Koko, "Tell me something you think is funny." She signs, "Nose there," pointing to a bird puppet's tongue. "That red," showing me a green plastic frog we had talked about. When I put a stethoscope to my ears, Koko smirks and puts fingers over her eyes.

She perceives right and wrong, but is touchy about blame. During a videotaping session, when I turn away, she tries to steal grapes from a bowl. I scold her. "Stop stealing. Don't be such a pig. Be polite. Ask me. Stealing is wrong, wrong, like biting and hurting is wrong."

Then I ask, "What does Penny do that's wrong?" Koko says, "Break things, lie, tell me 'polite' [when I'm] hungry pig."

Koko is ill, a mild respiratory disorder. I ask her, "Where do you hurt?" Koko signs, "Underarms."

Finally, Koko is learning self-esteem. A reporter asks about Koko as a person. I turn to Koko: "Are you an animal or a person?"

Koko's instant response: "Fine animal gorilla."

Questions for discussion:

1. How intelligent does the author feel gorillas are? How do you know this?
2. Do you find the evidence in the article about gorilla intelligence convincing? Why or why not?
3. If gorillas are as intelligent as Patterson believes, should they be treated differently than they are now?
4. Have you ever had a conversation with an animal?

Marginal questions: How is Koko's recent progress astonishing? What is a stethoscope? How is her smirking a sign of sophistication? How is understanding right and wrong a sign of progress? Why doesn't Koko say she is a "fine gorilla person"?

WRITING CHECKLIST

Checks (✓) in the columns below indicate areas in which you need extra work.

Writing Activities by Number

Editorial Mark	Meaning of the Mark	Page Number	Diag.	1	2	3	4	5	6	7	8	9	10	11	12
ad	Misuse of adjective or adverb	142–43													
agr	Error in Agreement: sub. - verb pron. - ant.	86–98 112–20													
awkc	Awkward construction	251–52													
awkt	Awkward transition	106–12, 258–66													
cap	Use capital letter	189–90													
comp	Comparisons	135–36, 142–43													
coord	Faulty coordination	224–25													
cs	Comma splice	17–18, 21, 230–31													
dev	Inadequate development	58–65, 207–17													
[ ]	Incorrect word division	276													
dm	Dangling modifier	174–75													
frag	Sentence fragment	19–21, 173–74, 231													
hyph	Error in use of hyphen	275–76													
ital	Italicize (underline)	274–75													
lc	Use lower-case letter	189–90													
mm	Misplaced modifier	174–75													
no ⌢,	Comma not needed	224–25, 278–79													
punc .?!	Error in punctuation: Period, question mark, exclamation point	188–89, 198–99													
⌢,	Comma	267–73, 277, 278–79													
‾⋀	Hyphen	275–76													
;	Semicolon	224, 267													
⋁,	Apostrophe	191–202													
⋁″	Quotation mark	273–74													
: - ( )	Colon, dash, parentheses	268–71, 277													
par ¶	Start new paragraph	26													

Writing Activities by Number

Editorial Mark	Meaning of the Mark	Page Number	Diag.	1	2	3	4	5	6	7	8	9	10	11	12
¶coh	Paragraph not coherent	101–12													
¶dev	Paragraph not developed	58–65													
¶un	Paragraph not unified	44–47													
rev	Proofread or revise	20–22, 29–31, 130–33													
run-on	Run-on sentence	17–18, 21													
shift vb	Inconsistent verb tense	171–73													
sp	Misspelled word	251–52													
sub	Faulty subordination	226–28													
+	Error in verb tense	162–69, 171–73													
vary	Vary sentence structure	219–30													
vb	Error in verb form	157–62													
ww	Wrong word	73–76													
//	Faulty parallelism	109–11													
×	Obvious error	251–52													
∧	Something missing	251–52													
℘	Delete	—													

Grade:

Index